CHICKEN SOUP
FOR THE SOUL®
OF AMERICA

Stories to Heal the Heart
of Our Nation

Jack Canfield
Mark Victor Hansen
Matthew E. Adams

Health Communications, Inc.
Deerfield Beach, Florida

www.hci-online.com
www.chickensoup.com

We would like to acknowledge the many publishers and individuals who granted us permission to reprint the cited material. (Note: The stories that were penned anonymously, that are in the public domain, or that were written by Jack Canfield, Mark Victor Hansen or Matthew E. Adams are not included in this listing.)

A Time of Gifts. ©2001 by *The New York Times Co.* Reprinted by permission. Originally published in *The New York Times,* September 26, 2001.

They Took a Vote. Reprinted by permission of Bill Holicky. ©2001 Bill Holicky.

Let Us Be United. Reprinted by permission of Kimberly Beaven. ©2001 Kimberly Beaven.

Do Unto Others and *A Hero for Our Time.* Reprinted by permission of Judith Simon Prager. ©2001 Judith Simon Prager.

Firefighter's Account from the World Trade Center. ©2001 by *The New York Times* Co. Reprinted by permission. Originally published in *The New York Times,* September 14, 2001.

(Continued on page 333)

Library of Congress Cataloging-in-Publication Data

Chicken soup for the soul of America : stories to heal the heart of our nation
/ [compiled by] Jack Canfield, Mark Victor Hansen, Matthew E. Adams.
   p. cm.
ISBN 0-7573-0006-5 (tradepaper) — ISBN 0-7573-0007-3 (hardcover)
   1. September 11 Terrorist Attacks, 2001. 2. Terrorism—United States—
Philosophy. 3. Victims of terrorism—United States. 4. Compassion.
5. Healing. 6. Kindness. I. Canfield, Jack, 1944- II. Hansen, Mark Victor.
III. Adams, Matthew E., 1964-

HV6432 .C43 2002
973.931—dc21

2002020898

Publisher: Health Communications, Inc.
          3201 S.W. 15th Street
          Deerfield Beach, FL 33442-8190

R-05-02

Cover design by Lisa Camp
Inside formatting by Lawna Patterson Oldfield and Dawn Grove

*This book is dedicated
to all of the people who make up
this great country we call America.
It is our hope that all can find peace
during this time of healing.*

Contents

2. AMERICA RESPONDS

3. THE WORLD RESPONDS

4. RENEWED PATRIOTISM

5. UNITED WE STAND

6. REFLECTIONS

7. WHERE NEXT?

Acknowledgments

Chicken Soup for the Soul of America was a book that was difficult to produce, yet a book we felt we had to do. Because we did it in one-fourth the time it normally takes us to do a book, it would have been impossible without the efforts of so many.

We would first like to acknowledge all of you who continue to love us and support us and allowed us the extra time and space it took to create this book—our families, who continue to be chicken soup for our souls!

Inga, Christopher, Oran and Kyle Canfield, and Travis and Riley Mahoney, for all their love and support.

Patty, Elisabeth and Melanie Hansen, for once again sharing and lovingly supporting us in the creation of yet another book.

Donna, Austin and CJ Adams for their patience.

Patty Aubery, for making sure the daily business at Chicken Soup for the Soul Enterprises continued with ease, and for being an integral part of the final process of editing and sequencing the stories.

Heather McNamara and D'ette Corona, who were more than senior editors on this project. Your names should be on the cover of the book. You were every bit as critical in creating this compilation as we, the coauthors, were. Your commitment to this book was awesome! Thank you so much!

Our publisher, Peter Vegso, for all of his love, support and commitment to the vision of this book. You continue to amaze us at every level.

To everyone at Health Communications, especially Terry Burke, Christine Belleris, Allison Janse, Susan Tobias, Lisa Drucker and Kathy Grant, for their complete support (which included reading and editing on their weekends) of this project. To Larissa Hise, Lawna Oldfield, Dawn Grove and Anthony Clausi—a big thank-you. You guys went way above and beyond for this one!

Leslie Riskin, for her care and determination in securing our permissions and getting everything just right under the worst time pressures ever!

Nancy Autio and the entire *Chicken Soup* staff, for helping us find truly wonderful stories and helping us take this book to completion.

Kathy Brennan-Thompson and Veronica Romero, for their unwavering commitment to this book. Thank you for handling so many little details that needed to be attended to with grace and excellence.

Dana Drobny, for keeping the wolves at bay so Jack could concentrate his full time on finishing this book, and for a wonderful job coauthoring one of our most favorite stories in the book. Thanks for going the extra mile on this one!

Maria Nickless, for her creative ideas and her enthusiastic marketing and public relations support.

Patty Hansen, for her thorough and competent handling of the legal and licensing aspects of this and all the other *Chicken Soup for the Soul* books. You are magnificent at the challenge!

Laurie Hartman, for being a precious guardian of the *Chicken Soup* brand.

Robin Yerian, Teresa Esparza, Vince Wong, Cindy

Holland, Stephanie Thatcher, Michelle Adams, Dave Coleman, Irene Dunlap, Jody Emme, Dee Dee Romanello, Gina Romanello, Brittany Shaw, Shanna Vieyra and Lisa Williams for your commitment, dedication and professionalism in making sure Jack's and Mark's offices ran smoothly throughout this project.

Marsha Arons, who flew to New York to interview several people so we could get the stories right. Thanks for being there when we needed you.

Barbara Chesser, Carol Kline and Janet Matthews who provided innumerable suggestions for editing, quotes, title changes and leads for stories.

Tom Lagana, who provided us with several fabulous stories.

Joyce Schowalter and Randy Cassingham of *HeroicStories.com*, who provided us with so many meaningful stories from their free online newsletter.

For Andrew Risner, our friend in Great Britain, for helping us track down a hard-to-find story.

All the *Chicken Soup for the Soul* coauthors, who make it a joy to be part of this Chicken Soup family—many of whom helped us out by finding stories and evaluating the final manuscript: Raymond Aaron, Patty and Jeff Aubery, Nancy Mitchell Autio, Marty Becker, John Boal, Cynthia Brian, Cindy Buck, Ron Camacho, Barbara Russell Chesser, Dan Clark, Tim Clauss, Barbara De Angelis, Mark and Chrissy Donnelly, Irene Dunlap, Bud Gardner, Patty Hansen, Jennifer Read Hawthorne, Kimberly Kirberger, Carol Kline, Tom and Laura Lagana, Hanoch and Meladee McCarty, Heather McNamara, Paul J. Meyer, Arline Oberst, Marion Owen, Maida Rogerson, Martin Rutte, Amy Seeger, Barry Spilchuk, Pat Stone, Carol Sturgulewski, Jim Tunney, Diana von Welanetz Wentworth and Steve Zikman.

Our glorious panel of readers who helped us make the

final selections and made invaluable suggestions on how to improve the book: Saskia Andriulli, Fred Angelis, Christine Belleris, Jacob Blass, Kathy Brennan-Thompson, Cindy Buck, Connie Carmeron, Barbara Chesser, Nancy Clark, D'ette Corona, Jennifer Dale, Patricia Drobny, Robin Dorf, Allison Janse, Melanie Johnson, Renee King, Tom Krause, Bob Land, Terry LePine, Barbara LoMonaco, Meladee McCarty, Linda Mitchell, Frank Mitchell, Heather McNamara, Maria Nickless, Ron Nielson, Steve Parker, Veronica Romero, Martin Rutte, Erin Saxton, Amber Setrakian, Lois Sloane, Bob Solomon, Jim Warda and Jeannie Williams. Your feedback and suggestions were invaluable!

And, most of all, everyone who submitted their heartfelt stories, poems, quotes and cartoons for possible inclusion in this book. While we were not able to use everything you sent in, we know that each word came from the bottom of your hearts—sometimes from experiences and emotions that were difficult to share.

Because of the size of this project and the speed at which we have put this together, we may have left out the names of some people who contributed along the way. If so, we are sorry, but please know that we really do appreciate you very much.

We are truly grateful and love you all!

Introduction

Although the events of September 11, 2001, were stunning, shocking and horrifying, they also brought out the best in us as a nation and as a people. As the days passed, the stories began to emerge—countless stories of heroism, selfless service, renewed patriotism and deepened faith.

A nation that was only months before divided over a deeply contested election came together around a single purpose and a single cause. Americans of every age, race, religion and location stepped forward in some way to offer their physical labor as well as their goods and services at Ground Zero in New York City and Washington, D.C., as well as their money to scores of charities that sprung into immediate action. Record numbers donated their blood to the Red Cross. Celebrities and noncelebrities alike gave their time and talents to the numerous benefit concerts that were performed around the country. Communities around the country and the world sent cards, posters, flowers and teddy bears to the surviving police officers, firefighters, soldiers and civilians, and gave their love and emotional support to anyone who needed it.

Rescue workers labored past the point of exhaustion in a desperate attempt to save those trapped beneath the rubble. People drove across the country to deliver needed telephone equipment and stayed for weeks—working for free—to help make it operational. Volunteers cooked food, delivered water, manned supply depots, gave massages and offered counseling. Children sold everything from lemonade to their own toys to raise money for the victims' families. Radio stations organized thousands of people into large human flags that were photographed and sent to the exhausted firefighters in New York. People dug out old flags and displayed them proudly in a fervor of impassioned patriotism and as a show of support for the members of our armed forces. Indeed, some people went as far as painting their whole houses red, white and blue. Thousands of cards and posters were produced by the schoolchildren of America and sent to the victims' families. Hundreds of new songs were written and performed on Larry King Live and on NPR Radio. Hundreds of thousands of e-mails were sent and forwarded around the country and around the world as people attempted to share their experiences and to comfort their friends and family members. And candlelight vigils were held in every neighborhood and town square across our great land.

As we witnessed, heard and read about, these inspiring acts at the site of the attacks and in our own communities, schools and homes, heroism began to take on a deeper meaning. Patriotism became something more tangible to all of us. Reaching out to members of different faiths and ethnic backgrounds, caring for our neighbors and spending time with our families became more pressing priorities. What it meant to be an American living in a free country became more precious to us than ever before.

As these stories of heroism, compassion and service began to emerge, so did the hundreds of e-mails urging and encouraging us at Chicken Soup for the Soul to compile them into a book.

With the many stories that are now coming to light of victims placing a last phone call of love to their family members or spouses, of the many individuals who gave up their own lives to stay back and assist others, as well as the heroic efforts of rescue workers, I feel it would be a moving tribute to these individuals if these stories were collected and bound into a book in their honor.

Lori M., Orlando, FL

I am writing from Canada, knowing of the heavy hearts of all Americans. We, your neighbors to the north, are also observing the tribute and remembrance of those who lost their lives in the atrocious acts of September 11. Our hearts and prayers go out to those who grieve the loss of loved ones. I think that a compilation of stories from those so affected would help bring healing to the nation and the world.

Denise S., Canada

And so we have responded with this offering. Compiling and editing this book has been a difficult and challenging task. We wanted it to be the best book we had ever done, and we wanted to get it to people as quickly as possible. While this put tremendous pressure on all of us, it became a labor of love like no other book we had ever done. We hope we have succeeded in creating a book that will honor those whose lives were lost, comfort those who survived them, acknowledge those who stepped forward to help their fellow Americans and contribute to the healing of the enormous wound that was inflicted upon our national psyche.

In compiling this book we collected and read thousands of inspiring and poignant stories that were worthy of publication. There simply isn't space to include all of them. We are also acutely aware that there are many thousands of other stories that didn't surface in our research that also merit telling. We can only hope that we have achieved our goal of representing the broad range of experiences that deserve telling with the ones we have chosen.

Our intention was to create a collection that would indeed facilitate the healing of our nation—both individually and collectively. We know that this book will not necessarily stop you from shedding a tear; in fact, many stories may make you cry. But know that when you do, you will not be crying alone. We hope that when you put down this book you will be uplifted, encouraged, inspired and a little more aware that we really are all in this together—one country, indivisible, with a passion for liberty and justice for all as we pursue the fulfillment of our individual and collective dreams.

Share with Us

We would love to hear your reactions to the stories in this book. Please let us know what your favorite stories were and how they affected you.

We also invite you to send us stories you would like to see published in future editions of *Chicken Soup for the Soul.* Please send submissions to:

Chicken Soup for the Soul
P.O. Box 30880
Santa Barbara, CA 93130
fax: 805-563-2945

You can also access e-mail or find a current list of planned books at the *Chicken Soup for the Soul* Web site at *www.chickensoup.com.* Find out about our Internet service at *www.clubchickensoup.com.*

We hope you enjoy reading this book as much as we enjoyed compiling, editing and writing it.

1

SEPTEMBER 11, 2001

*Today our nation saw evil . . . and we
responded with the best of America.*

George W. Bush

A Time of Gifts

No act of kindness, no matter how small, is ever wasted.

Aesop

The patterns of human history mix decency and depravity in equal measure. We often assume, therefore, that such a fine balance of results must emerge from societies made of decent and depraved people in equal numbers. But we need to expose and celebrate the fallacy of this conclusion so that, in this moment of crisis, we may reaffirm an essential truth too easily forgotten, and regain some crucial comfort too readily forgone. Good and kind people outnumber all others by thousands to one. The tragedy of human history lies in the enormous potential for destruction in rare acts of evil, not in the high frequency of evil people. Complex systems can only be built step by step, whereas destruction requires but an instant. Thus, in what I like to call the Great Asymmetry, every spectacular incident of evil will be balanced by ten thousand acts of kindness, too often unnoted and invisible as the "ordinary" efforts of a vast majority.

SEPTEMBER 11, 2001   3

We have a duty, almost a holy responsibility, to record and honor the victorious weight of these innumerable little kindnesses, when an unprecedented act of evil so threatens to distort our perception of ordinary human behavior. I have stood at Ground Zero, stunned by the twisted ruins of the largest human structure ever destroyed in a catastrophic moment. (I will discount the claims of a few biblical literalists for the Tower of Babel.) And I have contemplated a single day of carnage that our nation has not suffered since battles that still evoke passions and tears, nearly 150 years later: Antietam, Gettysburg, Cold Harbor. The scene is insufferably sad, but not at all depressing.

Rather, Ground Zero can only be described, in the lost meaning of a grand old word, as "sublime," in the sense of awe inspired by solemnity.

In human terms, Ground Zero is the focal point for a vast web of bustling goodness, channeling uncountable deeds of kindness from an entire planet—the acts that must be recorded to reaffirm the overwhelming weight of human decency. The rubble of Ground Zero stands mute, while a beehive of human activity churns within, and radiates outward, as everyone makes a selfless contribution, big or tiny according to means and skills, but each of equal worth. My wife and stepdaughter established a depot on Spring Street to collect and ferry needed items in short supply, including face masks and shoe inserts, to the workers at Ground Zero. Word spreads like a fire of goodness, and people stream in, bringing gifts from a pocketful of batteries to a ten-thousand-dollar purchase of hard hats, made on the spot at a local supply house and delivered right to us.

I will cite but one tiny story, among so many, to add to the count that will overwhelm the power of any terrorist's act. And by such tales, multiplied many millionfold, let those few depraved people finally understand why their vision of inspired fear cannot prevail over ordinary decency. As we left a local restaurant to make a delivery to Ground Zero late one evening, the cook gave us a shopping bag and said:

"Here's a dozen apple brown bettys, our best dessert, still warm. Please give them to the rescue workers."

How lovely, I thought, *but how meaningless, except as an act of solidarity, connecting the cook to the cleanup.* Still, we promised that we would make the distribution, and we put the bag of twelve apple brown bettys atop several thousand face masks and shoe pads. Twelve apple brown bettys into the breach. Twelve apple brown bettys for thousands of workers. And then I learned something important that I should never have forgotten—and the joke turned on me. Those twelve apple brown Betties went like literal hotcakes. These trivial symbols in my initial judgment turned into little drops of gold within a rainstorm of similar offerings for the stomach and soul, from children's postcards to cheers by the roadside. We gave the last one to a firefighter, an older man in a young crowd, sitting alone in utter exhaustion as he inserted one of our shoe pads. And he said, with a twinkle and a smile restored to his face, "Thank you. This is the most lovely thing I've seen in four days—and still warm!"

Stephen Jay Gould

They Took a Vote

Valor is a gift. Those having it never know for sure whether they have it until the test comes.

Carl Sandburg

The strength of a country comes from its people. It always has and always will. No matter what pomp and bravado a government shows, the solidity of the nation is directly determined by that of the individual citizen.

America has been shaken to its core by acts of terror. Many, including our president, have said we are strong, that we have resolve and that we will persevere. These words mean nothing to terrorists. Terrorists wait to see the actions of people, of individuals, to see if they will buckle and cower.

The cowards who killed our sisters and brothers, our mothers and fathers, our sons and daughters should know what happened on the flight they unsuccessfully tried to turn into a bomb over Pennsylvania. So should the rest of our fellow countrymen and women. In the history of this country of freedom, there has never been an event more emblematic of the values and heroism of the United States of America.

The flight had been hijacked, and was being turned around to be used as ammunition against innocent civilians at some unknown target in Washington, D.C. After some hurried cell phone calls to their loved ones, passengers learned of the World Trade Center attacks. They considered the consequences, then they took a vote together.

In that instant, they validated the great experiment of the United States of America. They voted. They affirmed the Declaration of Independence, the Constitution, our entire history of freedom, and gave meaning to every soldier who's ever died in the service of this country. Faced with all of the threats that this country stands against, and in their own last hour, these Americans determined their path with a simple act of democracy, of freedom. They voted.

They voted to give their lives to save the innocent people for which the plane was headed.

Think about that for a moment. It's the very definition of heroic. There is something else in that story, however, something incredible that should fill every American with pride. None of those American passengers took command. Nobody ordered them to attack the terrorists. Nobody forced them to follow along with the heroic insurgence.

Faced with death, tyranny, and terror, those Americans voted to sacrifice their lives for others.

September 11, 2001, is a day, as was said of Pearl Harbor, that will live in infamy. Thousands perished at the hands of cowards. We should never forget, however, that it was also the day that a few heroic patriots thousands of feet above Pennsylvania farmland sent a message to the entire world—our commitment to freedom and democracy, in the United States of America, is not wavering, it is not shaken, and it cannot be taken away by any act.

America is freedom.

Bill Holicky

Let Us Be United

September 10, 2001, was our eighth wedding anniversary. My husband, Alan, was leaving the next day for a week back in California to try his last Clean Water Act case. He'd decided to give up a thriving environmental law practice for a year's sabbatical spending more time with family and offering volunteer work in India. We spent the day celebrating our love for each other, planning our future and counting the blessings in our lives. We were so grateful for our life together. Alan always said, "When we wake up each morning, we should feel gratitude for being alive." And we did.

Alan woke up at 4:30 on Tuesday for his morning flight to San Francisco. As he kissed our five-year-old daughter Sonali and me good-bye, I pulled him toward me, knocking him over. He laughed heartily and said, "I'll return with the pot of gold."

"You are my pot of gold, Alan," I said. "Come home safe and sound."

He assured me he would, and at 7:00 A.M., he called to say he had checked in, he loved us, and he'd be back by the weekend.

And then it all began. . . . The CNN announcer confirmed

that Flight 93 bound for San Francisco had crashed in a field in Pennsylvania. In that instant, I felt a crushing blow. Devastated, with the wind knocked out of me, I could barely get a sound out as shock and disbelief poured through my veins. My heart literally stopped beating and I had to will myself to live. How could my husband, my best friend who I'd kissed good-bye hours earlier, be dead?

When Sonali came home from school, I let her play for an hour before I told her the news. I wanted to savor the innocence of her not knowing Daddy was dead. When she heard Alan's plane had crashed and he was not coming home, she wailed a cry so deep and heartbreaking, a cry I pray I will never hear again from any living being. She sobbed for an hour straight, and then she looked me in the eyes and said, "I am so sad. But I'm not the saddest girl in the world. Some children have lost their mommy and their daddy, and I still have you."

A few days after the crash, Sonali's brother Chris, concerned that Sonali might not understand what was really happening, asked her, "Do you know where Daddy is?"

"Yes, he's at work!"

Chris was wondering how to handle this, when she continued. "Silly, he's in court. Defending the angels."

Sonali's courage in the following weeks continue to amaze me and remind me of her dad. One of Alan's final contemplations was a sentence he'd heard in a recent workshop, *Fear—Who Cares?* I know these words helped guide him on September 11.

Sonali and I attended a memorial service at the crash site in Pennsylvania with her older brothers Chris and John. Standing at the fence, staring out at the field and the scorched trees, I couldn't help but notice what a beautiful place it was for him to die. Such an expansive countryside with golden red trees—this is where it all ended for Alan.

Sonali picked up some dirt in her hands, folded her hands in prayer and began singing a beautiful hymn she learned in India the previous winter. Everyone stopped to listen to her. Then she held the dirt to her heart and threw it toward the plane.

As the sun peeked momentarily through the thick cloud cover, Sonali looked up and said, "There's Daddy!" She drew a heart in the gravel and asked for some flowers, which she arranged beautifully around the heart with one flower in the center for her daddy.

News of Sonali's courageous, sweet voice reached California, and we received a call from the governor's office. Would Sonali like to sing at California's Day of Remembrance?

"No, I don't think so. She just turned five a few weeks ago, and there will be too many people."

Sonali heard me and asked, "What am I too young to do?"

She listened to my reasons why not and simply said, "I want to do it." I agreed. And in the next few days, Sonali's repertoire of mostly Disney tunes expanded to include a beautiful prayer from the *Rig Veda* that we heard at the Siddha Yoga Meditation Ashram in New York where we were staying. Clearly, "Let Us Be United" was the perfect song for Sonali to sing:

> *Let us be united;*
> *Let us speak in harmony;*
> *Let our minds apprehend alike;*
> *Common be our prayer;*
> *Common be our resolution;*
> *Alike be our feeling;*
> *Unified be our hearts;*
> *Perfect be our unity.*

On the flight back to California, our flight attendant heard about where we were going and asked if Sonali wanted to sing her song for everyone on the plane.

A bit concerned, my mother asked Sonali, "Do you know how many people are on this plane?"

Sonali had no idea. So she took the flight attendant's hand, walked up and down the aisle, and then came back with her guess. "About a thousand," she said. "I can do that. I'll be fine."

In a clear, strong voice, Sonali sang to her fellow passengers. She then walked up and down the aisle with one of the crewmembers, receiving the smiles, thanks and love of all the United passengers. At the end of the flight, who stood on top of a box at the door with the flight attendant, thanking everyone and saying good-bye? Our Sonali!

When Sonali sang on the steps of the state capitol, her voice was unbelievably strong. It was as though she wanted to fill the whole universe with this impassioned prayer so it would reach her daddy. As she sang, I felt it also become a pure prayer to everyone gathered—a prayer that painted a vision. I was delighted when she asked me if she could sing again, this time for Alan's memorial service at Grace Cathedral in San Francisco.

That wasn't Sonali's last singing prayer. When the Golden State Warriors awarded a check to the Beaven family at a fundraiser in their honor, guess who sang to thousands of people in their stadium? When asked how she was able to sing in front of so many people, Sonali said, "I wasn't afraid because Daddy was singing with me."

October 15th would have been Alan's forty-ninth birthday, and Sonali wanted to have a birthday party for him. "Daddy's favorite place is the ocean, so let's go to the beach and have a big fire. Everybody can write a prayer on a piece of wood and when we put the wood in the fire, the prayers will rise to Daddy in heaven."

And so we did. As sweetly as Sonali's voice reached the heavens and so many hearts, so, too, our love rose into the moonlit sky. Alan's courage and spirituality are so strongly reflected in Sonali's ability to rise above her own heartbreak and loss and uplift people. Just as Alan didn't sit back in his seat with shaking knees but rose fearlessly to help save thousands of people's lives, so, too, Sonali chose not to bury herself in grief, but to sing her dad's vision of love and courage. I am grateful for them both!

Kimi Beaven

[EDITORS' NOTE: *When Manhattan singer/composer Anne Hampton Callaway heard the Vedic prayer, "Let Us Be United," she was inspired to put it to music. Later, Anne recorded the song with Sonali and members of the Siddha Yoga International Choir. "Let Us Be United" is available through the SYDA Foundation at (888) 422-3334 or at* www.letusbeunited.org *where you can hear a preview. All proceeds will go to support the work of non-profit organizations, including Save the Children, the SYDA Foundation and The PRASAD Project. For specific information regarding these organizations, please see the previously mentioned Web site.*]

Contributions to The Alan Beaven Family Fund can be sent to 2000 Powell St., Suite 1605, Emeryville, CA 94608.

Sonali sings at the California Day of Remembrance.

San Francisco Chronicle/Darryl Bush.

Do Unto Others

Courage is not the absence of fear, but rather the judgment that something else is more important than fear.

Ambrose Redmoon

Of all the sadness that came out of September 11, one story shines like a jewel in the dust. It is a story of giving and receiving—a story of saving and being saved and not knowing which is which—the story of the firefighters of Ladder Company 6 and Josephine.

More than three hundred firefighters perished in the tragedy of the World Trade Center. On September 29, at a time when the country was desperate for good news, NBC *Dateline* reported "The Miracle of Ladder Company 6." By the time I sat around their table in the back of the fire-house two weeks later and heard them recount it, the fire-fighters of Ladder 6 had said these words many times, but every word was still flooded with the vibrant sound of their gratitude.

They had gone to the World Trade Center that day to give. To rescue. That's what firefighters do. They run into burning buildings against instinct and nature, while the rest of us are running out, trying to save our own lives. They had entered the building at Number One, as had so many of their brothers, after the first plane had mortally wounded it. People were streaming down beside them, saying words of thanks and encouragement to them, offering them drinks from the machines and telling them they should get a pay raise.

They, in turn, offered words of encouragement back. "It's over for you," the firefighters said to those lucky enough to be exiting. "Go out through the lobby and go home now. You're okay."

The stairwells were narrow, only room enough for one person to move past another in either direction. Each of the firefighters climbing the steps carried at least a hundred pounds of equipment. At the twenty-seventh floor, some of them learned that the other tower had gone down, and the effort to save the building was rejected for the more pressing job of saving the people. Somehow in all the confusion, somewhere between the twelfth and fifteenth floors, the men of Ladder 6 were entrusted with the safety of a sixty-year-old bookkeeper named Josephine Harris. Josephine worked on the seventy-third floor, and she had been trudging down those sixty flights of steps through smoke and heat until her desire and ability to go on seemed completely exhausted.

Now getting her safely out was their assignment. So, despite her unwillingness to continue down the stairs, the firefighters encouraged her on. They reminded her of her grandchildren, who were waiting for her when she escaped the building. They told her she could do it. They cajoled. They encouraged. They promised to get her out if she would just keep moving.

On the fourth floor, she finally stopped in her tracks. She could not take another step. Would not take another step. She seemed willing to let them go on without her, but she was done walking. Never even thinking about leaving her, the firefighters began looking around for a chair on which to carry her down the rest of the stairs.

They were tired, too, and burdened by the heat and the weight of their equipment, and they were anxious to evacuate the building. But because some of them were not aware of the other building's collapse, and because the towers had always seemed somehow immortal, they did not feel at that moment that there was great urgency.

None of them expected the terrible, otherworldly, thunderous sound; none of them expected the rumble that, in an instant, signaled catastrophe. Time stands still at moments like that. They stretch out long enough to give people pause, to consider what dying would mean. Bill Butler thought, *I didn't even get to say good-bye to my wife and kids.* Clearly, this was it. They had done their best, and now it was over. They prayed for it to be over quickly; they repented and asked for forgiveness; they thought of loved ones.

And then everything turned to dust around them. One hundred and five floors above them came tumbling down, each crushing the one under it with greater force. Within seconds the proud, shiny tower had been turned to sand-sized pieces of rubble, taking thousands of lives in its shattering wake.

From all vantage points, there was no way for anyone to survive this disaster, and no obvious reason why the staircase at which Josephine had halted should have been spared. But miracles have their own reasons. And as the dust settled, Captain John (Jay) Jonas, Sal D'Agostino, Bill Butler, Tommy Falco, Mike Meldrum, Matt Komorowski and Josephine, thrown wildly through the debris, were left whole, if not exactly standing, seemingly buried alive.

For four hours they were trapped in the rubble,

wondering what was happening around them and how long they would be trapped. D'Agostino found a can of Sunkist orange soda, which seemed a drink of the gods to the thirsty team. Josephine was "a trooper," D'Agostino said of her. He offered her a drink and she declined, being brave and stoic. When, after a while, she said she was cold, Falco gave her his coat and even held her hand when she said she was scared. They had no idea what was happening around them; they could only hope that there were efforts being made to find survivors. Little did they know how ecstatic firefighters would be to discover that anyone had survived this disaster. Little did they know that the search for them was frantic and urgent for all concerned— those lost and those desperate to find them.

While they waited, some of them methodically repacked the rope in case they would need it later, a routine that now gave them something to do. A cell phone played a part in the outcome, as it had in the tragedy of Flight 93. This time it was when Butler, who couldn't reach the firehouse through all the chaos of the phone system, called his wife. She called the firehouse and let them know of the plight of the missing men.

Finally, they were found. Rescued.

But it had been an intense time that they had shared with Josephine, and the six were not ready to turn her over to another company. D'Agostino said that when a firefighter finally discovered them there, he was so pumped up that he rushed to take Josephine from them, calling her "Doll" and saying, 'We'll take care of you, Doll. We got you."

But after all those hours of sharing the limbo between life and death with her, it seemed to them inappropriate not to give her the honor due her. D'Agostino said he grabbed the rescuer's arm and explained, "Her name isn't Doll. Her name is Josephine." When he thinks of it now, he shakes his head. Even in the midst of the excitement of recovery and the terrible fright through which each soul had journeyed, the other firefighter recognized the holiness of the moment and apologized, saying, "Sorry, Josephine, we'll take good care of you.'"

Ultimately, because special equipment was required to remove her from the wasteland that Ground Zero had become, Josephine was taken away from the men of Ladder 6 and they parted.

As I sat around the table with Sal and Mike and Bill and Tom and listened to them tell it one more time, I could see that the talking about it was part of the process—that we understand so much through stories. They had a reunion with Josephine at a later date, gave her a special jacket and called her their "guardian angel." While she says that they saved *her* life, they contend the opposite. They believe that by insisting that they stop there at that spot, at the only place left standing at Ground Zero, holding it as a sacred space, Josephine had saved *their* lives.

Judith Simon Prager

Reprinted with permission of Marshall Ramsey. ©2001 Copley News Service.

A Hero for Our Time

It was New York City's worst week.
But it was New York City's best week.
We have never been braver.
We have never been stronger.

Mayor Rudolph Giuliani

In the days before September 11, 2001, America was a little short on role models. Oh, we had basketball players, rock stars and millionaires, but there was a dearth of larger-than-life, genuine heroes. In those carefree, careless days, we had no one to show us how to *be:* how to be brave, how to be kind, how to be generous, how to be valiant.

Soldiers had come home from Vietnam, not war heroes but burned out and angry, and among them was one— bedecked in medals—whose inner need for an outlet for the fury inside found its expression in the blaze of fire-fighting. I remember the first time I met Lieutenant Patrick Brown. It was in 1991, and by then he had become one of the most decorated firefighters in New York City. It was over dinner with a mutual friend in a restaurant where the staff knew and respected him. I was enchanted by his easy charm, the contrast between his ordinary-guy demeanor and his perceptive philosophy. And then, within days, I turned on CNN to see Patrick and another firefighter lying on their bellies on the roof of a building holding a one-inch rope in their bare hands, anchored to nothing, as another firefighter swung on the rope and rescued first one and then another frightened man from the window of a burning building. "The guy was going to jump if we didn't act right away, and there wasn't anything to tie the rope to," Patrick explained, his hands abraded to shreds as he accepted another medal.

In 1999, *Time* magazine did a cover story on "Why We Take Risks" and featured Captain Patrick Brown among extreme skiers and race-car drivers. It was an odd juxtaposition from the start. Patrick's picture was a bit formal, but his quote was typical Pat. He said that in the F.D.N.Y. you were trained not to take "stupid risks." It was never about money or thrills, he said, only for "the greater good." When the article came out, he sent me a copy with a note that showed he was a little mystified at the honor . . . and the company.

As his legend grew, so did his spirit. He was relentless in his efforts to save those in need. It was said that if there were children or animals trapped in a burning building, Patrick was the one to send in. He had a special radar for the weakest among us, as if his heart were a magnet. The other firefighters admired, even loved him and called him "Paddy." The women loved him—he was so handsome. I thought he looked like a young Clark Gable—and we called him Patrick.

The more intensely he desired to help others, the more expansively he grew inside. He began to study yoga, saying it helped him find "the beauty of life again." He even tried, to no avail, to get the other firefighters to practice with him. In an article in *USA Today*, his yoga teacher, Faith Fennessey, called him "an enlightened being."

He trained for and received a black belt in karate, and then turned around and taught self-defense to the blind. He became incandescent, and yet if you had said so to his face, he would have shaken his head and changed the subject.

In 2001, I was writing a book with my partner, Judith Acosta, about words to say when every moment counts— words that can mean the difference panic and calm, pain and comfort, life and death. And when I thought of life and death, I thought of Patrick. So I gave him a call. "What do you do, what do you say," I asked, "when you encounter someone who's badly burned, maybe dying?"

He became thoughtful, almost shy, as he said that when things are at that terrifying pitch and lives are on the line, he tries to "spend a moment with the victim in silent meditation. Sometimes for just a few seconds, sometimes longer. It depends on the situation," he said. "With some victims, I will put my hands on them and do a little meditation, breathe into it, think into the universe and into God. I try to connect with their spiritual natures, even if they're dying. It helps to keep me calm as much as I hope it helps them."

On September 11, Patrick Brown arrived at the World Trade Center, focused with a clarity of vision that bore through smoke and flames. It is said that someone yelled to him, "Don't go in there, Paddy!" and it was reported that he answered, "Are you nuts? We've got a job to do!" I knew him better. Those weren't his words. So I was relieved when I talked with the men at Ladder 6 and they told a different story. One of the firefighters told me, "When they shouted to him not to go in, he said, 'There are *people* in there.'" Of course.

Another firefighter, who also spoke of how much they

all admired Patrick, said, "I saw him enter the lobby and his eyes were *huge.* You know how he gets." Yes. Drawn to battle. Drawn to serve. X-ray vision at the ready.

I visited Ladder 3, his company that had been devastated by the loss of twelve of their twenty-five brothers, and asked about Patrick. Lieutenant Steve Browne told me that, before he met Patrick, he had been a little worried about the new captain because he was such a legend. Surely he could be full of himself and difficult. And then Patrick walked in. "And he was so . . . modest," Browne said. "He was just too good to be true. He always stood up for his men, no matter who he had to stand up to. You can't teach what he knew." Another firefighter said of him, "He touched a lot of lives."

I knew as a friend that he had never gotten over the deaths of some of his men in Vietnam. The medals never helped him sleep one bit better. By the time we met, he had also lost men on the job, and each loss tore at him like the eagle that tore out the liver of Prometheus (who, it happens, was punished for stealing fire from the gods to give to mankind). When Patrick went into the World Trade Center that fateful day, those who knew him agreed that he could not have lived through the grief of losing men one more time. If his men had died, and he had not, we believed, he would never have recovered.

And so, as we waited to hear the names of those lost in the tragedy, we hardly knew what to feel. A week later, the friend who had introduced us finally, against her own better judgment and wracked with fears, walked over to the firehouse to learn his fate. There sat Patrick's car, where he had left it before the disaster. It hadn't been moved. There was no one to move it. She turned away and went home. Hesitating again, she dialed his number. The phone rang and the message—in his wonderful, gravelly Queens-accented voice—answered and, she told me, "I knew I was hearing a dead man." And we both cried.

These days, since September 11, people have come to recognize that heroes aren't necessarily the richest, most popular people on the block—they are the most valiant, selfless people among us. A Halloween cover of the *New Yorker* magazine featured children dressed up as firefighters and police officers.

America has a new kind of role model now, one who has shown us how to *be*. After the evacuation order, as others were leaving the building, someone heard Patrick call out over the radio, "There's a working elevator on 44!" which means he had gotten that far up and was still and forever rescuing.

And then the apocalyptic whoosh.

I know it must be true that if you died with Patrick by your side, you died at peace. That was his mission. He was where he had to be, where he was needed, eyes wide, heart like a lamp, leading the way to heaven.

Judith Simon Prager

Reprinted by permission of Mike Luckovich and Creators Syndicate, Inc.

A Firefighter's Account
of the World Trade Center

*We are shaken, but we are not defeated. We
stare adversity in the eye and we move on.*

Fire Commissioner Thomas Von Essen

The South Tower of the World Trade Center has just col-
lapsed. I am helping my friends at Ladder Company 16,
and the firefighters have commandeered a crowded 67th
Street cross-town bus. We go without stopping from
Lexington Avenue to the staging center on Amsterdam.
We don't talk much. Not one of the passengers complains.

At Amsterdam we board another bus. The quiet is broken by a lieutenant: "We'll see things today we shouldn't
have to see, but listen up, we'll do it together. We'll be
together, and we'll all come back together." He opens a
box of dust masks and gives two to each of us.

We walk down West Street and report to the chief in
command. He stands ankle-deep in mud. His predecessor
chief earlier in the day is already missing, along with the
command center itself, which is somewhere beneath

mountains of cracked concrete and bent steel caused by the second collapse of the North Tower.

Now several hundred firefighters are milling about. There is not much for us to do except pull a hose from one place to another as a pumper and ladder truck are repositioned. It is quiet: no sirens, no helicopters. Just the sound of two hoses watering a hotel on West Street—the six stories that remain. The low crackle of department radios fades into the air. The danger now is the burning forty-seven-story building before us. The command chief has taken the firefighters out.

I leave the hoses and trucks and walk through the World Financial Center. There has been a complete evacuation; I move through the hallways alone. It seems the building has been abandoned for decades, as there are inches of dust on the floors. The large and beautiful atrium with its palm trees is in ruins.

Outside, because of the pervasive gray dusting, I cannot read the street signs as I make my way back. There is a lone fire company down a narrow street wetting down a smoldering pile. The mountains of debris in every direction are fifty and sixty feet high, and it is only now that I realize the silence I notice is the silence of thousands of people buried around me.

On the West Street side, the chiefs begin to push us back toward the Hudson. Entire companies are unaccounted for. The department's elite rescue squads are not heard from. Just the week before, I talked with a group of Rescue 1 firefighters about the difficult requirements for joining these companies. I remember thinking then that these were truly unusual people, smart and thoughtful.

I know the captain of Rescue 1, Terry Hatten. He is universally loved and respected on the job. I think about Terry, and about Brian Hickey, the captain of Rescue 4, who just the month before survived the blast of the

Astoria fire that killed three firefighters, including two of his men. He was working today.

I am pulling a heavy six-inch hose through the muck when I see Mike Carter, the vice-president of the firefighters union, on the hose just before me. He's a good friend, and we barely say hello to each other. I see Kevin Gallagher, the union president, who is looking for his missing firefighter son. Someone calls to me. It is Jimmy Boyle, the retired president of the union. "I can't find Michael," he says. Michael Boyle was with Engine 33, and the whole company is missing. I can't say anything to Jimmy, but just throw my arms around him. The last thing I see is Kevin Gallagher kissing a firefighter—his son.

Dennis Smith

Two Heroes for the Price of One

When I saw her on the *Good Morning America* show being interviewed by Charles Gibson the morning of December 11, she looked pretty much like the other widows I had seen since September 11: Her face still registered that awful sadness, that deeply etched worry for herself and her family left behind since the death of her husband, Harry Ramos. And, yes, there it was that bittersweet pride when others referred to her husband as a hero. But what struck me about Migdalia Ramos was something else. She was angry.

Migdalia Ramos was sitting next to the widow of the man that her husband had rushed back into the World Trade Center to try to save. Both of them died. Harry Ramos was the head trader at the May Davis Group, a small investment firm on the eighty-seventh floor of Tower One. All the other employees of May Davis got out. I understood immediately why Migdalia Ramos seemed angry. I felt anger too at the television program that had brought these two women together just for a good story. Didn't they see the pain here?

The television program centered on the coincidences between the two men—things I thought were really irrelevant—like the fact that Victor Wald, the man Harry Ramos had tried to save, had the same name as the best man at the Ramos's wedding or that both couples had a child named Alex. The only relevant link between these two women was the fact that they both had husbands who died just because they went to work that morning.

But one of them had had a chance to save himself and had not taken it. Migdalia Ramos spoke about her anger— not at Rebecca or Victor Wald but at her own husband. She just couldn't understand then why he had gone back in. I understood how she felt. How could he leave her and his children with all the responsibilities that they had to face? Couples should be there for each other, should cleave to one another. And if everyone else at his firm had gotten out, why hadn't Harry? He made a choice and the conse- quences of it didn't just affect him. It affected his whole family.

Then Migdalia Ramos told about another incident in her life. Her mother had died on September 1. The manage- ment of her mother's apartment building had told Mrs. Ramos that she would have to clear out the apartment by September 30. So, on September 30, Mrs. Ramos together with other family members went to her mother's apart- ment. While they were hauling out boxes and furniture, the fire alarm sounded. The hallway quickly filled with smoke. Mrs. Ramos did what every mother would do, what every right-thinking responsible person would do— she got her child and her relatives to safety.

But then, without thinking, she did something else: Migdalia Ramos ran right back into a burning building, up seven flights of stairs, to get her mother's blind neighbor out.

She did what Harry did. And, probably like Harry, she did it without thinking, reflexively, because whatever was in Harry that made him act that way was in her, too. That "something" made her forget every other aspect of her life and focus on someone else, someone who needed help.

Migdalia didn't use the word "hero" once in her interview. I don't think she thinks of herself that way. She just did what needed to be done. A lot of people called her husband a hero. He was, but not just because he went back into the World Trade Center. To Migdalia and her family, Harry Ramos was probably a hero just because he got out of bed every morning.

Migdalia Ramos lost a lot—her husband, her lover, her best friend. But maybe Migdalia Ramos found something, too. Maybe she found that the best qualities in her husband had rubbed off on her.

Personally, I think they were there all along.

Migdalia Ramos said that what happened at her mother's apartment building made her understand her husband's motives. She thought he was sending her a message.

I heard a message from this woman on my TV screen. There's something inside some of us—inside, I think, most of us. It's something good and decent and brave and unselfish. It's that best part of ourselves, that part that rises to the surface unquestioning, without thought, the simple act of caring for and about another human being. In a world where there are those who only exist to cause pain and terror, Mrs. Ramos' message is timely. It is a message for all of us, of hope.

Marsha Arons

FYI

New York City Transit puts a lot of faith in paperwork. At times, it seems to have missed the whole computer revolution, or at least mistrusted it. In fact, in a dusty file room in downtown Brooklyn, there are boxes containing minute-by-minute records of the daily movements of your subway line, going several back years—all handwritten on paper.

But in the weeks since September 11, 2001, weeks that have generated enough paperwork to wrap every subway car like a Christmas gift, there are three pieces of paper that have survived consignment to the oblivion of a cardboard file box.

Instead, they have been copied and copied again and passed around like Soviet *samizdat* [a means of expressing oneself and communicating with one another in a sphere outside the censor's supervision.] They were written by a fifty-five-year-old man named John B. McMahon, who works as a superintendent over several stations in Manhattan. The pages are dated and stamped, and start like any transit memo, heavy on military accuracy and acronyms, like "F.O." for field office.

"While at my office at Forty-second Street and Sixth

Avenue at approximately 0900 hours," it begins, "the F.O. notified me . . ."

But as the memo continues, recounting Mr. McMahon's journey on September 11 from his office to the area around the World Trade Center, it quickly becomes apparent that it is something other than official correspondence.

It is the soliloquy of a man trying to figure out what happened to him that day. In essence, it is a letter from Mr. McMahon to himself.

That morning, he rushed downtown to get into the Cortlandt Street Station on the N and R line to make sure that no passengers or transit employees remained inside the station. When he found none, he went back up onto the street and, as debris began to rain down from the fires in the towers above him, he took refuge under a glass awning in front of the Millennium Hilton Hotel.

At 9:58 A.M., he looked up.

He saw what appeared to be a ring of smoke form around the south tower. "Except," he wrote, "that this ring was coming downward . . ."

There was a truck parked next to him in front of a loading bay at Cortlandt and Church Streets, and he dove between the truck and a roll-down door, grabbing onto the bottom of a wall.

He wrote: "There was an upward, vacuum-type of air movement, followed by a 'swoosh' of air and then . . . NOTHING. Not a sound, but pitch darkness with a powder-like substance covering every inch of the area. It also filled my eyes, ears, face and mouth."

He struggled to breathe. He scooped ash and dust from his mouth. But as soon as he did, his mouth would fill up again. He felt other people around him, and he remembers hearing himself and the others count off, signifying that they were still alive.

"Then," he wrote, "the strangest thing happened."

"While I was facing this wall, I turned my head slightly to the left because I saw two lights that were too big to be flashlights and there were no automobiles around. Although I thought I was losing my battle to breathe, I was comforted by the lights, which gave me a sense of peace. We yelled, 'help,' and joined hands, walking toward the lights. The more we walked, the lighter it became, until finally I saw images of cars and people."

But as he emerged from the cloud of ash, he wrote, he looked around him and realized that he was not holding anyone's hand. He was alone. He has no idea what happened to the other people. He still has no idea what the lights were, and no idea how he found his way out of the debris.

"I'm a Catholic," Mr. McMahon said. "But I only go to church about once every five years. I don't know what that was that day. I don't know how to explain it. Somebody got me out," he said.

Mr. McMahon wrote the memo to his boss on a yellow legal pad at the end of that week, sitting in his backyard in Westbury on Long Island. When his fiancée read it, she cried.

"I wrote it," he said, "because I had to get it off my chest."

The day it happened, as Mr. McMahon recounted in the memo, he wandered until he came upon New York University Downtown Hospital where nurses pulled him inside and checked his vital signs. He rinsed out his mouth and took a shower. Then he had his fiancée buy him some new clothes at Macy's so he could, as he wrote, "finish out my day performing my duties."

He is taking some time off now, struggling with hearing loss and problems with his right eye, which was injured by the dust. More than those ailments, he said, he is struggling with his own mind.

"When I tell my psychiatrist, I know it all sounds crazy to him, but that's the way it happened," he says.

Mr. McMahon's memo ends like thousands of others. On a line by itself are the words:

"For your information."

Randy Kennedy

What Can Be Said?

10:32 A.M.

I am writing this from downtown New York. In a per-
verse reversal, I have no way to contact anyone except
through my high-speed wireless Internet connection—
phones are out, and electricity in the area is intermittent.

The media will ultimately tell the story better than I, but
I can tell you that there is massive loss of life. The sky is
black with ash, and the people have been panicking and
fleeing in unadulterated terror. I have never seen anything
like it. It is very difficult to breathe, even with your mouth
covered—the ash blows down the streets and burns your
eyes. It feels like the world has ended. When the screaming started and the crowds began to run after the second
plane struck, it was a horror film running in overdrive,
jumping frames and cutting in and out. Time got lost—I
don't know how long this went on. I have a cut on my leg.
I ended up in a Wendy's where a huge number of us took
refuge. I don't know where the workers were—I helped
get water for people.

I am starting to see emergency workers, and the streets
are clearing somewhat—at least the first waves of panic

are passing. I've seen bodies draped in white sheets—it took me time to realize those were bodies, not injured people; they must be out of room or not be able to get them to the morgues or the hospitals.

I'm headed for the Brooklyn Bridge to walk out of the city. I'm going to stop at any hospital I find to give blood before leaving. If anyone reading this can, please donate blood—I heard from a medic that the hospitals are already running out.

3:50 P.M.

I am writing this from my home in Brooklyn after leaving Manhattan. I have signed up for a time slot to give blood later this evening and have a few hours available before then.

After my last posting I made my way east through an urban moonscape—everywhere there is ash, abandoned bags in the street, people looking lost. I managed to get a cell line out to Jean-Michele, who is still in Seattle, and she helped me navigate with online maps as I plotted my exit strategy.

Bizarrely, I caught a taxi cross town. I was standing at a corner, I'm not even certain where, and a taxi was sitting there. A very pushy woman, whom I will always be thankful for, barged her way into the cab.

In a moment, without thinking, I climbed in, too. The driver, a Pakistani guy who had an improbable smile, immediately took off.

The ash blocks out the sun downtown—it is like driving in an impossible midnight, made even more impossible because I'm in a cab with this woman who won't stop trying her cell phone and another man, my age, who looks like he's been crying. Maybe he just has ash in his eyes, I know I do—I feel like I will never see properly again, though that's probably just trauma. I don't even know where the driver is going. The crying man got someone on *his* cell phone and started explaining what he's seeing out the window. It's like having a narrator traveling with us. I only notice the things that he is describing as he describes them.

God bless that taxi driver—we never paid him. He let us all off, and I think he got out as well, near the Brooklyn Bridge. There are cops everywhere, people are herding themselves quite calmly, mutely, onto the bridge. We all walk across the Brooklyn Bridge, which is unbelievably beautiful, the wires and stone of the bridge surrounding us and the bright sun ahead, passing out of darkness.

No one is talking to each other, but there is a sense of warmth. Everyone has their cell phones out, fishing for a clear signal. Those who catch them talk hurriedly to families, friends, people in other cities, children in their homes. It is comforting to hear their voices, telling how they are, "Okay, shhh, it's okay, I'm okay." As we walk out into the sunlight, I am so happy to be in this company, the company of people who are alright, those who walked out.

I was in the city today to turn in some of my book. I had stayed up all night writing and I was so worried—is it ready, have I done my work? Those questions seem small today—not unimportant, but smaller, in a new proportion. I kept thinking of how much I have left to do in my life, so many things that are undone, people I haven't spoken to in years. It's overwhelming to feel everyone around me thinking the same thing, the restless thoughts trickling over this bridge as we come back to Brooklyn.

From the Promenade, I stand with hundreds of others, listening to radios, watching the plumes of smoke and the empty holes in the skyline. People stand there for a long time, talking to one another in hushed tones. Someone hands out a flyer for a vigil this evening, which I will go to after I give blood.

What can be said? Just this: we will emphasize the horror and the evil, and that is all true. It is not the entire story. I saw an old man with breathing problems and two black kids in baggy pants and ghetto gear rubbing his back, talking to him. No one was rioting or looting. People helped each other in small and tremendous ways all day long . . . a family was giving away sandwiches at the Promenade. Everyone I talked to agreed to go give blood. If a draft had been held to train people to be firefighters, there would have been fights to see who got to volunteer.

No matter how wide and intricate this act of evil may be, it pales in comparison to the quiet dignity and strength of regular people. I have never been more proud of my country.

Mike Daisey

Twin Saving at the Twin Towers

We are like one-winged angels. It's only when we help each other that we can fly.

Luciano de Crescenzo

Through the vivid blue eyes of middle-aged Kenneth Summers came one of the most inspirational stories of a citizen saved by an instantly heroic volunteer after the September 11 terrorist attack in New York.

Summers was one of the few people who were seriously injured and lived to see another day, only because someone stepped forward in sacrifice.

An early bird, Summers arrived at his desk on the twenty-seventh floor of the North Tower at his usual time around 7:15 A.M. After clearing up his busywork, he took the elevator down to the soaring glass lobby of the World Trade Center to mail some personal bills that were perilously close to being late. *What a perfect day*, he thought. *Crystal clear sky, cool air. The kind of day you feel happy to be alive.*

"I wasn't outside for more than ten seconds when I thought I heard something like a massive train rushing past. Then boom! I looked to the right and saw someone I knew from upstairs racing for cover," he recalled. "I don't even know if I took the time to look up."

To take cover for himself, he rushed back to the revolving door leading into the North Tower. Inside that swirling door, Summers immediately noticed the space around him filling up with orange-yellowish colored fumes. "A second later, all hell broke loose," he continued. Shards of glass were flying everywhere as the force of an explosion lifted him up and out onto the street.

"I was on my back and on fire. I frantically looked to see if I had fingers or toes. I was lying next to the big planters outside and I kept saying to myself, *I'm okay. I'm okay.* Then I realized I was bleeding from my hands to my head, and I was covered with burns."

He beat his clothes and his hair with his hands to extinguish the flames that engulfed him. Once he put the fire out, he staggered across the street, looked up and saw the black smoke billowing from the top floors of the Tower. *Was it another bomb, like in 1993?* he thought. *Or maybe a plane had hit one of the towers.* People on the sidewalk around him seemed frozen. Summers pleaded with strangers to help him, but understandably everyone seemed too stunned to respond.

A split second later, there was a whoosh over his head, and he heard a second explosion. Suddenly the South Tower was ablaze. Fiery debris rained down, and Summers began to run. His skin was smoking and smoldering, peeling off in sheets. He was charred black and going into shock.

That's when a stranger with a kind face started calming Summers. "I want to help you. My name is Stephen Newman. I want to be your guide," he offered.

A thirty-six-year-old banker for Merrill Lynch, Newman had taken a car service to work from his home on the

Upper East Side. When the first plane hit, he was stopped in traffic two blocks south of the World Trade Center. After he got out of the cab, he headed for the Twin Towers. "I was racing to reach my office to make sure everybody knew what was happening," he said. Just as he saw the singed Summers, the second plane hit the South Tower.

While he wasn't sure what motivated him, Newman knew Summers needed medical attention fast. "We have to get across the river," he said to the badly injured man who was getting weaker by the moment.

Staggering, Summers slumped more and more with every step. But Newman's calm persistence pushed him on. They finally made it to the pier near Wall Street where thousands of usually steely New Yorkers were quite animated as they pushed to board boats for New Jersey. Although Newman had only been across the Hudson River a couple times in his life, he wasn't about to abandon the needy stranger he had taken under his wing.

The hobbling man and his newfound guide were the last two people to board the ferry leaving for Jersey City. As the ferry pulled away, the South Tower collapsed. "It was like a volcano," Newman remembered. "An avalanche that was weaving its way all over the World Financial Center."

Since the captain of the ferry had called ahead to have medical help waiting for the critically injured Summers, rescue workers took him immediately to the burn unit at Saint Barnabas Medical Center in Livingston, New Jersey.

Summers was one of the few lucky ones. He lived. Had Newman not stopped amidst all the panic that surrounded them, Summers is certain he would have perished.

"If he hadn't led me, directed me and pushed me, I was so woozy I would have probably sat down and lost consciousness. Who knows what would have happened?

"Steve saved my life," Summers said. Yet, in a startling revelation, Newman made the same declaration to him.

"You probably saved my life, too," he replied. "If I hadn't helped you, we both might have been there when the buildings fell." Through the sacrifice of one, two lives were saved. It was volunteering of the tallest order.

Robin Gaby Fisher

More Than Chocolate

I arrived at Ground Zero as part of the Emergency Animal Rescue Services (EARS) team on September 19, a week and a day after the terrorist attacks. Although there were plenty of agencies providing food and drink to the rescue personnel, everyone was still mostly running on adrenaline. There was so much to do, so much chaos and wreckage—so much energy tied up in helping in any way it was possible.

The devastation at the WTC area was unimaginable. Over three hundred search-and-rescue canine teams had come from all over to help find survivors, and when it became obvious that there were precious few of those, the teams looked for bodies. Many of the human/dog teams weren't strictly search-and-rescue; if someone had a drug- or bomb-sniffing dog, they came, too. Everyone wanted to do *something*.

EARS helped at a triage area for the dogs working at the site. When a team came off a shift, they brought the dogs to us for cleaning and decontamination. There was a lot of asbestos in the omnipresent dust that covered the animals' fur. Plus the dogs had to trample through pools of foul and unsanitary water that collected as a result of the rain and the hose jets directed at the rubble to keep the dust out of the air.

After the dogs were clean, veterinarians did exams, paying particular attention to the dogs' eyes, noses and feet. Many of the dogs needed eye flushes because of the abrasive nature of the dust. Others had minor cuts on their feet that in that environment could have become easily infected.

One man, a police officer from Canada, had heard the news and decided to drive down immediately. He and his large German Shepherd, Ranger, had arrived on the 12th and, within hours, had begun that amazing duet called search-and-rescue work: the dog's instinct and intense concentration combined with the handler's keen attention and response to the dog's cues. Back and forth, over and over, the pair scoured the surface of enormous piles of broken concrete, twisted metal and shattered glass.

When the police officer's days off from his job at home were finished, he didn't want to leave what he felt was such important work in New York. He called his police station up in Canada and requested to take his vacation time. They refused his request.

"Then I quit," he told them and hung up.

When the people in his community heard about this situation, they immediately took up a collection to show their support of this man. The police station received so much flak over their unfortunate decision that they called the man and told him to stay as long as he liked; his job would be waiting.

It was late in the afternoon on the day I arrived in New York when Ranger and his handler came to our triage area. We scrubbed Ranger down and passed him over to the veterinary team. I noticed Ranger's handler sitting in a chair close by, staring straight ahead. He was a large man and looked like a combination of Arnold Schwarzenegger and Rambo—bald head and camouflage fatigues. The adrenaline had finally run out and the reality of the disaster around him was finally catching up with him. He had that look on his face I recognized from the over fifty disasters I've witnessed—a look that said, "I don't think I can do this much longer."

It was probably the first time the man had sat down in a very long time, and he didn't look at anyone or talk except to answer questions the veterinarians asked about his dog.

The doctor asked, "When was the last time your dog ate?"

The man answered, "Last night," in a voice as blank as his face.

Someone put some food in a bowl and placed it at Ranger's head. The big dog was lying on the pavement and, although he sniffed at the food once or twice, it seemed he was just too exhausted to eat.

I found a dog biscuit, squatted down near the dog, scooped up some of the gravy from the dog food in the bowl and offered it to Ranger. He lifted his head and slowly licked the liquid from the biscuit, so I dunked the biscuit in the bowl again, bringing up a little of the food with the gravy this time. Once more, he licked the food and gravy from the biscuit. I continued "spoon-feeding" Ranger while the triage workers and veterinarians looked on.

While I was feeding Ranger, I had the thought that someone should probably ask Ranger's handler the same question. After all, we were here to help people, too. When I finished, I turned to ask the man when he had eaten last, but before I could open my mouth, he looked directly at me and said, "Do you know how I get through this?"

I shook my head.

He reached his massive hand into his pocket and pulled

out a small plastic baggy with two chocolate kisses, two dog biscuits and a note inside.

I recognized it as one of the "care packages" children at the local school had made for the handlers and their dogs. What could be inside that had sustained the large and powerful man in front of me through this tremendously draining and demanding work? I knew from experience that it would take a lot more than chocolate.

He handed it to me, his eyes bright with tears. "Read it."

I took out the note, and unfolded it. There, written in a child's handwriting, were the words, "Thank you for helping to find people. I know Lassie would be so proud of you."

Terri Crisp
As told to Carol Kline

E-Mails from Manhattan

On this Earth, though far and near, without love, there's only fear.

Pearl S. Buck

September 11, 2001
A Tragic Day: The Walk Uptown

Probably more for my own sake than anything else, I wanted to try to describe this morning to you. My office is in the building of United Jewish Community and Jewish Education Service of North America, located at Fourteenth Street just a couple of subway stops before the World Trade Center. When I reached my stop at about 9:00 this morning, the first thing I heard was the announcement that there would be no connecting or continuing service: There was an emergency at the World Trade Center. Basically, get out. I walked up the subway stairs and smelled smoke but didn't know why. By the time I got upstairs, officials at UJC were already gathering everyone in the conference room. The room was not filled, despite the hundreds of people who generally work on the floor. Many had seen the planes crash and had never come upstairs. Others were stuck on the bridges, tunnels and subways, all of which had already been shut down. They advised us that the Consulate had not closed and that UJC was also not going to evacuate. Together, we saw the flames from our windows. We recited a couple of psalms. We heard the leaders speak. We knew that many of the people in the room had family and friends working in the World Trade Center. Within five minutes, we heard of the collapse of the second building. And then we heard that the Pentagon was struck. And finally, we heard that the Consulate had closed and we should leave the building.

But there wasn't really anywhere to go. Those who came in from outside of the city were stuck, and even those from within the city were without public transportation. Outside, the streets were filled with everyone from the surrounding buildings. Traffic was stopped. Smoke filled the air. And the sirens blared.

So I started walking, along with most of the other residents of Manhattan. During my four-mile walk, I noticed the different tones emerging from downtown to midtown and finally to uptown. The sea of people for the first mile might be indescribable. The mood was quiet, actually. Some people were speaking softly to each other, most were on their cell phones, and then they lined up at pay phones once the cells were no longer working. It seemed like most of the callers were telling family and friends that they were okay. My calls were to people who were not downtown—trying to find people calmer than me to tell me what to do next.

At midtown, people were gathered around stores and parked cars that had news radio shows playing loudly. The phone calls took on a different tone: People were searching for friends and family. From block to block I heard, "I don't know which building he works in," "I don't know if she

went to work today," "I can't find him." And still, "I don't
know where to go" and "I can't get home." It seemed to me
that people were walking more quickly past popular buildings, not wanting to be near a potential target. Amazing,
really, how quickly your mind-set can shift. I saw types of
emergency vehicles that I had never seen before. All of
them had sirens, and all the sirens blared.

Uptown, there were far fewer people. Anyone now on
pay phones was yelling at operators, trying to find loved
ones, able to get fewer and fewer dial tones. Mostly, the
people on the streets were parents picking up their kids
from schools that had decided to close for the day. The
conversations now were mothers trying to answer the
unanswerable questions of their young children. "Why
aren't I in school?" "Did people die?" "What happened?"
And even uptown, "Why are there so many sirens?"

I'm in my apartment, with my roommates, watching the
same news coverage as all of you. We have found most of
the people we were most worried about and probably
can't fathom the hundreds of people we should be worrying about—all of you, your friends and family, parents of
schoolchildren, spouses of coworkers, people who may
have been on those airplanes. We appreciate that so many
of you have called (or tried to call) here. I'll send this message as soon as I can, but our phone service is sporadic
and outgoing calls have been difficult. For those of you we
haven't been able to call back, know that we're okay—just
can't get a dial tone.

More than anything, I hope this message finds you safe
and that those closest to you are well.

Love,
Meredith

September 12, 2001
The Next Day

The news coverage is endless, and the stories are many, but writing to all of you is helping me to process and to stay connected to everyone.

The volunteer efforts of New Yorkers have been astounding. Red Cross centers have actually had to turn people away, asking them to come back later or tomorrow, pleading with them not to forget that in two weeks this will still be a tragedy that needs their attention.

My friends and I started walking towards Red Cross at 3:00 yesterday afternoon, not yet prepared to take public transportation (only buses were running). We picked up other friends along the way, teachers who had been in their classrooms all day and had only heard bits and pieces of what was going on. We told them to walk with us, and we'd talk on the way. We returned home five and one-half hours later, not having been able to give blood—they couldn't possibly process all of the donors that were lined up. We were quickly interviewed to become volunteers, and soon after we became experts in conducting that same interview process. As a social worker, I waited to hear where they wanted to send the mental health profession-als. Some were sent to the site of the towers to talk to res-cue workers, others were bussed to morgues, and still others were sent to shelters. My roommate got on a list to watch after kids whose parents had not yet been found.

I spent today at Channel 13 with about sixty other men-tal health providers, probably none of whom felt prepared for our task. The television had donated space and phones to allow the Red Cross to run a missing persons hotline. It looked like a telethon, reversed. The phones rang nonstop as we wrote down the names of the people called in as missing. Later, I switched roles and called families. I had to quickly squelch their optimism of hearing from a Red Cross volunteer and let them know that I had no new information. I needed more details from them. "Are you sure they were in their office?" "Do you know what they were wearing?" "Are there any distinguishing dental features . . . scars . . . tattoos?" And the responses: "He works on the 104th floor and wears a silver chain." "She has a tiny scar on her right cheek." "She was at Windows on the World." "He was working on the roof." "She's a single mother—please find her." Children screaming in the background. Parents crying. "How old is your fiancé?" ". . . your brother?" ". . . your daughter?" Twenty-six. Twenty-four. Thirty-one. "His wife is stuck in Paris. Can you get a government plane to get her home?" I can't do anything. You know more than I do. I haven't even seen the news today.

My last call was to a twenty-six-year-old woman who has a voice like me. She is missing her fiance, whom she described while she looked at his picture. She told me what he was wearing based on what she knew was not in his closet. "He only has one brown pair of shoes and they're not here," she told me almost laughing. "He was so handsome," she said. He worked on the 101st floor. She knew he was in his office. He brought his breakfast to work. That was my last call—I couldn't hear another story.

My roommate is volunteering the night shift tonight, delivering food and blankets to the rescue workers on site. They've been detained, though. Buildings are still falling.

I think it's important to tell the stories. These people have already died for nothing. Thank you for all of your messages. Everyone here is gathering together, taking care of each other in order to balance the difficulty of taking care of ourselves. We are grateful that we are all still here.

Love,
Meredith

September 13, 2001
The Best and Worst of Humanity

I left the phone hotline last night thinking that I was going to return this morning, or at least go back to the Red Cross to find out where they needed people today. By the end of last night, although day and night distinctions have become blurred with on-call volunteerism and night-long shifts, I recognized that I wouldn't be able to handle two consecutive days. I was comforted by the absolute certainty that there would not be a hole because of my absence—quite the opposite, people here are itching to volunteer. When turned away at 7:00 in the morning, they return at noon. If space is full at noon, they go back at 6, prepared to work through the night, knowing that the next shift will probably begin at midnight. For many, the opportunity to deliver bottles of saline solution or water, or to buy groceries for drop-off sites is what they need to feel like they are helping. We all feel helpless and need to find ways to fill the days. Nobody is looking to be a hero—everyone I know realizes when they need a break.

What can I say about Manhattan right now? The pace of the city has changed. Everyone is moving slowly, quietly, often with dazed looks on their faces. People sitting by themselves on buses spontaneously break into tears. More stores were open today, and friends were able to gather at Starbucks and restaurants, most of which had been closed for the previous day and a half. The only conversations are those of the tragedy. My roommate and I sat outside and told each other we could only talk about unrelated topics. We found ourselves sitting in silence, listening to the tales of those around us.

Most people I know sleep limited hours, keeping the television on, with friends at each other's apartments and the smell of smoke wafting through our buildings even on the Upper West Side. We remind each other to turn off the news, to take a break, to go outside, to eat. We keep track of where our friends are going, who they are with, when they'll be back. We have somehow managed to break down at different times, at one point offering support and at the next point getting the support. My extended circle of friends has been extraordinarily lucky. None of us are missing, nobody close to us is gone. Everyone knows someone with a story of having been late to work on Tuesday. It feels like everything here has turned into a shelter. People are sleeping on the field at Shea Stadium. Battery Park City, a neighborhood between Wall Street and the river that borders Manhattan, has been completely evacuated. We heard they were brought to New Jersey. We don't necessarily think we're in danger, but as New Yorkers the sirens that we once learned to ignore suddenly make us jump.

A flag hangs from the doorway of our building. On either side of my apartment (7C and 7E) we have representations of the best and the worst. On our left is the third grader whose class is making sandwiches for the rescue workers tomorrow. Their goal is to reach one thousand. But on our right, two women are missing their roommate. She worked on the 104th floor of Tower One.

Things are not going to return to any type of "normal" for quite some time, and we pray for even one more missing person to be found alive. As I was talking to someone about tonight, each of us is dealing with this in our own way, and we each have our own way of thinking about the events of this week. My messages to you are just one person's perspective, and I thank you for allowing me to process it in this form.

Best wishes for a peaceful New Year and a Shabbat Shalom.

Love,
Meredith

October 12, 2001
A Memorial

Last night I went to a commemorative memorial which, upholding the Jewish tradition of *shloshim,* marked thirty days since the attack on the World Trade Center. About seven hundred people gathered at this particular memorial on the Upper West Side, a service that brought together rabbis from Reconstructionist, Reform, Conservative and Orthodox synagogues, and united all of my friends and neighbors, who are usually spread out over the plethora of *shuls* that the West Side has to offer. For more than two hours, the rabbis and community leaders spoke, offered prayers, eulogized their lost congregants and paid tribute to the heroes of September 11, the ideals of America and the strong spirit of New Yorkers.

As I sat there wondering how much more the American psyche can withstand, I was struck by an intense challenge we are facing: the constant tug of opposites.

In my first e-mail to all of you, I wrote of the blaring sirens I heard throughout the walk from downtown to uptown. I couldn't help but think of them again last night—this time not because of the noise, but because of the piercing silence in the room. Each rabbi spoke and sat down, and in between each there was nothing but silence. Several things were palpable: the tears falling down almost everyone's cheeks, people looking around the packed room toward their friends for comfort, relief of seeing acquaintances we never thought to worry about, the solemn prayers of the rabbis, the touching words of community leaders and the silence. And then we heard from a firefighter, who wanted this job ever since he was a little boy. He lost two of his closest friends one month ago, and after he spoke about them and the people who do this every day, he said sweetly, "Next time you see a fire truck, smile and wave, and say a prayer." All of a sudden, our silence became a thunderous applause and a standing ovation. The contrast was startling, overpowering, remarkable.

Two days ago we celebrated Simchas Torah. Usually on that night we get to feel like we've taken over the city. The police close off about twelve blocks of West End Avenue, we dance in the streets, we run into just about everyone we've ever met. A couple of weeks ago we were told that there would be no outdoor celebration, so we coordinated with our closest friends and decided which synagogues and apartment parties we would meet up at. We didn't compromise our spirit for this night that comes once a year. We put aside our sadness, ignored our emotions, took a break from our World Trade Center conversations, and, well, drank until we were free to dance and smile and laugh and remember what our New York lives were like until a month ago. Two days later, just as quickly as we had created that mood for Simchas Torah, we found ourselves back in the midst of memorials, missing persons posters, vigils, banners, flags and the eerie calm of the city that used to be anything but.

We promise that we are moving on with our lives—that things are getting back to normal—and we know that neither is true. We feel the tug of opposing forces, of mutually exclusive emotions, of our strong ability for, and our strong resistance to, compartmentalizing our experiences. It's a strange new way to live, but I guess all over the country we each look for the good and attempt to strike our own balance.

Shabbat Shalom.

Meredith Englander

Prayer Flags

They were everywhere in my downtown New York neighborhood: countless flyers announcing those missing after the September 11 attack. Like many of my neighbors, I spent much time in silent and sympathetic contemplation of these heartrending pieces of paper. There were pictures of people just like me and my friends, cradling their newborns or standing proudly on their wedding day. Written on them were desperate and loving words penned in moments of almost unimaginable anguish by people whose husbands, wives or parents had simply not come home—or, maybe worse, who had called and said they were getting out and coming home but never did. The flyers reminded me of Tibetan prayer flags, flapping in the warm breeze. [Prayer flags (also called "wind horses") are common in Tibetan Buddhism. Their purpose is to purify the air with the prayerful words written on them.] It was all almost too much to bear. And yet we, the neighbors and friends of these people, felt duty-bound to bear witness, to pay respect, to send love and light.

As I stood there, a simple and haunting melody came into my head, and the words I was reading practically flew off the page and rearranged themselves in stanzas in my mind. The next day I took off from work, booked an afternoon in the studio and recorded this song live.

Although "Prayer Flags" is a very sad song, I like to think of it as a healing song, and one that is very respectful to the people who helped it come to be—and to whom it is dedicated:

Prayer Flags

have you seen him
have you seen him
brown hair blue eyes 5 foot 10
have you seen her
here's her picture
she's my wife
she's my best friend

have you seen her
have you seen him
he's got a mole on his left hand
if you've seen him
here's my number
please call as soon as you can

have you seen him
have you seen her
she's wearing a yellow dress
a tattoo on her right shoulder
says baby I am the best

have you seen her
have you seen him
he's wearing a wedding band

and the words on the inscription:
may 12, 2000, forever, ann

have you seen him
have you seen her
he was on the 100th floor
she's my mother
he's my brother
she called me at 9:04
from the stairway
from the hallway
from her cell phone
from the roof
if you've seen him
won't you tell her
please
we love her so

have you seen them
have you seen them
walking in the by-and-by
from the rubble
through all the trouble
into the beautiful blue sky

Marc Farre

One mile from Ground Zero, the flyers that inspired "Prayer Flags."

New York Cabbies

New York cabdrivers are legendary. Countless jokes have been made at their expense about the way they zip through traffic, narrowly missing other cars and fixed objects, coming within inches of any pedestrian foolish enough to think he can make it on a flashing "don't walk" sign. And anyone who has ever been a passenger knows that wrenching feeling of speeding up to go one short block then stopping short to avoid a car stopped ahead. Somehow, cabbies never seem able to remember the adage that you can only go as fast as the guy in front of you. And no New Yorker is ever surprised when a cabbie leans his head out the window of his taxi and offers some important comment on another's driving ability or indeed on his personal attributes or lineage!

But three months after September 11, when I spent a week in New York City, the cab rides I took were slow, the cabbies quiet, subdued. I asked a few of them where they were and what they did on September 11. One driver didn't want to talk about it; then he did. In fact, he had so much to say that when we reached my destination, he put up the meter and I just sat there listening.

"Traffic came to a complete stop that day. No busses or cabs or cars could go anywhere. Which is just as well because it was a hell and no one knew where to go to be safe. I was at midtown, stopped in traffic, and I had a fare when the first plane hit. We heard it first, then saw it. Both of us thought it was an accident. Who knew . . . ?

"But then the second plane hit. I dropped my fare and got out of my cab. By then there were so many sirens and emergency vehicles headed south, you couldn't move. So, like everybody else, I watched from the sidewalk. Then . . . then they started to come down! It had been a beautiful sunny day but the air changed in a minute. Suddenly it was black and gray and you couldn't breathe. I turned my cab around to head north. People banged on my window. I told them to get in and we just drove away from it. I don't remember where I left them off.

"Someone flagged me down—stood right in front of my cab. He flashed an ID. He was a doctor and he wanted me to take him to NYU Med center. I did. There was a line of cabs at the hospital. The police wouldn't let us leave. So we all went in and gave blood. Later, the only vehicles allowed out were ambulances. I said, 'I'm a good driver. Let me help.' They put me on an ambulance with another driver. We started taking supplies down to NYU Medical Center downtown.

"Later that day, I got my cab and drove around. There were people all over, just walking dazed and crying. I couldn't do anything for them except give them a ride so I did. Many of them were going from hospital to hospital trying to find a family member who had worked in the WTC. I took one group—a father, mother and two sisters—to five different hospitals. At the last place, I left them because there was someone who fit the description of their loved one. I never found out if it was him. . . ."

I tried to take notes the whole time the man was talking

but I couldn't write fast enough. So I just listened. I know I got the whole story. It wasn't one I could forget.

Another cabbie told me how he spent his time trying to take people home. "They were walking, walking any-where—across bridges, in the middle of the streets. People were leaning on each other. I stopped and took an elderly man and the person he was leaning on to the Upper East Side. They looked like walking dead. . . . We picked up some others along the way. One lady said she had to stop to tell her son that she was okay. Her phone wouldn't work so we stopped at his office around Fiftieth Street. He was outside, just staring south. When he saw his mother, he started crying. The lady decided to stay with him. So I looked for some more people to take."

I had heard that in the hours and days that followed, New York came to a standstill. There was no public trans-portation available for days. But every one of the cab drivers I spoke with was busy in those hours—taking people home, carrying medical supplies, and transporting emergency personnel. Whatever any of these able-bodied people could do with or without their cabs, they did. They found ways to help. Of course I didn't have to ask if they ever let the meter run during any of those trips. They would have been insulted if I had.

The cabdrivers of New York City are a microcosm of society. They are black, white, Indian, Muslim, Hispanic—every race, creed and color imaginable. They go about their day like most people, earning a living, getting the job done. For the most part, they are ordinary people. And ordinary people find ways to do extraordinary things when called upon. A lot of people did a lot to help others that day. They used what skills they possessed to save lives, give hope, help others. Those skills included being able to perform emergency surgery and being able to drive a cab. Each was needed and important in the aftermath of the horror of September 11.

It's absolutely true what they say about New York cab-drivers—they are legendary.

Marsha Arons

Anxiously Awaiting

There are only two ways to live your life.
One is as though nothing is a miracle.
The other is as if everything is.

Albert Einstein

As usual, I was dozing on the bus on my way to work on Tuesday, September 11, 2001, when I heard someone say, "My God, look at the World Trade Center!"

We were still in New Jersey. I looked in the direction of the Twin Towers and saw smoke pouring out of all the windows of the upper quarter of the North Tower. Someone else on the bus was listening to a Walkman and said a plane had crashed into the World Trade Center. I asked if they said which tower it was, and he said he thought they said it was Tower Two. Tower Two was not visible from the angle we were looking, so I knew he must be mistaken.

I said, "My husband works in the World Trade Center. I know that is Tower One. Of all the days to forget my cell phone."

I was in a state of shock. I don't know how long I sat staring, but I turned to the woman next to me and asked if she had a cell phone I could borrow. She smiled and said she had just asked if I would like to use hers, but I did not hear her. She was kind enough to dial my husband's number and hand me the phone. All I heard was a recording that all circuits were busy. I handed her back the phone and started to pray: "Dear God, please keep him safe."

I did not realize it, but she had continued to try to reach my husband by hitting the redial button. She finally got through and handed me back the phone saying she had my husband's voicemail. I don't remember what I said, but I left a message and handed her back the phone.

By this time we were in the Lincoln Tunnel, and all I could think of was getting to my office and checking my voicemail and e-mail for a message from my husband. As soon as we got out of the tunnel, I got off the bus with well wishes from everyone on the bus saying they would pray for us.

Running to the bus stop to catch the cross-town bus, I saw people's mouths moving, but I could hear no sound. All I could think of was getting to my desk and hearing a message from my husband.

As I arrived at the Chrysler Building, I walked through the lobby and could hear the guards saying, "We are evacuating." I kept walking as fast as I could, afraid I would be stopped from going up to my office. I reached an empty elevator and got in, praying the door would close. One of my coworkers, Verne, got on and said, "Did you hear about what's going on at the World Trade Center?" I broke down and said through tears, "My husband works there." I did not hear his words but felt his support as he put an arm around me for comfort.

We arrived on the sixteenth floor, and I heard my boss from his office saying, "Rosemarie, have you heard from your husband?"

I said I had not and ran to check my messages. Jeff asked if my husband had a cell phone or a beeper. I told him Eddie did not have the cell phone with him.

There were no voicemail messages from Eddie.

The first person to call was my sister, Carmel. She was in tears as she asked if I had heard from him. I told her I had not. We were both on the verge of hysteria. She said she was fine. (She worked one block from the World Trade Center.) She also told me my niece, Sharon, was fine. (She worked in the South Tower.)

My other sister, Mary Lou, called also inquiring about Eddie. I again said there was no word from him. She hung up asking me to call as soon as I heard.

I turned on my computer and scrolled through my e-mail messages hoping to see my husband's name. No e-mail messages either.

I spotted an e-mail message from my youngest daughter, Jillian. She and my second daughter, Jessica, attend the University of Scranton in Pennsylvania. It said, "Please e-mail back as soon as you get this and let me know what is going on with the World Trade Center. I tried calling you and Daddy, but I can't get through. I need to know if Daddy is okay. Please get back to me as soon as you can." I called her and told her I did not know anything yet.

Everyone in the office was very supportive and concerned. My boss asked the secretary next to me if she would answer my phone if I was away from my desk. She agreed and offered me a cup of coffee. My supervisor came to my desk and asked if she could do anything to help.

The fire alarm went off, and they announced on the PA system that they were evacuating the building. My mind was in turmoil. I did not want to leave. I did not know where to go or what to do. My boss started telling me what to do, and I responded like a robot. I felt like I was watching what was happening from outside my body. Jeff instructed me to change my voicemail message to say that I was not in the office due to the incident at the World Trade Center and to tell my husband, if it was him calling, that I would be at my mother's, to give my mother's phone number, and as an alternative, to contact my boss on his cell phone and give his number.

At that point my other daughter called, and I told her I had not heard from Daddy and that I was going to my mother's because we had to evacuate the building. I told her I would call her when I got to my mother's. We all just kept praying.

The phone rang again. I picked it up. I heard a voice on the other end say, "Hi, Ro. It's me."

Eddie was sitting in a conference room, facing a window near his office on the seventy-fourth floor of the North Tower when he heard the plane crash into the building above him and felt the building move about a foot. He saw flaming debris falling and smelled the jet fuel. He went to the nearest emergency exit and started down the stairs. He met one of his coworkers, and they stayed together. He said everyone was very orderly and acted in a calm manner. They stayed to the right of the stairs, allowing the injured people to go down past them. When they were approximately halfway down, they met firemen coming up. The firemen assured everyone that it was safe down below and to remain calm and to continue going down to safety. He was still in the stairwell on the way down when someone with a radio said a second plane had hit Tower Two. That's when he realized it was an attack and not an accident.

When my husband reached the Plaza Level, he was not able to exit because of the flaming debris falling outside. He proceeded down the steps to the Concourse Level and walked through several inches of water, which was coming from the sprinkler system, and was finally able to exit the building. He walked to the subway station and got on a train going uptown. He was probably on the last train to ever leave from there. He did not stop to make a phone call until he was in Grand Central Station.

When I heard his voice, I went completely weak. "Eddie, where are you?"

He said, "In Grand Central Station." I could not believe my ears. He was right across the street.

I said, "Thank God!" He said he was coming to my office.

As I hung up the phone, it rang again. It was my second daughter, Jessica, again. She told me not to go to my mother's because she had heard the first tower collapsed, and my mother lives about ten or fifteen blocks from the World Trade Center and is in direct line with them. I did not give her a chance to finish. I said, "Daddy is okay, and he is on his way to my office." I also told her I did not know what we were doing, but I had to evacuate the building and would call her later. I told her to tell my other daughter. I quickly called both my sisters to let them know Eddie was okay, and I was going to meet him downstairs.

When I got downstairs, I saw him standing in front of the building. I just hugged and kissed him and could not believe how fortunate we were. I was so grateful he acted as he did. Even though it seemed like an eternity, this all took place within a little more than an hour.

We decided to go to my cousin's apartment about four blocks away. Since the bridges and tunnels had closed, we would not be able to get a bus home. When we arrived there, we again called my sister and my daughters to let them know where we were. My husband told my youngest daughter to e-mail our oldest daughter, Judie, who is in medical school in the Caribbean. We later learned she had heard of the attack and was frantically trying to contact us.

My story has a happy ending. We pray all the time now for those who were not as fortunate, for those who did not make it and for their families. They are now in heaven— the only place greater than the United States of America.

Rosemarie Kwolek

A Day in D.C.

We all have big changes in our lives that are more or less a second chance.

Harrison Ford

"Don't go, Mom," my ten-year-old daughter pleads while she watches me pack my bag for Washington, D.C. "I've got a bad *feeling* about this." I have to go, I try to explain, I have an important meeting on Tuesday, September 11.

At the airport, I walk into the jetway to board the American Airlines plane and glance back. My nearly teenage son waits to leave the gate. I give him a reassuring look—the kind that says everything will be all right—and take a deep breath. I, too, am having second thoughts.

As my flight approaches Reagan National Airport, I am in awe by the sight of our majestic national monuments piercing the darkness of the warm night in a bath of glorious light. This is my first trip to our nation's capital—my first business trip for an editorial position that I have had merely five months.

Early Tuesday morning, September 11, I find myself in the House office buildings participating in my employer's lobbying effort. As we ride the elevator, a legislative aide says that a plane has hit the World Trade Center and there is a "big hole in the side of the building." Although I question for details, he only knows this. I make a mental note to watch the evening news.

By 9:20 that morning, a coworker and I are walking toward the Senate office buildings for my scheduled meeting with the senator. We hear a noise that makes us look at each other and ask, "What was that?" We glance around. No one seems concerned, so we walk on toward Capitol Hill.

Near the Capitol, we stop to take photographs and watch a senator give a press conference. Our diversion is interrupted by the frantic screams of a woman, desperately calling out a name. My first thought was that she had lost a child. Trouble seems to be stirring—something is wrong.

We step closer to the Capitol and listen to a man in a military uniform give a press interview. We are shocked to hear him say that the Pentagon is on fire as he gestures in the direction of a dark tongue of smoke in the near distance.

Then a woman runs by crying uncontrollably—with a cell phone to her ear and a hand over her mouth. In the chaos, I look in every direction—trying to figure out what is happening. Reporters and cameramen are sprinting out of the Capitol, and they keep running. Then we hear shouts again—this time from security guards and police officers.

"Run!" the guards command with exaggerated arm motions pointing away from the Capitol. "Run!"

People scramble, scanning the sky for an unseen danger. A stranger tells us that it was a plane that hit the Pentagon, that a low-flying aircraft was in the area and they think that the Capitol might be a potential target.

We run. We are not positive from what, but clearly know that we are in the wrong place. My heart thumps in my chest, and I wish this wasn't happening.

The world around me is surreal. My thoughts swirl from the illogical—wondering if this means my appointment with the senator was off—to horrific visions of foreign airplanes dive-bombing our nation's monuments. In the numbing confusion, my mind fills in its own answers—answers straight out of wartime movies. I struggle to fight back visions of the entire city being leveled.

Many blocks away, the crowds slow to a walk and people look around. I notice two uniformed guards, who seem like the right people to ask just what on earth is going on. They tell us the Twin Towers in New York City were "hit," the Pentagon was "hit," and they had heard that the White House Old Executive Office Building was "hit" as well. I gasp. We were just at that part of the White House! (Later that day, I would learn the information about the White House was, of course, incorrect.)

Then the guards tell us the horrific news, that those planes that crashed in New York City and D.C. were hijacked American commercial airliners, filled with passengers. *Unbelievable.* I pause for a moment, slowly realizing that the smoke I saw coming from the Pentagon was wreckage where many innocent people just died. I say a silent prayer.

This was beyond belief. I wonder if the entire nation is under full attack. I begin to think that I just may not make it out of this city alive and grab my cell phone to call my husband. The call doesn't go through. I then try to call other coworkers in D.C. No use—none of the cell phones seem to be working. I ask myself: *All this for a job?*

I continuously hit the redial button on my cell phone and clearly understand why people in dangerous situations call home. The feeling is overwhelming to communicate one last message—to let your loved ones know you're fine . . . or not fine. I want to tell someone what is happening and how much I hate being where I am now. I want to tell my kids that I am sorry for not heeding their warning not to go. Then I wonder if those airliner passengers tried to call home too.

We begin to walk, following the crowds, but to where we don't know. Police officers are directing traffic. We walk by a senator who had gathered together what appeared to be his office staff. We stop for a moment to see if we can glean any more information, then walk on.

At a traffic light, my coworker recognizes a congressman who has rolled down his vehicle window and is talking with people—telling them the latest information as he knew it. My coworker urges me to take his photograph and I suddenly remember—I am a journalist. For a brief second, I wonder if I should head back into the action for "a story." Images of my family fill my mind, and I immediately know that I am not a hard-core reporter.

The streets are crowded with honking cars, and sirens blare everywhere. I begin to cross, and my coworker yanks on my arm as a car speeds recklessly around the corner. The irony—would I survive this morning, only to be hit by a car?

Yet the people in the streets were surprisingly calm and orderly—following the police officers' directions. My coworker and I head back to our hotel and regroup with the others.

The first thing nearly everyone does is phone home—to get word out that we are all right. I felt desperate to have my children know that their mother is alive, and I need assurance that they, too, are okay.

Crowds gather around any available television to watch the horrific events unfold before our eyes and to comfort one another.

I go to the lounge and find it full of people, their eyes glued to the television. I am asked if I'd like a glass of wine. No, I reply, I need something a little stronger today—the news report had just flashed a list of commercial aircraft unaccounted for. We feel like "sitting ducks." We wonder what this might be the beginning of—or what might come next. Our hotel is in the same building as the Federal Emergency Management Agency and other federal office buildings surround us. I want out of there.

As the afternoon drags on, I cannot sit idly in my hotel room. I walk, observe people playing cards in the lobby, and make my way to the rooftop pool to look around the city. Several people are swimming, as if it were a normal day. A plane flies over and people cringe. "It's just our fighter jets," a man loudly calls out to the group on the roof.

On the street corner, a family with packed suitcases holds a sign with their anticipated destination—desperately trying to find a way out of town. Several groups with their buses readily available are boarding and leaving town.

Back at the hotel room, my coworker arranges for our own quick departure via Amtrak. There is no way either of us will get back on an airplane any time soon—especially on the East Coast. I wonder how this day has changed the world in which we live.

I don't sleep that night. At 1:00 the next morning, six of us pile into a taxi that takes us to Union Station to catch the 3:00 A.M. train home. The sooner we leave D.C. the better.

Many long hours later, the train pulls into the midwestern farm town where my family awaits me. I am back home. I step off the train, grab my children and hug them . . . as if I have been given a second chance. Yes, it is going to be all right.

Maria Miller Gordon

Last Call

As smoke and heat diminished from the mangled steel
  and glass,
The hope of rescue workers faded in and out so fast.
These heroes of our nation working tirelessly to find
A sound, a breath, some proof of life, to keep that hope
  alive.

The victims were so innocent, just doing their life's work,
In a nation called America, the most free on this Earth.
Suddenly, a worker finds a cell phone flashing red.
He plays the "last call" message, and this is what it said:

"Hello, it's me. I'm calling to tell you I'm all right.
I've made it up to heaven; I tried to call last night.
The group that I arrived with is strong and brave and tall,
And proud to be Americans while answering God's call.

"I love you all and know I've been in all your thoughts and
  prayers.
You need to know I felt no pain and safely made it here.
Now let me say a prayer for you of closure and of life,
Move on with courage and with faith that we will reunite.

"I know it's sad; I'll age no more, but in this you can trust:
My dreams were put back on the Earth in particles of dust.
That dust is in the air you breathe; I've passed it on to you.
So please breathe deeply every day and make my dreams
   come true."

Dave Timmons
Submitted by Tom Lagana

The Vigil

In the darkest hours of the night, Judith Kaplan, dressed in her Sabbath finery, sat in a tent outside the New York City medical examiner's office, singing the haunting repertoire form the Book of Psalms. From midnight until 5 A.M., within sight of trucks full of body parts from the Word Trade Center, she fulfilled the most selfless of Jewish commandments: to keep watch over the dead, who must not be left alone from the moment of passing until burial.

Normally, this orthodox ritual, known as sitting *shmira*, lasts for only twenty-four hours, and is performed by one Jew, customarily a man, for another Jew. But these are not normal times. Thus, the round-the-clock vigil outside the morgue on First Avenue and Thirtieth Street is already in its eighth week. The three sealed trucks may or may not contain Jewish bodies. And the *shomer*, or watcher, is just as often a young woman as an old man.

Ms. Kaplan, twenty, a senior at Stern College for Women (a division of Yeshiva University), is one of nine students who has volunteered for this solemn task on weekends, working in shifts from Friday afternoons until nightfall on Saturdays, the holiest part of the week. The rest of the time, the task is performed by scores of volunteers from an

Orthodox synagogue, Ohab Zedek, on West Ninety-Fifth Street.

Devout Jews cannot ride on the Sabbath, putting the subway or taxis off-limits for the long trek from Ohab Zedek to the morgue. So, the Stern students, whose dormitories are within blocks of the morgue, have filled the breach. They were recruited by Jessica Russak, twenty, a student who takes the dawn shift, peeking out of the tent as the sky brightens to time her morning prayers.

Ms. Russak, Ms. Kaplan, and others have won blessings from Christian chaplains at the site, and their dedication has moved police officers and medical examiners to tears. The burly state trooper who guards the area has learned the girls' names, and a bit about their religion.

At first, the trooper demanded identification, not knowing that carrying anything on the Sabbath was prohibited for Orthodox Jews. Now, he keeps an eye on the prayer books and snacks that the Stern students drop off before sundown on Friday and retrieve Saturday night. The trooper once called Ms. Russak at home when she was a few minutes late, in case her alarm clock had not gone off.

The young women have the full support of Dr. Norman Lamm, prescient of Yeshiva University, who agreed without hesitation that the normal gender rules—women can sit *shmira* only for other women, while men can sit for any deceased person—could be waived under the circumstances. The school is also providing security guards to escort those who sit the late-night shifts.

While the tradition is a peculiarly Jewish one, Dr. Lamm said he felt that the *mitzvah,* or good deed, reached across denominations. "The idea that you can have companionship even in death is a very consoling thought, whether you are Jewish or not," he said. Dr. Lamm called "the loving watching of the corpse a very human act," and noted that the *shmira* is "the truest and most sublime" of the 613 *mitzvahs* "because there can never be reciprocity."

But there are other rewards, which the Stern students discussed on Friday, at Mr. Kaplan's apartment, while preparing their Sabbath dinner—four different kinds of kugel, pepper steak and honey-glazed chicken.

All of them had felt so helpless after the terrorist attacks. They donated money to the Red Cross, but were turned away as blood donors or volunteers because those needs had quickly been met. Then came the pleas for Sabbath *shomers.* "This is something I can do," Ms. Kaplan said. "And it's surreal. You absolutely feel the souls there, and you feel them feeling better."

Each volunteer said she had begun with fears about sitting within sight of the trucks full of remains. Instead, they said, they have found peace and a kind of joy.

Ms. Russak does not sing the psalms as Ms. Kaplan does, but rather mutters them, in whatever order moves her, often starting with Psalm 130, which she knows by heart. The effect is meditative. "The meter and the rhythm one after the next after the next, it calms you," Ms. Russak said. "That's the magic of the psalms. They put you in the right place."

Ms. Kaplan made up slow, sad tunes for each psalm and sings them in a clear soprano, sweet as birdsong. If she mumbled them, without melody, Ms. Kaplan said, she might lose a word here and there and thus the full meaning of each line. By singing, she said, she is fully mindful.

"Time completely stops," she said. "Now I understand what it is to pray with your heart."

Two weeks ago, during their regular four-hour shift, Ms. Kaplan sang 128 of the 150 psalms and grudgingly gave up her place to Ms. Russak at 4 A.M., begging her to finish the cycle. Last week, determined to do the full canon on her own, Ms. Kaplan pleaded and won an extra hour.

"It's very completing for her," Ms. Russak said. "Like finishing an entire book of the Torah."

But before Ms. Kaplan's middle-of-the-night vigil on the brown leather benches in the tent, others had taken their turns, among them Anat Barber, the newest recruit, who was full of nervous questions. "The bodies there, do they know who they are?" Ms. Barber asked, as Ms. Russak escorted her to the site of the first time.

Ms. Russak did her best to be reassuring, telling Ms. Barber that she would be fine, that "the irony is that it feels too easy." Outside the tent, the last of the men, a volunteer from Ohab Zedek, was rushing toward his Sabbath observance in Brooklyn. It was time for the women to begin their watch, to fill the night with poetry and prayer.

Jane Gross

A Picture and a Friendship

Tim Sherman spotted the photograph near the end of his first day of digging, the Friday after that Tuesday. The time of day, he recalls, was "after dark." He had been on the move since dawn. A gang from his job at the Middlesex Water Company had come to New York to help, with strong backs and water main know-how and willing spirits. In a way, there was nothing to do.

Around them, smoke heaved from shapes no human hand could form. However many tons of stuff were on the ground, the landscape fell heavier and longer on the eye. *There is no God,* he remembers thinking.

The Middlesex crew grabbed hand tools and faced the wreckage at Liberty Plaza. Digging. Bucketing. Whatever needed to be done.

Late that day, he raked a pile of ash, then saw the picture. Frozen in time and in eight-by-ten inches of vibrant colors, three cute kids stared at him from the ground: one boy just old enough for braces, another boy a few years younger and a toddler sister.

The picture was sopping. He stuck it on a wall to dry, but it slid off. "If you put it back up there, it'll just fall again and get lost," a coworker told Mr. Sherman, so he stashed it away. "This could be the last thing a mother or father saw before they died," Mr. Sherman would say.

Over the next two weeks or so, the fraternity of hard work, warm meals and caring people changed Mr. Sherman's opinion about God. Back in New Jersey, his hometown paper, the *Home News Tribune,* ran an article about the water company crews helping out. The paper also published the picture Tim Sherman had saved.

All day after Brian Conroy saw the salvaged picture in the newspaper, he had a hard time concentrating on his job, managing a sales territory for Arnold Bread and Thomas's English Muffins. He knew those faces—knew the kids. Those were George Tabeek's children, and George worked at the Trade Center for the Port Authority.

Years ago, a decade or more, Mr. Tabeek owned a piece of a restaurant in Edison. Mr. Conroy tended bar there once a week. The Tabeek boys would visit their dad while he was watching the register. At closing time, the two men would share a pizza and news about his children. They were good friends, but work friends, so when the restaurant closed, they went about their lives.

Photo reprinted by permission of George Tabeek

Mr. Conroy recalled that the Tabeeks lived in Brooklyn, and he found two listings for them. On one call, an answering machine picked up. Mr. Conroy put the phone down. At the second number, a woman said hello.

"Yes, this is the Tabeek household."

Mr. Conroy explained who he was, but fumbled trying to state his business. He cannot say if his heart was pounding or had simply stopped.

The woman finally figured

out whom Mr. Conroy was talking about.

"Oh," she said. "Oh. George. He's right here. Do you want to speak to him?"

Mr. Conroy fell silent. The little hairs rose along his arms.

About ten years ago, George Tabeek took his children to the Sears where his sister worked the photography department and had the children sit for a portrait. Dana would have been about three; Steven, eleven; and young Georgie, fourteen.

The picture of the children followed him as he moved through jobs at the Port Authority, as Georgie became a New York City police officer, as Steven went to St. John's University and as Dana started high school at Bishop Kearney.

Mounted in a gold frame, the portrait sat on the edge of his credenza, in his office on the thirty-fifth floor of 2 World Trade Center. Mr. Tabeek, an engineer, was one of the people with the keys to everything. When he looked out the window across the plaza to the great spread of New York, in the corner of his view was an eight-by-ten picture of his children.

That awful morning, he had the good luck to be stopping for a doughnut in the plaza when the first plane hit. He then tested that fortune, running up twenty-two floors with firefighters to rescue people. He was inches from a fireman, Lt. Andrew Desperito, when the second building fell and took Lieutenant Desperito.

He told all this to Brian Conroy, the old friend he had shared pizza with in the life before. Mr. Conroy then told him about Tim Sherman the water worker and the wet picture he had found buried in the ash.

For the first time in weeks, Mr. Tabeek said that yesterday, he thought about the picture that sat in the corner of his window view, the small piece of his remembered sky.

Jim Dwyer

Memento

"I want to buy something in New York," my friend David says, as we drive through the Lincoln Tunnel to our favorite place on earth. "You know, take something away, a memento." This is our first trip to Manhattan since September 11.

We park where I used to live, on Thomson Street and shop at the first place we see.

"How about this?" I say, holding up a trinket.

"No, it just doesn't feel right," he answers.

He buys some T-shirts for his kids, I give in to my favorite jewelry vendor, but his special memento is not found.

We walk toward Ground Zero, soon realizing that the hundred copies of "Dust," a piece he wrote to share with rescue workers, is still in the car, which is now in the bowels of a parking garage.

As we near the site, there is uncharacteristic silence and no traffic, except for the occasional shriek of an emergency vehicle. Police stand at barricades looking exhausted and sad. Residents of the attacked area straggle out from the empty blocks dragging suitcases, carrying stuffed animals, wearing devastated expressions.

We stroll in silence, then stop for a drink in a corner pub and sit like we are part of a window display, watching people, talking, the lights of Ground Zero glowing in the distance.

"I didn't get my memento," he says with sadness.

On our final journey of the day, we pass the parking garage and see our car, front row center. The folder holding his piece, Dust, beckons us from the back window. We collect his thoughts, his feelings, his words, and take them with us to hand out as we pay tribute at Washington Square Park.

We stick some under candles; wax sealing them to the ground, blurring the ink. We hand them to strangers who share stories of loved ones lost in terrorist attacks years before. We give one to a solemn state trooper from Syracuse, New York, and stand silent, listening to him tell stories of what the loss of the last two weeks means to him. We give one to a teacher from the Bronx and help him hang a long banner done by eighth graders who watched the towers burning from their school windows across the river. His friend helps us seal one to hang on the chain-link gravestone. We slip one into the crippled hands of a woman, sitting in her wheelchair in the dark, listening to the music of mourners. We give them to the police, and to gay men walking arm in arm, and to newlyweds, and to huge neckless bouncers at clubs. As we leave the city we pass them through the windows to homeless and confused and forlorn faces curbside. We hand out his words-on-paper and hugs and support until we are too exhausted to go on.

Riding home we tell shared stories and recall the faces, the touches. He expresses despair, then resignation over not getting a memento to mark the day. He didn't buy a shirt, or a picture for the wall, or a ring to wear, but he has his memento.

You will hear it in the stories he writes. You will see it when he looks at a child. You will feel it in his touch. His memento won't wear out, or fade, or tarnish. He will wear it, hanging heavy in his heart, polished and ready to share.

Mary Sue Mooney

Dust

A few Fridays back I was in the car listening to the radio. A member of the scientific community, when asked what constitutes the dust we find on our tabletops and under our beds, responded with an answer that has been swirling in my mind. "Bits of everything." he said, "fragments of tree trunks and manmade objects, even dinosaur bones. Anything might be in that dust, from the beginning of time."

I've been thinking about this when I dust or see the tiny particles float through a ray of light coming in my kitchen window. The entire history of the universe is under my bed. The thought made me smile, until last week. To my horror, I watched the Twin Towers turn to dust across my television screen. Floor by floor they collapsed onto each other after two jets and their thousands of gallons of fuel ignited the catastrophe. There were flames and screams and falling debris and sirens and clouds and clouds of dust. People ran up the avenues and down the streets being chased by mountains of billowing dark dust. It rushed into open windows and around corners, down stairwells and into subways. It snuck into pockets and clung to shoulders and the linings of nasal passages. It balanced on electric wires and spiraled up into the wind, which carried it away.

Under my bed, and yours, within the collage of time

is a new ingredient. I don't mind the dinosaur bones. They were over and done long ago. I have no fear of Tyrannosaurus Rex jumping out from a dark corner when my back is turned. But this new dust is different. It holds the paperwork and electronics of a financial capital, tons of steel and glass, copper wire and concrete, infinitesimal shreds of thousands of lives and the potent, microscopic seed of hate.

The dust lays heavy these days. It covers up patterns and bright colors. It clouds the vision. So much is in the air. I blink it away with tears that keep coming and coming again. If ever there was a time to see clearly, it is now. Next to my bed, on my knees, in absolute stillness, it came to me. Dust needs to settle before it can be swept.

David C. Page

2

AMERICA RESPONDS

*I cannot do all the good that the world needs,
but the world needs all the good that I can do.*

Jana Stanfield

THE FAMILY CIRCUS   By Bil Keane

"When I grow up I wanna be a
SUPERHERO—a fireman or a policeman."

Reprinted with permission of Bil Keane.

A Night at Ground Zero

We were stunned and confused after the attacks. We were not, however, shaken. Rather, the best of us donned hard hats and workman's gloves and face masks to deal with this horror as decent, civilized human beings. And the rest of us supported them, applauded them and prayed for and with them.

Cardinal Edward M. Egan

After hearing the reports on television that no one could get down to the epicenter of this tragedy, I basically had reserved a spot on the couch for my third night in a row of watching and waiting, wishing I could "do more."

Randomly, one reporter invited some teenager on the air to say what supplies were needed down at the scene, and the boy said, "The firefighters need coffee." So I looked at my friend who was similarly camped on the couch next to me, and we both said, "We can get coffee."

One can of coffee became four cans . . . and three pizza pies and gallon jugs of water, which we shepherded into a taxi to head down to Chelsea Piers, where this boy said coffee was needed. Chelsea Piers are huge—there's an ice skating rink, golf practice area, community gyms. . . . I wasn't sure where to stop, but when we saw some fire-fighters standing among some boxes, we thought they might like some pizza. It turns out that this area was a loading area for community stores to donate goods—sup-plies of paper towels, cloth towels, immense packs of bottled water, vast quantities of Quaker Chewy Granola Bars. Individuals also brought supplies—a six-pack of soda, clothing like T-shirts and pants for the firefighters, boxer shorts. One young boy came over with his parents, struggling under the weight of a gallon cranberry juice bottle, label half peeled off, which he proudly said he had filled with water for the "policemen who fight fires."

Without being told what to do, everyone fell into line, the "pass the bucket" variety in which you grab from your right and pass to your left, to get everything off the trucks and into piles on the pier. One by one, NYC Police Department Harbor Patrol boats would drive up to the pier to be loaded with supplies to be brought down to the firemen and policemen working at the site. With three big tins of heated ziti in hand, I boarded the boat . . . and only when I was handed a filtered mask did I fully realize where I was headed.

The trip down the Hudson River was short . . . and it was a beautiful, warm night. Any other night it would have been gorgeous. Any other night the New York City skyline wouldn't have had a giant cloud of white smoke billowing up into darkness. The air quality definitely worsened as we approached the dock. The last time I had been on that exact dock was a few years ago when my project threw a dinner cruise for a client. This could not possibly have been more different from that evening, when the windows glistened, and the flags along the har-bor flapped wildly in the wind. Now, the flags were still, at half-mast. The buildings were covered in white-gray dust. Paperwork of those who used to work so far above lay strewn all over the pier. Whole chunks of buildings near the towers were peeled out from their place, sides of a building looked like a banana peel of window frames and twisted metal. The World Financial Center glass atrium, the Winter Garden, was a ghostly metal frame with some window panes still intact—but the only lights reflected on the few remaining windows came not from the internal lights, but the eerie refraction from the bright work lights being used at the site. With dust on everything, with buildings cut and windows blown out, it looked very much like a movie set—the glass atrium like the model for the *Millennium Falcon* from *Star Wars,* and the rest like a set that was painted in the same matte colors without differentiation. Almost like a science fiction cartoon picture.

We took the supplies off the boat and brought them to the principal loading area by the pier. Since we expected rain, everything had been moved under the building ledges where restaurant outdoor cafés once stood. Piles of clothing and towels, medical supplies, work supplies like shovels and pick axes, and food lay arranged in their proper area . . . and from there as needed would be taken from their large storage areas to the "up front" area. Clutching pans of pasta, I sloshed through the mud puddles and navigated around the fire hoses that lay all over the ground, through what was once the World Financial Center complex. Volunteers had written messages in the dust that covered windows: "Let's Show the World," "America Stand Strong" and "Thank You." I walked through the building and emerged on the plaza side, facing what was once the World Trade Center towers. The mass of twisted steel, heaps of concrete and huge polished metal sidings of what was once the WTC . . . it's just like what's on television, but it's huge. Firemen were climbing all over these huge piles, covering the mounds of rubble, passing buckets of rubble one-by-one. It was unreal. The sheer volume of volunteers milling around was so impressive—and the horribly immense pile of material to be cleared was unimaginable. Just when you might have thought you were at a construction site, or a junkyard, you'd find a shoe. Just laying there.

After passing out food briefly, I spent the next nine hours reorganizing their supplies inside what was once One Financial Center. The escalators were still, and dirt was everywhere, but the roof was solid . . . and would provide needed protection from the expected rain. I was humbled by the police and firefighters who were volunteering. When I asked one fireman if he wanted to lie down to rest, he pointed at a picture of his wife and daughter, which was taped to his arm. "Every time I get tired, I think of them, and I have the energy I need." A number of policemen there were "off-duty"—the force didn't want them to risk injury, so they aren't allowed to work there while on the job. On their off hours, however, they can do as they like . . . and after working twelve- to sixteen-hour shifts, they're back at Ground Zero, ready to help. One policeman has a compromise with his terrified wife that he'll call her every hour to tell her that he's okay.

The rain came pounding down, and still they stayed out there. We ran out of rain gear, and I hated to tell them we didn't have anything to keep them dry. We even ran out of garbage bags for a while from which they had been fashioning slickers. Rather than get all huffy or mad, they simply shrugged and said, "That's okay, thanks for your help." We ran out of long-sleeve shirts for a while, and though they must have been freezing, when I gave them the news they said, "Okay, thank you for looking." I don't know any of their names, because they all referred to each other as "Brother." They helped me to carry my carts of clothing over the fire hoses and were incredibly polite. They made sure I wasn't cold and continually asked me if I had eaten anything. I couldn't believe with everything they were doing, they took the time to check on me.

I had no idea what kind of wonderful, caring people we have protecting our city. These people will not give up. They just keep going out there. They nap for a few minutes, and then they're right back on the pile. It was a privilege to help out, even just for a little while, to "do more." They were there when I arrived in the evening and they remained after I left in the morning . . . they will not leave . . . and they're simply remarkable. My heart goes out to them.

Erin Bertocci
Submitted by Fr. Brian Cavanaugh

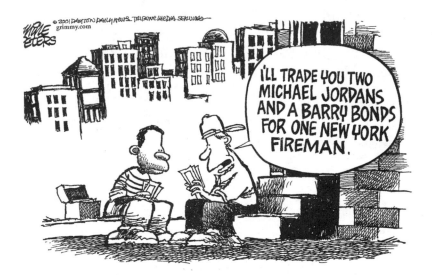

The Only Thing
We Could Think Of

*We must have perseverance and above all con-
fidence in ourselves. We must believe that we are
gifted for something and that this thing must be
attained.*

Marie Curie

My singing group, The Sirens, was invited to New York
City to sing at an awards ceremony for Helen Thomas (the
White House correspondent). Only five of us could make
it, but it turned out fine. We were excused from all of our
classes for the day so we decided to make use of our time
off. After the ceremony, we hopped on the subway and
headed to Ground Zero. As soon as we stepped onto the
sidewalk, the mood was completely different. It was dark,
quiet and it smelled strange.

What we saw was devastating. The buildings were still
burning, and the air was filled with smoke. The area was
fenced off, but you could see pretty much everything. I
have never seen such destruction in my entire life; not

one person there could look at it without feeling horrified. There were candles, pictures, posters and letters posted all along the fence that separated us from the remains. Hundreds of people stood watching and crying. I have never felt so hopeless. We decided to do the only thing we could think of and that was to sing. We have been preparing many patriotic songs that are beautifully written and well arranged (for a cappella music).

The girls and I stood up against the wall, faced the people, and with the remains behind us, we sang for two hours. People videotaped us, took pictures, hugged us, sang with us, and about five people called home and held up their cell phones to our music.

At one point, a woman in front of us broke down and started bawling, and all of us girls felt her pain and lost it in the middle of the song. The most amazing thing was that the crowd joined in and finished it for us; it was absolutely surreal. CNN showed up and taped our group and the people responding to the music. In our last song, "The Star-Spangled Banner," firemen began to fill the streets. There were about forty of them, and they had just walked off Ground Zero from working there all day. They removed their hats and began to cry. It was so sad; I cannot begin to describe how it felt. At the end they applauded us, and we applauded them. We walked into the streets and hugged them and thanked them. They were crying and tried to explain how horrible it is there, but told us how important it is that people support each other.

I will never forget that day as long as I live.

Elizabeth M. Danehy

Playing for the Fighting 69th

After silence, that which comes nearest to expressing the inexpressible is music.

Aldous Leonard Huxley

I had probably the most incredible and moving experience of my life. Juilliard organized a quartet to go play at the Armory. The Armory is a huge military building where families of people missing from Tuesday's disaster go to wait for news of their loved ones.

Entering the building was very difficult emotionally, because the entire building (the size of a city block) was covered with missing posters.

Thousands of posters, spread out as high as eight feet above the ground, each featuring a different smiling face. I made my way into the huge central room and found my Juilliard buddies. For two hours we sight-read quartets (with only three people!), and I don't think I will soon forget the grief counselor from the Connecticut State Police who listened the entire time, or the woman who listened only to "Memory" from *Cats*, crying the whole time. At 7:00, the other two players had to leave; they had been playing at the Armory since 1:00 and simply couldn't play anymore. I volunteered to stay and play solo, since I had just arrived. I soon realized that the evening had just begun for me: A man in fatigues who introduced himself as "Sergeant Major" asked me if I'd mind playing for his soldiers as they came back from digging through the rubble at Ground Zero. Masseuses had volunteered to give his men massages, he said, and he didn't think anything would be more soothing than getting a massage and listening to violin music at the same time. So at 9:00 P.M., I headed up to the second floor as the first men were arriving. From then until 11:30, I played everything I could do from memory: Bach's B Minor Partita, Tchaikovsky's Concerto, Dvorak's Concerto, Paganini's Caprices 1 and 17, Vivaldi's "Winter and Spring," the theme from *Schindler's List*, Tchaikovsky's "Melodie," Meditation from Thais, "Amazing Grace," "My Country 'Tis of Thee," "Turkey in the Straw," "Bile Them Cabbages Down." Never have I played for a more grateful audience. Somehow it didn't matter that by the end, my intonation was shot and I had no bow control. I would have lost any competition I was playing in, but it didn't matter. The men would come up the stairs in full gear, remove their helmets, look at me and smile.

At 11:20, I was introduced to Colonel Slack, head of the regiment. After thanking me, he said to his friends, "Boy, today was the toughest day yet. I made the mistake of going back into the pit, and I'll never do that again."

Eager to hear a firsthand account, I asked, "What did you see?"

He stopped, swallowed hard and said, "What you'd expect to see." The colonel stood there as I played a lengthy rendition of "Amazing Grace," which he claimed was the best he'd ever heard. By this time it was 11:30, and I didn't think I could play anymore. I asked Sergeant Major if it would be appropriate if I played the national anthem.

He shouted above the chaos of the milling soldiers to call them to attention, and I played the national anthem as the men of the 69th Regiment saluted an invisible flag. After shaking a few hands and packing up, I was prepared to leave when one of the privates accosted me and told me the colonel wanted to see me again. He took me down to the War Room, but we couldn't find the colonel, so he gave me a tour of the War Room. It turns out that the regiment I played for is the Famous Fighting 69th, the most decorated one in the U.S. Army. He pointed out a letter from Abraham Lincoln offering his condolences after the Battle of Antietam ... the 69th suffered the most casualties at that historic battle. Finally, we located the colonel. After thanking me again, he presented me with the coin of the regiment. "We only give these to someone who's done something special for the 69th," he informed me. He called over the regiment's historian to tell me the significance of all the symbols on the coin.

As I rode the taxi back to Juilliard I was numb. Not only was this evening the proudest I've ever felt to be an American, it was my most meaningful as a musician and a person. At Juilliard, kids are hypercritical of each other and very competitive. The teachers expect, and in most cases get, technical perfection. But this wasn't about that. The soldiers didn't care that I had so many memory slips I lost count. They didn't care that when I forgot how the second movement of the Tchaikovsky went, I had to come up with my own insipid improvisation until I somehow (and I still don't know how) got to a cadence. I've never seen a more appreciative audience, and I've never understood so fully what it means to communicate music to other people.

And how did it change me as a person? Let's just say that, next time I want to get into a petty argument about whether Richter or Horowitz was better, I'll remember that when I asked the colonel to describe the pit formed by the tumbling of the towers, he couldn't. Words only go so far, and even music can only go a little farther from there.

William Harvey

Reflections from the Pit

We have been called to heal wounds,
To unite what has fallen apart,
And to bring home those who have lost their way.

St. Francis of Assisi

It is exactly 227 miles (as the crow flies) from Peace Ledge, our home in New Hampshire, to Ground Zero. I know because, last night when we got home, I checked the distance on my global positioning satellite (GPS) gadget. But it might as well be a distance of several light years from here to there. The contrast between the two places is striking.

Twenty-five years ago, we named our home Peace Ledge because it sits in the woods, up on a hill, and smacks of tranquility—a place where God is very present to us. How many times we have come back to this place in fatigue, in gratitude, even in personal defeat, and found restoration here.

Peace Ledge is a dark place at night if the moon isn't shining. Only if the breeze is right can you pick up the slight noise of a truck going through its gears on Route 106 five miles away.

Not so 227 miles away. There the brilliant halogen lights shine all night long and light up the smoke still percolating up from fires deep in the rubble (someone told me the temperature in the hot spots remains at seventeen hundred degrees). The noise in the pit is constant and sometimes painful to the ears. And the constant antlike, rushing motion in the pit by hundreds of men and women leaves one in almost a manic state of mind. Here at Peace Ledge there is something akin to an oasis; there I can think of no better description than the impression I have always had of Dante's Inferno.

Yesterday we left New York and drove Interstates 95 and 93 north to our home in New Hampshire and began to unload the car. If it were not for the smells that linger on our clothes, our boots and my knapsack with which I carried special materials that Gail had purchased each day, it would be virtually impossible to believe that we have spent a week at the lip of the pit and worked with the people of the Salvation Army we've become privileged to know.

Before we left, Gail and I both spoke in a worship service at the Salvation Army Training Center. When I began my talk, I held up my Salvation Army cap that says Disaster Services, and I told the officers and cadets that of all the hats and caps and helmets I'd worn during my life, this one brought me the most pleasure. I would keep it, I said, for the rest of my life as a symbol of an extraordinary experience where I felt I saw the spirit of Jesus at work like never before.

On our last day at the pit, Gail and Colonel Rader had walked into the disaster area ahead of me. After finding a place to leave our car, I followed. Having the required credentials, I decided to walk through the pit (sort of a shortcut) from one entrance point to where our station was located. On the way, I stopped frequently to talk to men and women and prayed for a few who seemed particularly open to speaking to a "chaplain."

Suddenly a foreman approached me and said rather

brusquely, "Put your hard hat on! This is a hard hat area!" I realized that I was wearing my cap and not the hard hat that still dangled from the back of my knapsack. I thanked him for the reminder and made the switch immediately. He was right, of course. There is still the danger of pieces of glass or stone façade falling from buildings that ring the WTC disaster site.

This morning I started my talk to the Salvation Army officers and cadets with a description of that encounter. And I suggested that ministry is, or ought to be, a "hard hat" job. We can't afford to let ourselves get sucked into the minutia of organizational life when a larger world beckons with all of its yearnings to hear a word of love and hope. But people who go out "there" better wear a hard hat of a kind because it's a lot more dangerous than life in religious territory. On the other hand, some may debate that.

I have always known that I preferred life "out there" rather than inside the religious world. Perhaps that's why, as Gail and I drove north, I felt a strong sense of melancholy coming over me, probably a kind of psychic and emotional withdrawal. After all, we have spent a week unlike any other week in our lives. Every moment was fraught with an intensity of experience that one can hardly describe to anyone who hasn't been there. At the site, no one seemed a stranger. But now, away from the site, all the old feelings and experiences of incivility begin to creep back.

Drivers on the interstate are posturing for position at the tollbooths; at the gas station the attendant doesn't even look at you when you try to engage him; and at the rest stop along the way, a young man lounges outside his car with his radio speakers turned up so loud that you can hear and feel his music pound on you fifty yards away. He doesn't care who is affected by his insensitivity.

Not so at the pit. There, everyone seems to connect. Tell the policeman who stands nearby that you need some ice, and fifteen minutes will not pass before a van drives up and a half dozen burly officers begin loading you up with more ice than you can use. And then, when you say "Thank you," they say, "No, thank you for what you're doing." Ask one of the "guerilla volunteers" if she's seen any Dr. Scholl's foot pads, and a case of them shows up rather mysteriously an hour later. From where? Ask any person who passes by how they're doing, and they'll talk to you as if you were lifelong friends.

I think life at this pit carries some hints of what combat veterans talk about when they reminisce, if you can get them to do it, about life under battle conditions. Stephen Ambrose was right: In such circumstances, we become a band of brothers (and sisters).

As we drive farther north into New England, we can see the first hints of fall coming on. There is relative cleanliness on the roads; there is greater order to the affairs of people; there is even the expectation of a hot bath when we arrive at home.

But somehow I prefer life at the pit. The pit is—if I dare to compare—a more real and more desirable place. It smells badly and its tumult pounds at you. But there is something awfully stimulating to the senses and to the soul at that place of human tragedy. And a part of me would rather be there wearing my hard hat and my Salvation Army chaplain jacket than be here.

I am reminded that missionaries often return home from hot spots where they have seen death, poverty, disease and great spiritual loss, and they often appear to be in shock and overly critical of the way they see Americans (American Christians) living. You can sense that they would like to say to many of us, "Get a life!" when they hear us talk about problems and needs that are really kind of petty when put in contrast to what they've seen. I suspect that Gail and I will struggle with that same kind of withdrawal for a while. Now I appreciate why many missionaries come to regard some Third World site as their real "home." There is a quality of life out there on that edge that tugs at our souls and calls from us a better quality of person. We find that the gospel works better there, if you please; that it is designed to fit best in the suffering situation and is powerfully transforming. And if I may say it this way: when we go to such places and give away everything we have, we like ourselves better.

Life at the pit this past week renewed my sense of genuine manhood. I was pleased to feel bonded to real men and women who were bringing out the best in each other. I loved being in touch with their intensity, their sorrow, their determination to be faithful to their lost comrades. We were all swept up in a cause much bigger than us.

On the next-to-the-last day we were in the pit, I was walking (I forget to where) in the street among a spaghetti-like maze of fire hoses and utility lines. People were rushing back and forth all over the place. Suddenly a firefighter called out my name, "Hey, Gordon," he yelled. Since my name is written in bold letters on the peak of my hard hat, I'm not difficult to spot. He came over to where I was and said, "Remember me? I'm Ken. You prayed for me the other day. I wanted you to know the prayer has been working. I'm okay!" As we embraced in that special manly way, my cheek brushed his, and I could feel the sweat and the grittiness of the dust and dirt on his skin. Perhaps at another time I might have recoiled from this. But not in this hour. I felt proud to share his smudges. I whispered a blessing into his ear as we stood there in the middle of the street, and then we parted.

Gordon MacDonald

Dear Mr. Cox

Dear Mr. Cox,

It has taken me too long to write you. I was delayed by my own fear that your son was lost at the World Trade Center and by the challenge of finding out the truth and then locating you. I hope I am right to believe that, as Fred's father, you would want to hear from me even as you endure his loss.

I am a writer who travels often on business. I met Fred in the last week of August on a flight from Los Angeles to New York with a stop in Las Vegas. We were both headed home, but he was intending to take a few hours in Vegas before catching a later flight to Kennedy.

For me, every flight is a chance to have a few precious hours of solitude, for reading, and just reflecting in a way that's almost impossible at home or work. I almost never engage in a long conversation with a seatmate. Instead, I use body language and a book to create some space between me and the other passengers in our tiny, shared space.

However, on this flight I got bumped to first class, where the comfortable surroundings made me more relaxed. My seat was in the last row, by the window. The young man who got up to let me sit down smiled warmly, offered to hand my coat to the flight attendant, and told me his name—Frederick.

In that short flight Fred told me how much he loved his work, especially travelling to meet with clients, and how his life seemed to be taking a shape that made him very happy. His choice to work at a smaller firm was an example. He believed it gave him a chance to learn much faster, and he was grateful for the opportunity. (He was also very proud that he had been accepted at the company even though he didn't have the advantage of a Wharton or Harvard degree.)

On the personal side, Fred said that despite his intentions, he had fallen in love with a young woman whom he admired deeply, and he was discovering that the values and lessons he had been taught as a child—be honest, care for others, listen to your heart—really worked in adult life. Fred possessed a rare combination of idealism, intelligence and innocence that was very appealing.

When I confessed to Fred that I am a writer, and that I have written a couple of books on golf, he began telling me about you, the times you had spent together on various courses, and how much it meant to him to share the game with you. When I mentioned I had been a caddy at Wentworth by the Sea in New Hampshire he told me, rather excitedly, that you had been a caddy as a boy and had worked in hotels in New Hampshire and elsewhere. "I just love caddies," he said. "You guys really play the game for the right reasons, and appreciate it in ways the rest of us really don't."

Fred told me how much he valued his relationship with you. He described how you had begun a search for the ideal place to live the next stage of your life. And he spoke of your sense of adventure with great love and admiration. It was clear to me that Fred was able to embrace life so vigorously because it flowed from you, and from his mother.

When we landed in Las Vegas, Fred said good-bye and I went looking for something to eat during the layover. But before I ate, I stopped at a phone and called my wife to tell her about this extraordinary young man who seemed to have his feet on the ground even as he let his heart soar.

After wandering the airport a bit, I boarded the plane to New York to discover that Fred was again in the cabin. He grinned, explained that his appointments had been canceled, and asked the person in the seat next to his to trade with me so we could resume our conversation.

On the flight to New York, Fred told me about his dream to convert his experience on Wall Street into a life of his own design. He talked about moving to a smaller town or city, opening a business—perhaps something in aviation—and devoting himself to both his own passions and his relationships with loved ones. What was most remarkable was Fred's commitment to real values—friendship, love, service to others—and his rejection of stark materialism and self-involvement. He said the most important thing he had learned on Wall Street was that money is a means, not an end, and that a single-minded obsession with work was almost suicidal.

I hope you will tell Fred's mother that he spoke at length to me about her as well. He talked about her teaching—he was genuinely awed by her ability to reach students—and about her unwavering love. At one point he reached for his computer, made a few clicks, and brought up a manuscript, complete with drawings, of a children's book she had written and illustrated. (It had something to do with nutrition and health.) He made it clear to me that like you, she had been a major source of the values that guided him. She had taught him to love, and he was deeply grateful for that.

When we landed, Fred and I exchanged business cards and e-mail addresses. (A first for me with a fellow traveler.) We agreed to meet for lunch, and to play golf with you on Long Island, where I live. A few days later an e-mail arrived. I answered, and we had begun to schedule our lunch. Though I am much older than Fred, I believed that I had met someone extraordinary, someone who would become a good friend. I knew that he was one of those rare people whose eyes were truly filled with light, whose heart was open, and whose mind was alert and ever at play.

I suspect that Fred affected everyone he met in the way that he affected me. Though he would likely have been the last one to say it, he was clearly a cut above the ordinary, a young man who gave freely of himself to others and approached life with a generosity and spirit that is exceedingly rare. You should know that he felt fully loved and supported by you and his mother. In turn, it was clear that he loved both of you very much. Indeed, I have never met a young man who seemed so certain about the gifts he had received, so happy with what he had, and so determined to share them with others.

Please accept my gratitude for your son and the time he shared with me. I am saddened by his loss, by the terrible fact that I won't have a long relationship with him. But I was blessed just to know he was in the world, and I hope you are warmed by knowing that he touched me very deeply.

Please share my thoughts with Fred's mom. And you can both feel free to contact me.

Sincerely,

Michael D'Antonio

Michael D'Antonio
Submitted by Tara Hitchcock and John Langbein

Dear Mike:

Thanks for your wonderful letter. As you know I have already faxed it to Annelise, his girlfriend, who has e-mailed you.

Your letter was one of the best communications that I have received since 9/11. I am sensitive to the time it took you to write your letter and I will treasure it for the rest of my life. For a complete stranger to take his valuable time and say the things you did has more meaning to me than you possibly can understand.

I look forward to meeting you.

Fred O. Cox

Fred O. Cox

A Patriot to the End

The only homage that counts is the homage of deeds not of words. . . . Justice among the nations of mankind . . . can only be brought about by those strong and daring men . . . who love righteousness more than peace.

Theodore Roosevelt

At eighty-four years old he found a way to serve.

On the last day of his life, eighty-four-year-old Anthony Bai dressed in his best day clothes, a brand-new gray flannel shirt and pressed jeans, slapped Aramis on his freshly shaved face and hugged his daughter good-bye.

Then he climbed into his gold Lincoln Town Car and drove from his Springfield home to serve his country.

His family had tried their best to dissuade him.

"Dad," his daughters said, "what in the world can you contribute—an old man who has heart problems, diabetes and is deaf?

"You served your country once before," they argued. "Leave it to others this time. There are enough volunteers at the Pentagon. There won't be anything for you to do."

But Mr. Bai had spent five days watching the horror on television, the crumbling towers in New York, the black hole gouged out of the side of the Pentagon, still smoldering just fifteen miles from his home. He had driven to the site on September 12, only to be sent home by rescue workers.

This time, he was sure.

"I have to go," he told them. "There has to be something I can do to help."

This time, his daughters knew better than to try and stop him.

Long before the terrorist attacks, Tony Bai knew pretty much all there was to know about hardship and sacrifice and war.

His parents fled Poland during World War I, before he was born, leaving behind two sisters, one of whom wound up in a concentration camp.

His mother died when he was two.

His father beat him so badly that he ran away at the age of fourteen, hopping trains across the country to the magical world of Depression-era Hollywood, where Ginger Rogers treated him to steak and eggs for lunch and Eddie Cantor teased him that he looked like Cary Grant. And young Mr. Bai believed in the magic and vowed he was going to create some for himself.

He didn't have much to go on, just an autograph book full of famous signatures and a dream of a happy home, a family who cherished him and enough money to take care of them forever.

Mr. Bai made his way back to the East Coast and made peace with his father just in time to go to war. When the military draft took effect, Mr. Bai was first in line to register. A faded newspaper photograph shows him sipping coffee, waiting outside the military recruitment center in the Bronx before dawn. It was a few months before the

Japanese bombed Pearl Harbor on December 7, 1941. He was twenty-four. But Mr. Bai badly damaged his eardrum in artillery training and never saw combat. Years later his family wondered: Did he feel guilty at surviving when so many others were injured or killed? Is that why he devoted the rest of his life to helping veterans, in the Teamsters union where he worked as a delegate, at the American Legion, in Polish-American clubs where he helped people with language and immigration problems?

"I think he felt this burning desire to give something back," said his youngest daughter, Deborah. "He had been so lucky in life himself."

Mr. Bai always said his luckiest break of all was the day he met Vickie Martin.

It wasn't the most auspicious start to a romance. Hot and sweaty and hungry, wearing dirty overalls, Mr. Bai rolled into a Howard Johnson's restaurant in the Bronx for lunch one day. The war had just ended and he was trying to make a go of a new trucking company.

An elegant Irish redhead served him coffee. Her name was Helen Alvera Victoria Martin. Mr. Bai's heart melted on the spot. But Vickie, as she was called, laughed when he asked her out. She was engaged to a firefighter.

Mr. Bai went home, showered, put on a new suit and went straight back to the restaurant. He told Vickie Martin that he wasn't leaving until she came with him. Thirty days later they were married.

"Tony Bai never took no for an answer," said Kenneth Cripps, his friend of fifty years. "And he was fearless when he knew he was right."

Mr. Bai knew he was right about Vickie. He knew he was right when he and Mr. Cripps, who both worked for a cement company, were subpoenaed to testify against Teamsters leader Jimmy Hoffa in the late 1950s.

"He never talked about it much," said his daughter Margaret, the eldest, who was in her early teens during some of the union corruption scandals and who remembers detectives being posted at their home in the New York borough of Queens. "He just said it was something he had to do."

There were other things that Mr. Bai felt he had to do. He needed an education. And so, in his fifties, he enrolled at Cornell University and graduated with an associate's degree in industrial labor relations. In 1971, when he finally could afford to, he went to Poland and met his two older sisters. A home video shows Mr. Bai, silver-haired and beaming, hugging and kissing his sister Mania as if he would never let her go.

A few years later, he paid for Mania and other Polish relatives to come to America.

He treated the rest of his family with the same boundless generosity, showering Vickie with gifts of fine furniture and china, a gleaming yellow Chrysler that was the talk of the neighborhood, and a house in Florida with a pool.

It was there that they spent their final years together, hosting dinner parties for the family on a yacht named *My Vickie,* traveling the country in a motor home named *My Vickie II.*

The only time the couple were apart was when Mr. Bai went to Washington for President Clinton's inauguration in 1993. Vickie was too ill to go. Mr. Bai himself had undergone quadruple bypass surgery a few weeks earlier. Still, he dressed up in his veteran's uniform and hung his silver Polish Legion of American Veterans medal around his neck.

He looked as handsome and patriotic as his family had ever seen him.

"A Democrat was being inaugurated president," Mr. Bai said.

He had a duty to go.

When Vickie died in 1998, everyone thought it would be just a matter of time before her husband followed her. But he struggled through his grief and hurled himself into life again, with gusto.

He moved to northern Virginia to be near Margaret and Cynthia. He bought a little condo, signed up for computer classes, threw himself into genealogy and began to map his family tree.

"He was as passionate as ever about life, about living it to the fullest," Cynthia said.

And as passionate as ever about his country. A month before the attacks, Mr. Bai drove his twenty-seven-year-old grandson, Chris, to an Army recruitment center and urged him to consider the military as a career. Chris said he would think about it.

He wasn't sure if his grandfather was joking when Mr. Bai asked if he could join up, too.

So when terrorists struck the Pentagon, it surprised no one that Mr. Bai wanted to help. Or that he refused to take no for an answer.

Turned back from the Pentagon, he searched for a place where an eighty-four-year-old veteran would be allowed to serve. He found his answer at the Salvation Army.

On Sunday, September 16, five days after the attacks, he was put to work on a medical detail, sorting drugs from large containers and putting them into smaller packages. He would rather have been driving a forklift or pulling bodies from the rubble. But at least he was contributing.

For hours, Mr. Bai sorted and filled and stamped dates on parcels. He didn't say much. He just glowed.

At the end of the day, exhausted, he signed up for another shift.

That night, Margaret cooked her dad's favorites: London broil, potatoes and asparagus salad. Over dinner, they sat on the deck with friends and talked about terrorism and tragedy and patriotism and pride.

"There were tears in his eyes as he talked about the outpouring of help and love, about being part of something so important," Margaret said. "It was as happy as I've ever seen him."

After dinner, Mr. Bai hugged his daughter and promised he would call when he got home.

He never made the call.

They found him the next day, in front of the television, baseball cap perched on his head, a tiny American flag pinned to it. He looked like he was sleeping.

In fact, he had died of a heart attack.

Helen O'Neill
Submitted by Alaine Benard

Beep if You Love America

The wolf will live with the lamb, the leopard will lie down with the goat, the calf and the lion and the yearling together; and a little child will lead them.

Isaiah 11:6 NIV

We become a large town during the summers when our tourist population swells. But after Labor Day, we have a population of about five thousand in Bradley Beach, New Jersey. On this day, September 13, 2001, we stood in front of a World War I monument, in honor of those who perished and those who survived September 11, 2001. Members of the clergy spoke to the crowd and so did the mayor. We lit candles and cried together and shared stories about the day and how it affected us. Many had stories about friends, about family, who did not come home. Over and over, we heard the same refrain, "They just never came home that Tuesday." There were children of all ages, holding candles and flags. They were listening.

Later, when the memorial service was over, the children

left the park to stand on the corner, and we stood around aching to do something more. We hugged. We talked. We told each other it would get better. But there were no smiles and there was no laughter.

Suddenly, we noticed horns honking up and down Main Street, as if a parade was passing through town. As if there was a celebration.

We couldn't imagine who would celebrate on a day like today.

And then we heard the children's chants. "Beep if you love America!" they shouted. Again and again. "Beep if you love America." They stood at a four-way intersection, on the curb, jumping up and down, waving their hands to get attention, holding the American flags in front of their chests, pleading, "Beep if you love America." And everyone did. The night air was filled with horns honking and people waving as the children jumped in the air, holding flags in front of them and shouting, louder and louder, "Beep if you love America."

Their energy galvanized the people standing there and those passing in the cars. Perhaps the drivers were coming from work or going shopping. Undoubtedly they had on their radios and were listening to the accounts coming in, lives saved, lives lost. And yet, there were youth on the corner and energy on the corner, shouting and waving over and over, "Beep if you love America."

It went on for a long time. The town resonated with honking horns.

People smiled from their car windows. We heard ourselves laughing with the children. We began to wave also to the passing cars. We let the children lead us that evening. Even though they had read the papers, looked at the television, watched the adults around them cry and vent their anger, even though they knew something really terrible had happened to their country, a new feeling had taken hold of them—one they couldn't even explain to themselves. It had something to do with the flags they were holding. It had something to do with their country, America. It had something to do with their love for freedom.

That night, for a while, we let the children lead us and heal us.

"Beep if you love America," we roared.

And we knew America would hear us.

Harriet May Savitz

The Face of America

In the faces of men and women I see God.

Walt Whitman

Mount Pleasant, South Carolina, U.S.A.

September 11 dealt a stunning blow to the American psyche. For many of us, dazed and shocked, the urgent question we asked ourselves as we watched the carnage pouring out of our television sets was *What can I do to help?*

Local and national news commentators urged us to respond to the Red Cross's call for blood donations by participating in a blood drive. I have donated blood in the past, but nothing has approached the urgency I felt to donate this time. Tuesday night I told my husband, "We've got to go tomorrow."

We equipped ourselves with books to read and snacks to munch while we waited, figuring the line might be, oh, maybe an hour or two. When we reached our local Charleston, South Carolina, Red Cross, we couldn't believe it. At 11:00 A.M. the line stretched around the block.

It might be eight hours before we reached the head of the line—still, we walked to the end. And while we waited, I looked at the faces around me—and I saw the face of America.

I saw young and old, women with children, Generation-Xers in T-shirts and tattoos, veterans, people leaning on canes and in wheelchairs, waiting to give what they had to our country. No one was impatient, no one argued or pushed ahead of anyone. We had a purpose and a goal—so we waited.

As we stood, local television and radio stations came out. They hooked up speakers for us to listen to music and the news from New York and Washington. They brought us American flags donated by locals to wave and stickers to wear that read AMERICA WILL PASS THIS TEST.

Red Cross volunteers brought out food donated by local merchants: pizzas, McDonald's cheeseburgers, sub sandwiches, delicious fried chicken, snack foods, fresh fruit, bottles of cold water and sodas. They fed us, answered our questions and told us what to expect when we finally reached the head of the line. They thanked us for coming out and for our "sacrifice."

One volunteer told us that television pictures of us waiting in line and giving blood were being transmitted to giant screens in the middle of the World Trade Center. He told us, "You don't know how much good it does for these guys to see you here. They come out of the rubble, exhausted. Then they see you on the screen and they go back in."

We were just Americans, doing what we do, finding another way to have fun, even in the midst of tragedy. We sang to the music from the speakers and we laughed, because Americans are people who love to laugh. We made friends and discovered common ground.

On a hot fall afternoon in Charleston, South Carolina, I saw the face of America. Our hearts are broken, but our spirit is roaring back. We have a common purpose and a common goal. We are once again the UNITED States.

Susan Halm
Edited by Joyce Schowalter
Reprinted with permission of HeroicStories.com ©2001.

FOXTROT. ©*Bill Amend. Reprinted with permission of UNIVERSAL PRESS SYNDICATE.*
All rights reserved.

READER/CUSTOMER CARE SURVEY

We care about your opinions. Please take a moment to fill out this Reader Survey card and mail it back to us.
As a special **"thank you"** we'll send you exciting news about interesting books and a valuable **Gift Certificate**

Please PRINT using ALL CAPITALS

First Name [_____]   MI [__]   Last Name [_____]

Address [_____]

City [_____]   ST [__]   Zip [_____]

Phone # ([____]) [____] - [_____]   Fax # ([____]) [_____] - [_____]

Email [_____]

CAA

(1) Gender:
- ○ Female
- ○ Male

(2) Age:
- ○ 19-29
- ○ 30-39
- ○ 40-49
- ○ 50-59
- ○ 60+

(3) Your children's age(s):
Please fill in all that apply.
- ○ 6 or Under
- ○ 7-10
- ○ 11-14
- ○ 15-18
- ○ 19+
- ○ 1
- ○ 2
- ○ 3
- ○ 4+

(8) Marital Status:
- ○ Married
- ○ Single
- ○ Divorced / Widowed

(9) Was this book:
- ○ Purchased For Yourself?
- ○ Received As a Gift?

(10) How many Chicken Soup books have you bought or read?

(11) Did you enjoy the stories in this book?
- ○ Almost All
- ○ Some
- ○ No

(12) How did you find out about this book? *Please fill in ONE.*
- ○ Personal Recommendation
- ○ Store Display
- ○ TV/Radio Program
- ○ Bestseller List
- ○ Website
- ○ Advertisement/Article or Book
- ○ Catalog or Mailing
- ○ Other _____

(13) What FIVE subject areas do you enjoy reading about most? *Choose 1 for your favorite, 2 for second favorite, etc.*

	1	2	3	4	5
Self Development	○	○	○	○	○
History	○	○	○	○	○
Military	○	○	○	○	○
Family and Relationships	○	○	○	○	○
Health and Nutrition	○	○	○	○	○
Sports	○	○	○	○	○
Business/Professional	○	○	○	○	○
Entertainment	○	○	○	○	○
Teen Issues	○	○	○	○	○

3727049068

(18) Where do you purchase most of your books?
*Please fill in your top **TWO** choices only.*

○ General Bookstore
○ Religious Bookstore
○ Warehouse / Price Club
○ Discount or Other Retail Store
○ Website
○ Book Club / Mail Order

(20) What type(s) of magazines do you SUBSCRIBE to?
*Fill in up to **FIVE** categories.*

○ Military / History
○ Religious / Devotional
○ Parenting
○ Business / Professional
○ World News / Current Events
○ General Entertainment
○ Sports
○ Other (please specify) _____

(25) Are you:
○ A Parent?
○ A Grandparent

Do you have your own Chicken Soup story that you would like to send us?
Please submit separately to: Chicken Soup for the Soul, P.O. Box 30880,
Santa Barbara, CA 93130

CAA

How the Children Help

When I woke up on the morning of September 11, it was to the sound of my mother crying, "My God, we're being attacked!"

By the time I reached the kitchen, most of my family was in tears, sitting around my sister's radio as the news interrupted her usual morning music. In the living room, the children who attended our in-home daycare sat huddled around the TV where they usually get to watch educational morning programs. That day, it was different. The cartoons had been interrupted by emergency broadcast news reports and dark images of smoke, rubble and pain. For the first time in my history of working with children, not one of them complained or cried for us to change the channel (news is "boring," you know). No, this time they all sat, staring intently at the screen. They obviously could feel the seriousness of that particular news broadcast.

When the image of the towers crumbling to the ground glowed from that gruesome screen, all the children turned to check the reaction on my face before looking back at the television. Not one of them made a sound the entire time, and I tried my best to hide any expressions of being upset. For their sakes, I smiled.

After skipping channels for an eternity, all I found were dark images of the many distraught people, smoke and rubble. I turned on a movie instead; I think it was *Bambi*. As I sat down on the couch, I immediately found myself buried by all seven children, from one to three years old.

That night, after all the children had been picked up, I went down to my local Red Cross to donate blood. I was amazed by the scene. The line was out the door, and the employees and volunteers were turning people away. Unable to donate blood, I returned nightly with a plate of homemade brownies, cookies or cupcakes to hand out to the donors.

The children loved baking "goodies" for the "people helping to save all the people that got hurt from the airplane crashes." It was not our job to explain what terrorists were, and the children wouldn't understand anyway, but they did know that planes had crashed and people were hurt, and they wanted to help more than anything. We baked every day, and each night I brought what we made to the people waiting to donate blood.

The children also made thank-you cards for the donors, and I handed them out with brownies one night. One elderly gentleman waiting in the line cried when I gave him his brownie and card. He had lost his daughter and granddaughter on one of the flights. I didn't know what to do other than to hug him and cry with him. Everyone else in the line began to cry, too. After a few minutes, we all wiped away our tears and started talking, sharing stories and finding common ground. They shared their cards with each other, smiled at the children's pictures and misspelled thank-yous and condolences. By the time I left, many were gathered around the elderly gentleman, arms around him, pointing out details on his thank-you cards.

On Thursday we received word of an assembly being organized for Friday afternoon. We were invited to gather in a local park to show our patriotism and support for the rescuers back East. We asked permission from the parents to attend. On Friday morning the children were dropped off wearing flag shirts and red, white and blue dresses. They had patriotic ribbons tied in their hair and around their wrists. One parent had even painted a T-shirt for her three-year- old to wear. It had a giant American flag on the front and in huge red, white and blue letters on the back it said, "THESE COLORS DON'T RUN." The little boy seemed very excited to be wearing it. He was determined to walk backward the whole time in case a camera was there; he wanted the world to read his shirt.

We baked cookies, packed a big picnic lunch, then went outside to decorate the three strollers most of the children would be riding in to the event. We used streamers and flags, cardboard cutouts and ribbon. We even had some beach towels with American flags on them that we used as blankets for the children's laps. With these strollers, holding two children each, we looked like a regular parade! As we passed houses on the way to the park, people came out to ask where we were headed in such glory, and each person we told grabbed the flag from the front of their house and joined us. It was a regular marathon of people and strollers, all carrying flags. We filled that park and overwhelmed the organizers.

I can't describe that entire afternoon, other than that we sang "God Bless America" four times, and the kids were more intent on waving their flags than eating their lunches. To top it all off, the elderly man from the Red Cross was there! He came and shared our picnic with us. I had been so worried that seeing the children might upset him, and I nearly clenched my teeth when they all ran up to shake his hand. They took a liking to him immediately, and they were all very excited to have him sit with us. In fact, they all offered their cookies to him.

He spoke to the children about the plane crashes, and told them that his daughter and granddaughter were on one of them. The children listened, and one little girl even asked, "Oh, you're a grandpa?" Instead of crying, as I thought he might, he smiled and the children hugged him. The three-year-old boy showed him his T-shirt, a little girl told him that it's happier in heaven than it is here, and a two-year-old offered the man her juice cup. Just as he was leaving, the little girl who spoke so highly of heaven shook his hand and said, "You know, even if they're both in heaven, you'll still always be a grandpa and a daddy." He smiled as he walked away.

Even though children feel the losses, they somehow know what is needed to go on. How lucky I am to work with such healers!

Ann Marguerite Swank
Edited by Joyce Schowalter

See contributors' bios for more information about the free online newsletter *HeroicStories.com.*

"Finally, a line I don't mind waiting in."

Answering His Country's Call

. . . Gold is good in its place, but living, brave patriotic men are better than gold.

Abraham Lincoln

The Nebe family and friends are gathered in the kitchen, holding plates laden with Mexican food, their heads bowed in prayer.

They have come on this recent Saturday evening to celebrate Justin Nebe's brief homecoming. Eleanor and Bill Nebe's baby boy, Nicole's kid brother, Beatrice Gomez's feisty grandson, is a U.S. Marine, stopping at home in Texas for a week before reporting to a California base.

Being the first Marine in his family makes him proud. His parents say it makes them proud, too. But since September 11, Justin's recent enlistment has stirred other emotions in his family. They want, of course, for him to serve his country. But now they are fearful, too.

When Justin decided to join the Marines nearly eleven months ago, America stood at peace. He and his parents knew that he might be called on to defend his country. For his parents, the possibility seemed remote. Besides, the military seemed the perfect choice for Justin. The Marines, in particular, appealed to him. He liked the discipline. The honor. The challenge.

Last December, he finished his high-school course work. In February, he attended boot camp. In May, he graduated from boot camp and attended his high-school graduation in his Marine uniform. Since then, he has been training at bases in Florida and North Carolina. And now Justin, who will celebrate his nineteenth birthday while home, is on his way to Marine Corps Air Station Miramar, near San Diego, where he will work as a helicopter mechanic.

All of this is ordinary—the experience of thousands of new enlistees each year. Except these are extraordinary times.

Outside the family home, the American and the Marine Corps flags are hoisted up the huge silver flagpole, flapping in the breeze. They once waved alone, the only flags on the block, flying to celebrate Justin's May graduation. But there are flags everywhere now, waving proudly in front of the neighbors' houses, marking the day America abruptly changed.

Justin's homecoming—and his leaving—is particularly bittersweet. Each time, in the last year, when Justin has come home or the family has gone to visit, he, too, has changed. Nicole, his sister, says he walks differently. His mother can no longer see the little boy who once broke all the pencils in confirmation class at church. The teenager who once cared more about his friends than his family has evolved into a young man who says that family is what matters most.

When Justin leaves this time, he and his family do not know when they will see each other again. When Justin arrives on base, he will be given a flak jacket, a canteen and other equipment needed if he is sent to war. Though it's unlikely he will be sent to the front lines soon, the possibility exists. And so does the uncertainty.

"I'm just worrying more and more," says Mrs. Nebe.

"I have mixed emotions, obviously," says Mr. Nebe.

"I want to fight for my country," says Justin, a refrain he repeats often.

At the dining room table, Justin, who weighs 207 pounds and stands over six feet tall, is eating a tamale.

Mrs. Nebe stands behind him, her hand stroking his crew cut. She suddenly smothers him with kisses.

On Sunday, Justin stands before the mirror in his mother's bathroom, trying to button up the collar of his dress uniform. The cloth is straining against the width of his neck. The material is stretched across his shoulders. The weight training has thickened his physique.

Once he has buttoned the jacket, he asks his mother to make his eagle buttons parallel with the deck. Mrs. Nebe carefully turns each button so that the eagle embossed on them has its feet parallel with the ground and its head pointed skyward. She tucks in a stray string. Justin pulls on white gloves. They are ready.

Dressed in his uniform, Justin moves differently. He stands straight and moves crisply. He says he has a different attitude.

"I walk more proud, you know?" he says.

In the parking lot of Trietsch Memorial United Methodist Church, Justin offers an arm to his mother and one to his girlfriend, and they begin to stride toward the church, past the small white crosses that the congregation has pushed into the grass to mark each of the nearly six thousand victims of September 11. Justin stops. He motions to the women to start with their right foot. They stride again, this time in step.

The Reverend Jim Ozier has known Justin for years. The pastor has him stand before the congregation, which

Justin does, his shoulders squared, his feet slightly apart.

"It seems just like yesterday when I scolded him for breaking all those pencils in confirmation class," Reverend Ozier says. "What a little twerp." There is laughter. "But look at him now." There is applause.

At the end of the service, the Nebes all stand in the pulpit with Reverend Ozier, their arms locked around each other as the minister gives the final benediction.

The week goes by quickly, and suddenly it is Saturday and Justin must leave.

On the closet door, fatigues hang from a knob. His bedroom is cluttered with half-packed suitcases. He has already said good-bye to his father and his sister, since they had to leave the house early.

His mother tells him over and over again to pack. But Justin is sprawled across the couch with his girlfriend Amanda, whispering in her ear, wiping away her tears. The pair have been dating for more than a year and have even discussed marriage, although both agree they have no immediate plans. On his bed, Amanda has placed a shoebox she has covered with colored paper. "My heart belongs to you," say the words on the lid.

He can't wait much longer to pack. Soon, his Marine buddy, Jason, will arrive from Plano; they will load up his truck and start the long drive to the base in California. Justin tears himself away and begins to throw clothes into open suitcases in his room.

An assembly line soon forms, and his mother, grandmother, and friend, Taylor, take the bags as they are packed and place them in the foyer.

In minutes, Jason arrives. The young men wedge suitcases into the flatbed of the truck.

"I need to leave," Justin says. He sounds as if he's trying to convince himself.

Mrs. Nebe keeps going back to his room and coming out

with stray items—his white hat, a pillow and a surge protector.

He hugs his mother and his grandmother. Mrs. Gomez walks silently away, her hand brushing away the tears. Justin sees her.

"Come here, Grandma," he says, and he stoops down and engulfs the petite woman in a hug.

Mrs. Nebe isn't quite ready to let go. Tears are slipping down her cheeks. "Do you have your wallet? All your money? Did you leave your toothbrush?"

Justin doesn't answer. He hugs her again. Then Amanda. Then Taylor. It's time.

Justin finally gets into the truck and Jason backs out of the driveway.

He leans out the passenger window. "Bye. Love you guys," he says. And the truck roars away.

Karen A. Thomas

Acts of courage shape human history. Each time a man stands up for an ideal, or acts to improve the lot of others, or strikes out against injustice, he sends forth a tiny ripple of hope.

Robert F. Kennedy

His Dream Came True

The temptation was to stop. Quit running. End the pain that wracks the body of every marathoner. But Erich Maerz heard the voice of his brother Noell urging him to finish the journey that Noell could not.

The New York City Marathon was a 26.2-mile trip through five boroughs and a dozen emotions. It began in sorrow on the Verrazano-Narrows Bridge as Maerz gazed across the harbor to his brother's burial ground at the World Trade Center ruins, still smoldering in eerie defiance and filling the gaps in the skyline with white smoke.

As Maerz ran through Brooklyn, he communed with his twenty-nine-year-old brother, Noell, a bond trader missing since the September 11 terrorist attacks. As he crossed the Queensboro Bridge, he concentrated on good memories instead of the burning sensation on the soles of his feet.

As Maerz ran in the shadow of Manhattan's skyscrapers, he thought about Noell's baby daughter, born and named Noel on Halloween, seven weeks after her father made a last frantic phone call to his wife. Four hours and forty-four minutes after he started, Maerz crossed the red, white and blue finish line under a canopy of fall color

in Central Park. He wiped away a tear, for a short life well
lived, for a long race well run.

"He was looking down on me," said Maerz, who ran
under his brother's name and registration number, 8334.
"In my mind, I ran ten, he ran ten and the crowd ran six.
Noell will be in the record book as the finisher. That was
his goal."

The 2 million spectators lining the course on a day as
crisp as a red maple leaf were so loud that runners said
they could hardly hear their labored breaths over chants
of "Go USA!" and "New York loves you!" For flag-waving
New Yorkers, the thirty-second annual event that began
with the release of white doves was a cathartic celebration
of New York's resilience, a giant pep rally for the city. For
many of the 30,000 runners wearing T-shirts imprinted
with the photographs and names of missing business-
people, parents, police officers and firefighters, the
marathon was a memorial in motion, a race of
remembrance.

Never has a marathon been such a powerful symbol of
man's desire to endure. Never has a finish line been so
emblematic of man's will to overcome suffering.

Noell Maerz had been ready to run his first marathon.
The former Hofstra quarterback was an accomplished
triathlete, kayaker and skier. He was a handsome, ener-
getic young man in the prime of his life, thrilled with his
job at Euro Brokers and anticipating the birth of his first
child and the first anniversary of his marriage to Jennifer,
who he had met on a subway. Why not cap it all with the
New York City Marathon?

"Noell loves people; people love him," said Ralph Maerz,
fifty-six, who mixes present and past tenses when speaking of his eldest son. "In the whole twenty-nine years I
raised him, I could never stay angry at him for more than
ten minutes. He always got out of trouble. That's why we

figured he'd get out of the Trade Center, too."

Just before 9:00 A.M. on September 11, Noell made three calls from his office on the eighty-fourth floor of the South Tower. He told his father a bomb had gone off but he was fine. He told Jennifer that the plane had not hit his building and not to worry, that he was getting out and he loved her. He called Erich and told him that people were jumping out of windows, but that he was down to the seventy-seventh floor. Minutes later, a second hijacked plane hit its target.

Erich Maerz, twenty-seven, decided to finish what Noell started.

He talked his father into joining him, and Ralph, an ex-smoker who hadn't run since high school, completed Sunday's race in five hours, thirty-one minutes. He said he borrowed Noell's energy.

"At mile twelve, I said, 'Noell, I'm so glad I can share this with you,'" Ralph Maerz said. "At mile twenty, I said, 'Noell, I hope you're enjoying this. I hope you can see all these people cheering.'

"And at the finish line I just looked up and said, 'Thank you, Noell.' I was so proud of him. Now I can say he's proud of me."

Erich and Ralph are putting their race numbers in a hope chest for little Noel so someday she will understand how her father's spirit endures.

Linda Robertson

The Unity of Strangers

Candles lit in a circle standing, agreeing, disagreeing but keeping each other's candles lit.

Gary G. Gach

Tonight a friend called. He was going by himself to a nearby park in Los Angeles with a bunch of candles to think and honor the victims of September 11. He wasn't sure if anyone else would show up. Nothing had been scheduled. I had been looking for some place to go to share my feelings with others. I gathered a few candles, a small American flag and met him.

At 7:00 P.M., we were the only people in the park, but a small group of people who appeared to be from a church were on the sidewalk handing out candles and lyrics to patriotic songs. We began to sing.

As darkness fell, we set up our candle shrine and more people came. They brought flags and more candles. People began driving by, honking, parking and joining. More people, more flags. Huge ones, tiny ones, one homemade and colored with crayons by a child when his local store ran out. Another friend showed up with her dog that was

wearing a red, white and blue kerchief. People started lining the streets and waving their flags. Across the street we
saw a long line of marchers carrying votive candles. They
had been called about the gathering in the park. The
crowd swelled, shouting "U.S.A.!" and waving their flags.
There was an older Armenian lady mourning a loss who
added her candle to our shrine. They kept coming: Latino
families, Asians, young and old, a man in a wheelchair and
a homeless man from the park with a flag stuck atop the
shopping cart that held all his belongings.

Then, the firefighters came . . . not to tell us we were a
fire hazard, but to park their massive trucks on each side
of the corner. We cheered these symbols of American
heroism and shook their hands. The ladder truck started
raising its tall ladder with a big American flag at the top
into the night sky. It swung out over the street as it
extended and the flag waved. We cheered as the firefighters climbed to the top of the ladder. Cops drove by,
honked and turned on their sirens. The corner was ablaze
with candlelight and we kept singing. People who never
knew the words, learned them. People I'll never see again
sang them with me. More people came. The blare of
continuously honking horns filled the air as flag-
decorated cars drove by and approved of our demonstration. I spoke to a female firefighter who had just returned
from digging for survivors for two days in the rubble of
the World Trade Center. She needed to see this kind of
support, and we were happy to give it to her.

Later, I met a young woman who had been eating at a
restaurant across the street. She saw our group, went
home to get her flag and returned. It was a huge flag and
she could only hold up one end of it, so I took the other
end. We stood in front of the people lining the street, waving the flag. We joined others chanting "U.S.A.!" and
singing "America the Beautiful" and "Grand Old Flag" as

more fire trucks passed and briefly put on their sirens. *CNN News* showed up and started shooting, a news helicopter circled overhead, and the ABC and CBS local vans pulled up. Photographers from many papers took countless pictures.

I hope those images are part of a huge patchwork that stretches across America to other cities and all the countries of the free world—to other corners and other strangers standing strong, defiant and steadfast together, heads and flags held high. Despite our many nationalities, religions and political differences, we are united in a sorrow, anger and determination that no ragtag army of madmen can ever defeat. This was a night I'll never forget, part of a time in history when, no matter how diverse, the people of Los Angeles were one . . . on one corner . . . where only a few had stood only a short time before. That's what the madmen didn't count on and what will, in time, defeat them.

Lynn Barker

The Cops from
Madison, Alabama

You cannot do a kindness too soon,
for you never know how soon it will be too late.

Ralph Waldo Emerson

I wondered when I would finally feel the sadness. I wondered why other New Yorkers I passed in the streets of Manhattan looked so pained while I felt so numb. I really began to wonder if I was human. I felt nothing at all. Nothing.

It started several days after the sky fell on September 11, when I looked out my living room window in Westfield, New Jersey, and saw friends and family visiting the pregnant wife of a thirty-one-year-old man who was missing in the rubble. I tried hard to cry, but—as much I would like to say I felt courage and resolve—what I really felt was an almost paralyzing fear brought on by the sheer audacity of the acts.

At work in Manhattan, I found it even harder to feel pain and sadness: I work across from the Empire State Building, and that building's new status as New York

City's tallest skyscraper gave all of us in the surrounding neighborhood a case of the jitters. It's hard to feel sad when you keep looking up at the sky waiting for something to come crashing down.

Several days later, my wife and I attended an interfaith service. I passed a sign with the names of a number of those from my hometown who had been lost. So many were parents of young children. I could feel a little lump forming in my throat. But I still could not cry.

The pent-up emotions finally hit like a ton of bricks when I least expected it: I was out walking in front of the Empire State Building. I wanted to simply be in the presence of the New York City police officers now guarding that building. And as I drew closer, I saw that the building's entrance was being protected by police officers from Madison, Alabama. And I lost it. I ran upstairs to my office and finally shed the tears that had eluded me for three weeks.

You have to understand. Most New Yorkers are hopelessly provincial, still living with the illusion that they live at the center of the universe, as if this wonderful complex, diverse universe could even have a center! Some are even still fighting the Civil War, with a view of the South that is as up-to-date as a Matthew Brady photograph. I know people who never even leave Manhattan, as if—having found paradise—they have no reason to go anywhere else.

Yet there they were out in front of the Empire State Building, a group of wisecracking, cynical New Yorkers who had surrounded these officers and were looking at them with the reverence usually reserved for members of the clergy. And these big, strong, confident, reassuring police officers from a place that no one had ever heard of were actually calming the nerves of people who had seen things that no one should see and felt things that no one should feel.

I don't know where Madison, Alabama, is. I don't know how many people live there. I don't know what petty disputes are currently being fought out in its city council, but I bet some group of citizens has been making a lot of noise lately about the lack of a stop light at some especially congested corner. I don't know if a peaceful river runs through town or where the lake is in which you can fish and swim. I don't know where in town you can taste the best barbecue, and I certainly don't know a soul that lives there. But I do know that on a fine, sunny day in my hometown, three weeks after it seemed like the world was collapsing around us, a bunch of courageous and compassionate cops from Madison, Alabama, were just what we needed at precisely the moment we needed it.

To the good and decent people of Madison: thank you for your sending us your bravest and finest. Just the sight of their Madison shoulder patch and the decency and confidence they demonstrated gave me an incredible dose of hope that—whatever comes along—our almost instinctive compassion as a nation will overcome any adversary.

And do me a favor: Promise that someone from Madison—wherever it is—will get in touch with me the next time a river overflows (is there a river nearby?), the next time a fire leaves some people homeless, the next time—God forbid—that a place of such obvious kindness and decency has its reckoning with pain and loss. I'd love to help.

Steven M. Gorelick, Ph.D.

In light of recent events, we're all New Yorkers . . .

Given the Choice

I will never look at a firefighter the same way again. What is in someone, hundreds of them, to compel them to run into a burning building while everyone else is running out, just to save people they don't even know? Their bravery has become part of our collective national legacy. Their bravery dignifies us all.

Reverend Bill Hybels

Somewhere in the darkness between Two Falls and Ogden, I eased my Ford F-250 off the freeway. I'd been driving nonstop since leaving Seattle, and I was tired. In the waning hours of September 12, I laid my head on the steering wheel for a few minutes rest.

When I closed my eyes I could see it clearly, jutting into the cobalt-blue Rocky Mountain sky. I'd known of the I.A.F.F. Fallen Firefighter monument for years but had never visited Colorado Springs until September 1995. My first visit to the national memorial had come as the result of a fiery warehouse collapse that took the life of my friend Jim and three other Seattle firefighters eight months earlier.

Every September thereafter, I'd trek back to "the springs" for the annual memorial observance. I'd always find a quiet moment to stand below the monument and gaze up in awe at the bronze image of a firefighter descending a ladder, cradling an infant in one arm. I'd run my fingers across the new crop of names etched on the smooth, black granite wall fronting the monument. Behind the wall, an American flag flew proudly, often at half-mast. Memorial staff members would lower Old Glory to the position of tribute each time a firefighter gave his life. A new flag would be hoisted and flown for each fallen firefighter and presented to the public servant's family in a triangular oak case at the September observance.

I lifted my head off the steering wheel and put my truck into gear. The diesel growled as I accelerated back onto the freeway toward Colorado.

Several hours later I was south of Ogden, finishing yet another cup of lukewarm coffee. In a moment of fatigue, a wave of selfish frustration passed over me. I seethed that terrorists on the other side of my continent could carry out such cruelty and simultaneously toss my life into such chaos. I had planned to make this year's trip with my wife, Kate, but our flight had been canceled along with everyone else's.

In the softly breaking light, my eye caught a solitary American flag fastened to a lonely fence post by some defiant patriot, hanging loosely in the predawn stillness. From Seattle southward I'd seen stars and stripes everywhere—stapled to car antennas, hanging from farmhouse rooftops and slung from office windows. As I considered the thousands now dead, their shattered families and the hundreds of sacrifices made by fellow firefighters, my frustration evaporated, and in its place I felt shame for my selfishness.

In his dying, Jimmy had given me a wonderful gift. For years I'd guarded a secret. I was a closet poet. After a particularly tragic accident or difficult shift, I would write, for hours on end sometimes, to soothe the pain and restlessness in my own soul. Ironically, it was at Jimmy's funeral, while reciting one of my poems that his mother had requested, that I discovered my fireground songs resonating in the hearts of many other firefighters.

Word traveled quickly, and soon I was wearing the nickname "firehouse poet" with a combined sense of embarrassment and awkward pride. In the years that followed, the I.A.F.F. Memorial had used several of my poems during their annual observances. They'd even published several on plaques. I was honored, but never more so than after the 2000 observance. The memorial's director had approached me with a special request. With the existing wall of honor nearly full of the names of fallen firefighters, a new wall was to be constructed. Would I, he asked, consider writing a poem to be etched on the new wall?

It hadn't been an easy project. For months I'd struggled to find the words, only to come up empty again and again. The question kept haunting me, *What can I possibly say to make this memorial any more meaningful?*

I had discovered the answer in early April on a family weekend getaway. As I leaned against a piece of driftwood and watched seagulls ride the ocean winds, a revelation struck me: the memorial wasn't complete. It contained monuments, memorial walls and names of our fallen, but there was no parting thought, no final message. The memorial lacked a statement from fallen firefighters. As I visualized the thousands of children yet to learn they would never see Daddy again, the mothers and fathers yet to bury a child, and spouses yet to become widows and widowers, the poem I'd been looking for was born. I scratched out the two dozen lines on a wrinkled scrap of paper, tucked it in my pocket and joined A. J. and Annie, my son and daughter, as they played near the surf.

By early mid afternoon on September 13, I was an hour north of Denver. Pulling into a gas station in Fort Collins, I nearly collided with a red, four-wheel Toyota pickup. Flapping proudly above the truck's cab were two massive American flags. Instead of an obscene gesture or a glowering scowl, the driver gave me a thumbs-up. I smiled and returned the gesture. How the world had changed in forty-eight hours! I'd never witnessed such patriotism, such camaraderie between strangers. Out of unspeakable evil, good was already emerging.

Arriving in Colorado Springs, I checked into my room and tossed my two suitcases on the floor. After nearly twenty-four hours on the road, the king-size bed looked inviting, but I had one final stop to make. I jumped into my pickup once again and turned the key.

From my parking space two hundred yards from the monument I could see the bouquets. Rainbows of flowers covered the memorial grounds, some carefully lining the top of the black granite wall, others strewn at random like toys abandoned by a toddler. Dozens of hardened wax puddles littered the cobblestone walkway encircling the site, each spent candle a token of a grateful citizen's respect and remembrance. Amongst the flowers were cards and hand-written notes: "We love you," "Thank you for your sacrifice" and "God bless your families." Another bore a meticulously colored picture of a Dalmatian and a stick figure crying. "I'm sad you died," it said simply.

Barely a whisper of wind moved the half-mast American flag. It hung like a sentinel over the original black granite wall with its new crop of freshly etched names, each a symbol of a firefighter's family sacrifice. I turned my attention to the newly constructed wall behind it.

Stretching out seventy feet, its rich ebony surface was blank except for a lonely poem. As I ran my hand over the stone plates, I realized the first names to be inscribed here would not be those of sixty, seventy, or even one hundred firefighters from a year's worth of tragedies, but those of more than three hundred of New York's bravest who died in a single, terrible ordeal. I leaned against the cold, smooth granite and cried.

As expected, firefighter turnout to the Saturday memorial service was sparse. On September 15, thousands of firefighters were mobilizing nationwide for rescue and support operations, and with air service 10 percent of normal, hundreds more had been unable to find a flight. But in the void created by absent firefighters, citizens streamed to the memorial from Colorado Springs and beyond. From Denver to the north and Pueblo to the south, from Cascade and Fort Carson, they came by the thousands, bringing with them their tears, their flowers, their hugs, their whispers of support. In our time of grief and remembrance, they had not forgotten us.

As I looked out over the thousands who had come to grieve firefighters they'd never known, I realized that, maybe for the first time, America truly understood. They understood that, for firefighters, the only difference between the unspeakable tragedy in New York and those that occur each week on our continent lies in the number of lives lost—never in the depth of commitment or pricelessness of the sacrifice. As I stood at the microphone and prepared to share my poem, I realized America did understand. We had been there for them. Now, they were here for us.

Battling tears and a rising lump in my throat, I shared the words etched on the new memorial wall—the words I'd jotted that early spring day on a coastal inlet as the surf had pounded the shoreline. Simple words, but powerful words, I hoped. Simple and powerful, like the breed of American they were intended to honor.

Given the Choice

If I'd been given the choice,
you know I would've stayed.
Grown a little more gray,
a lot more wise,
fought a few more fires,
saved a few more lives.
If I were given the choice,
I'd come back one more time
to see and touch
the ones I miss
I'd dry one tear,
steal one kiss.
And if I were to choose
where you'd etch my name,
I'd ask, this field
beneath the Rockies,
where mountains tower
above the plains.
Carve my memory
in this granite,
here with these
who teach the world
what lion-hearted bravery is,
each time another flag's unfurled.

Captain Aaron Espy

Artizans Syndicate: Michael De Adder

Reprinted with permission of Michael De Adder. Artizans.com.

Taking Control

It was the morning of Friday, September 21, 2001. I was walking through the expansive United Airlines terminals at O'Hare International Airport noticing that the normally busy terminals were unusually quite. As a person who flies regularly, I would have guessed that it was early on a weekend or holiday and not a regular Friday business day, if not for the sad reality as to why the airport was so sparse.

After checking in and going through security, I began my long walk to my gate. Along the way I enjoyed listening to Copeland's "Appalachian Spring" over the airport sound system, and unknowingly I started to whistle along with the song. As I was descending the escalator a voice to my left said, "Catchy tune, isn't it?" It was the voice of a United pilot.

"Yes, Captain," I said.

Unsolicited, the captain turned to me and said, "There are two ways to stop all of this," instantly knowing exactly of what he was speaking.

"One way is the fact that in my hands I control an extremely powerful piece of equipment, and if I have to, I can cause that plane to have so much turbulence that you couldn't hold down your lunch, not to mention hold a weapon."

"Indeed," I replied, knowing he needed no prompting to continue.

"The second way is when the passengers become fed up," clearly implying the counterattack methods used by passengers on Flight 93.

I was stunned by the power of his words. He at once appeased my fears and empowered me to control my own destiny. How settling was his admission that he would virtually shake any assailant into submission, and if that was not enough, admonishing me and all passengers to fight, if not for our own well-being then for the thousands of lives we could be saving on the ground.

Now, I am not a person who advocates violence, but the thought that a knife-wielding assailant might have to contend with my laptop holding shoulderbag used as a sling gave me resolve.

Once seated on the plane, I again heard the same captain's strong voice, this time over the plane's PA system. After welcoming all aboard he announced to the entire plane what he had shared with me earlier. In addition, he added that he was a combat-experienced pilot and a veteran of a hijacking some thirty years ago.

Here we were in the face of all that anxiety and fear, and this wonderful captain made us all realize that we need not be passive victims, but that our fate is at least partially in our own hands and his.

Matthew E. Adams

Operation Teddy Bear

*I am only one, but I am one. I cannot do every-
thing, but I can do something. And I will not let
what I cannot do interfere with what I can do.*

Edward Everett Hale

I was driving the children to school when I first heard
the news. My initial thoughts were that it was a small
plane that had undoubtedly caused damage, but it was
early and surely there were not many people at work yet.
I thought *How awful,* and I hoped that there were no fatal-
ities. Then I put it out of my mind. To be honest, I was too
busy wallowing in my own pity to dwell on something
that happened so far away from my little world in a tiny
town in Tennessee. My husband was out of work nearly a
month now and still he had found nothing. We were so far
behind on bills I doubted we would ever dig out of that
hole. I had made an appointment to see if I could get state
assistance just to put food on the table for our three children. I was missing my mother, who had passed away in
1997, and had no one to share my woes. I remember thinking that things couldn't get much worse.

I made it back home, and after tidying up the house a bit, I settled in to nurse the baby and catch a bit of television. The images that flashed across the screen on every channel horrified me. I went from shock and disbelief to absolute horror, then came the anger, and finally I just went numb. I had cried for hours and hours and couldn't sleep at all that night. All my petty thoughts of debt and self-pity were gone. True, I was in the same predicament that I had been in hours earlier, but that seemed somehow trivial in the face of such tragedy. So many lives, so much destruction and an entire nation in mourning. *Who cares if the car payment is made?* I sat in my bed that night and I cried. I cried for the mothers who lost their children, and for the firefighters, EMTs and police who paid the ultimate price in the name of service. I cried for the children who lost their parents. I cried for our nation, and I cried for my children. I cried because I was fortunate enough to have a home and bed to go to that night and because my children, husband and family were all safe and sound. I cried out of fear that we may go to war and my children would have to be raised during war time. I cried until no more tears came.

The next morning I went through the usual motions of getting the children ready for school. They asked very few questions about the previous day's events, but the few they did ask started me thinking.

"Why did God make bad people, Mommy?" asked my six-year-old.

"God didn't make them bad, honey," was my mumbled response. Thankfully that appeased him.

"Mom, can't we go and help them?" my eleven-year-old pleaded.

"Oh baby, I wish that we could, but it is so far away and we just don't have any money to send," came my shame-filled reply.

Once the children were in school, their questions continued to flutter in my mind. *Why? Why? WHY?* I didn't
have any answers, only more questions of my own. I
stopped at Wal-Mart to pick up diapers, and while there, I
saw some red, white and blue ribbon. It was only forty-four
cents for a roll, so I figured I could afford that much to
show my support for those who were dealing with such
horror. I made unity ribbons for the entire family and
even had enough ribbon to make a few extra that I carried
to the school and gave to the teachers. That night my
daughter removed her ribbon and pinned it to her
favorite teddy bear, I assumed for safe-keeping. Then to
my surprise she brought the bear over to me and said,
"Mommy, can I send this to New York to one of the
people who were hurt?"

With tears in my eyes I said, "Sure, honey, I think we
could do that." From there the wheels began to turn in my
head. *Why couldn't we do that?* I thought I could collect bears
and attach a unity ribbon and a handwritten message to
each one to send to New York City and Washington, D.C.
I can do that! So the 911 Teddy Bear Brigade (Operation
Bear Hugs) was born.

I got on my computer, and I told as many people as I
could. One of the online groups called "Mom writers" was
especially supportive. This group of mothers is one of the
most compassionate group of people I have ever had the
pleasure of knowing. Before I knew it, I had suggestions
coming in and offer to help write a press release, and
within a few days, over forty bears from around the world
had been delivered to my doorstep.

Once the press release and flyers were ready, things
really took off. I was interviewed first by the local paper,
then on television by our local public access television
show, "Tullahoma Living." Then the newsleader Channel 6
had us on briefly. I e-mailed several network news channels, and a few of them mentioned our project. Girl Scout

troops sent us bears with notes that would tear your heart out. With each new bear and every precious message attached, our hearts were filled to overflowing and we cried. Oh, how we cried.

By October 5, we had in our possession about three hundred bears. Some of them didn't have notes, and for those we asked local fire and police departments if they wanted to write messages, and for the others we wrote them.

We have a target date of December 11, 2001, to send the bears to New York City and Washington. We don't know how many we will end up with, but our target is five thousand.

We will be giving the bears to the volunteers. We noticed that much was being done for the victims and families, so we wanted to honor the volunteers who have worked so tirelessly, sleeping on the street and returning to work at daybreak. I cannot imagine the horror of the scene at Ground Zero, but I am so thankful for the people who are there giving so selflessly of themselves to help others. They deserve our thanks and so much more. I know you may be thinking a bear is nothing in the scheme of things, but it isn't really the bear that counts. It is the messages attached, the love and gratitude and the simple gesture that count. The volunteers are the backbone of the rescue and clean-up efforts and should not be overlooked. I think this quote says it best: "Volunteers are NOT paid, not because they are worthless, but because they are priceless."

I just wanted to show that if I can do something to help make a difference, then anyone can. I am simply a stay-at-home mommy on a tight budget. I had no money to give, but I gave what I did have: my love and eternal gratitude.

Tina Warren

No Words

In the days that followed the bombings of the World Trade Center, New York stayed at a standstill. Those who managed to get to work did so with a sense of purpose but also with fear. Some thought that by going back to work, they were making a statement, "We're Americans. We aren't cowed, beaten." But fear lurked everywhere—in the horrific images on TV, among survivors and their friends and acquaintances, in the faces of passersby on the streets.

Rowland Henley, who works for Philip Morris, needed to go back to work on Thursday. "Everything seemed surreal. I thought if I went back to work, I could shake that pervasive terrible feeling of loss. I couldn't." Philip Morris received a bomb scare on Thursday and the building was evacuated. People poured into the streets. Some were talking on cell phones, saying good-bye to loved ones. Rowland headed south toward the Brooklyn Bridge hoping to get home. He ended up in a bar with other evacuees, a hodgepodge of humanity—professionals, cab drivers, construction workers, firemen, and emergency workers. Their common link was their need to comfort and be comforted.

Rowland, like thousands of others, felt that the only

way to mitigate the sadness growing inside him was to help in some way. When his company offered opportunities for any employee who wanted to volunteer with the Red Cross, Rowland did. His job was to provide support to the workers at Ground Zero.

"We were told to make an effort to cheer these people up. 'Ask about the Yankees, smile big, take their mind off things. . . .' Making small talk was just that—small and these people were giants, every one of them. I stopped trying and just threw myself into the manual labor."

Rowland and other volunteers were put to work carrying boxes of supplies, setting out food, cleaning tables, emptying trash, filling things, hauling things, doing whatever was needed to support those doing the terrible work of clearing Ground Zero.

"They kept thanking us!" Rowland said incredulously. "They were thanking us when they were the ones who should be thanked. I wanted to say something, anything that would convey to these unselfish, caring human beings what I felt.

"I thought if I could just find the words. . . ."

But there were no words.

Even when a body was recovered, when everyone stopped and placed a hand over his heart as a processional slowly brought its precious cargo to the staging area to be taken to the makeshift morgue, even when tears fell, they fell silently. There were no words.

For some, like Rowland, that silence was the worst. One young woman whose husband or lover or friend was one of those whose body had been found stood alone inside a Salvation Army tent after the memorial. She stood there a long time just staring into space. After a time, she noticed on a table in a corner, a small stuffed animal. It was a teddy bear with a red ribbon.

"I had stopped near the opening of that tent," said

Rowland. "I had passed by before on one of my errands and seen this woman standing there. I don't know what made me stop then and watch her. But I did. And then I was glad."

The woman picked up the teddy bear, clutched it tightly to her and began to cry—big deep gulps of sobs. It was as if she needed something to release what was pent up inside of her. That something had to be a normal thing, a soft, lovely child's toy sent by someone whose only intention was to offer comfort, kindness, and appreciation. And, there amidst all that devastation, the bear wasn't the slightest bit out of place. Because all the workers—those on the pile and those, like Rowland Henley who had volunteered to go to support them—were there for the same reason.

Someone had sent this bear (and I later learned that many more were on the way) in the hope that it would provide some comfort to someone, anyone, who needed it. Its softness, its bright red ribbon against the gray, sad surroundings shown like a beacon of what it was meant to show—compassion and hope.

Sometimes words aren't enough. And sometimes, they aren't even necessary.

Marsha Arons

Send Beauty

On the morning of Tuesday, September 11, Kate Cain-Bell was fully immersed in teaching "something important" to her first-grade class at Richboro Elementary School in Richboro, Pennsylvania.

Not long into the day, the principal asked her to step out of the classroom for a moment. There, in the hallway, she heard about the devastation in New York and Washington, D.C. It was difficult for her to grasp the news, let alone try to explain it to innocent minds, so she agreed with the school's decision not to inform the children.

When Kate returned to her waiting students, the class work seemed to pale in comparison to the significance of the day's events. As a deeply spiritual woman, she felt compelled to impact the world in a positive way during the time of such a crisis. An idea leapt to mind. She drew in a breath, walked to the front of the class and made a request.

"I want each of you to imagine the most beautiful thing you can think of. Hold that thought in your mind and then send it out to the world. Can you all do that?"

A sea of young faces nodded.

"Okay. Let's do it."

And with that, a wave of beauty was sent out into a world of ugliness.

At the end of the day, Kate wanted her class to be prepared with some knowledge that they wouldn't be walking into the same world they'd left that morning. Another idea blossomed. She stood in front of the class again.

"Remember when I asked you to send out your beautiful thought to the world?"

After pausing to accept their nods, Kate continued. "Well, while you were sending out your beauty, someone else sent something not-so-beautiful into the world."

Kate paused again, to see if her young students understood.

A little girl named Allie piped up, "Well, when I get home, I'll send them something beautiful right back!"

In the midst of tragedy, triumph comes in many forms. This time, it came in the form of a young child who learned a lesson that was truly "something important."

Send beauty.

Teri Goggin

Repaying an Old Kindness

A group of South Carolina schoolchildren have raised nearly half a million dollars, exceeding their goal to buy New York City a fire truck and help repay a 134-year debt of kindness.

Efforts by White Knoll Middle School students to replace one of the fire trucks lost in the September 11 attacks got a boost when it was discovered that New York firefighters had given a fire wagon to Columbia two years after the Civil War. Columbia officials at the time promised never to forget the favor.

"It shows we care about people in New York," said eighth-grader Laurin. "It also shows we keep our promises."

The children plan to present a check for $447,265 to New York Mayor Rudolph Giuliani during the Macy's Thanksgiving Day parade. That covers the $350,000 cost of the truck and any other equipment firefighters wish to buy.

South Carolina Governor Jim Hodges hopes the truck will wear a little South Carolina pride. At Tuesday's announcement, he gave students a blue Palmetto State flag to take to New York.

White Knoll Principal Nancy Turner said she was

surprised the students were able to raise the money so quickly. But she said the children never doubted it.

When she told adults about buying the fire truck, they all asked, "How much will it cost?" All the students wanted to know was, "Who was going to drive?"

It was Turner who stumbled across records of New York's long-ago gift while doing research about the cost and what type of truck to buy.

In 1867, Columbia was still struggling to recover from the devastation of the Civil War when the New York Firemen's Association heard the city was still using bucket brigades to fight fires.

The New Yorkers—many of them former Union soldiers—took up a collection to buy Columbia a fire wagon. When the wagon was lost during shipment, they took up another collection and bought yet another wagon.

Former Confederate Col. Samuel Melton was so overwhelmed that he promised on behalf of South Carolina's capital to someday return the favor "should misfortune ever befall the Empire City."

Inspired by the historical link, William Murray, a New York attorney with South Carolina ties, pledged $100,000 to the campaign if the students could raise the remainder. Columbia Fire Chief John Jansen, a native New Yorker, also joined in to help lead the fund-raising efforts.

While emphasis had been put on the repayment of the nineteenth-century kindness, several officials Tuesday focused on the lessons of giving.

"This is the ultimate example of character education," said state Education Superintendent Inez Tenenbaum. "These students have given a gift to the people of New York, but they have also given a gift to all of us."

Associated Press

The Crumpled Blue Ribbon

*We won't always know whose lives we touched
and made better for our having cared, because
actions can sometimes have unforeseen ramifi-
cations. What's important is that you do care
and you act.*

Charlotte Lunsford

Mrs. Green, a fourth-grade teacher, was grief-stricken as
she watched the news on TV. She had been teaching for
more than twenty-two years, but she had never been
faced with such disaster. She was overwhelmed with
despair, until suddenly she recalled the "Who You Are
Makes a Difference" story she had read in the first *Chicken
Soup for the Soul* book, in which a fourteen-year-old boy's
life was saved when his father honored him with a blue
ribbon.

"That's the answer," she shouted. *We don't have to focus all
our energies on the terrorists. I can teach my students how to love
one another and make the world a healthier and more peaceful
place right now.* She immediately called to purchase the
"Who I Am Makes a Difference" blue ribbons.

As she held the blue ribbons in her hands, her eyes twinkled as she announced to her students that today they would not be learning reading, writing and arithmetic. Instead, they were going to have a hands-on experience of love, life and what it means to be truly a great human being. One by one, she approached each of them, telling them how very special and unique they were to her. Then she placed a "Who I Am Makes a Difference" blue ribbon just above their heart. The sadness and pain of the recent days faded.

Her students' faces glowed, chests swelled and spirits soared. If only for those thirty minutes, the usual gloom and doom of the recent days had lifted, and she was convinced that something very special had occurred on this day.

As her students left her classroom, she handed out extra blue ribbons saying, "Go home and tell your parents, brothers, sisters—everybody—how much you love them. Tell them today! Place a blue ribbon above their heart." The bell rang, her students raced out with a new vigor. She sat at her desk, crying with happiness. She felt such a relief. Love was definitely what needed to be taught in this world right now. At least she had done her part.

Now she hoped that her students would be able to pass on this love to others. But she could not have imagined the difference this exercise would have made to one father.

Less than a week later, a parent stormed into her classroom unannounced.

"I'm Timmy's father," he declared. "Was this your idea to do this blue ribbon project?"

"Yes," Mrs. Green answered.

"Well," the father mumbled, pulling out a crumpled blue ribbon from his pocket, "my son came home the other day and told me how much he loved me and what a good father I am. I've come here to tell you that I'm not a good father. I'm an alcoholic. But something happened to me when my son told me how much he loved me. At that moment, I decided to go to AA for the first time. I even attended church this past Sunday. You see," he said as he turned toward the door, "the world might be hurting, but I don't need to add to the pain. In fact," he said, "from now on, I'm going to become the father my son thinks I am."

Mrs. Green gasped as she watched the father go out her classroom door, knowing that the healing had begun and the world was going to get better . . . because she taught at least one child to love.

Helice Bridges

BOWS Across America

When events occur that we don't expect, they increase our faith, strengthen our ability to endure, and bring forth our hidden talents, abilities and strengths.

Iyanla Vanzant

Like so many of us, I was stumbling around on the Saturday after the September 11 attack on our country, wondering what to do. How could I help, and was it really true that someone had leveled the World Trade Center with a couple of hijacked airplanes?

It was not a time to sit around the house, so I headed into town. The local firefighters were out collecting money for New York, flags were flying on buildings and cars and motorcycles, and banners hung on bridges and around horses' necks. People were walking around the lake, heads down, and the town was unusually quiet and yet just as active as every other Saturday in a tourist town in the Rocky Mountains.

I stopped at the coffee shop and went from crying at the sight of a four-year-old with American ribbons in her hair to a sudden and immense pride in the country where I lived. In a moment's time I found myself at the fabric store searching for some way to display my American pride. One small piece of flag fabric, a pin, and some red, white and blue ribbons were left in a basket in the corner, so I bought what they had and wondered to myself why I never had owned a flag to fly. In a time of national crisis, with a renewed sense of patriotism, there was not one to be had in the entire city of Denver. I felt somewhat ashamed of myself.

The fabric and ribbons turned into a bow that I wore to church the next day. Before the service was over, ten people wanted a bow just like mine. I found myself saying, "I'm selling them for five dollars, and all of the money goes to the New York Fire 9-1-1 Relief Fund. How many would you like?"

The next day I wore my bow to work and quickly realized that this was a way I could help. After one hundred orders, I went to the nearest fabric store and bought the only bolt of flag fabric and all the pins and ribbon they had. It took three nights of making bows before I could get through the evening without tears. This simple process of creating with my hands was helping me to heal. Not that any more sense was being made out of the attacks—just that each bow represented a positive energy to replace the worn-out sadness.

This project needed a name and a mission. I woke up one morning with the acronym "BOWS Across America— Bracing Others With Support." The mission was then to make a bow in memory of the people who had lost their lives on September 11. *If we made 10 or 50 or 150,000 bows, our pride would just grow and expand, and there would be no need to stop making bows,* I thought. Just as not having a flag to fly when I most needed it, why wouldn't people display a red, white and blue bow on their chest whether it was Christmas, the Fourth of July, Tuesday or St. Patrick's Day?

Within a week, teachers from seven elementary schools requested materials to make bows. Local grocery stores allowed the kids to sit outside their doors and sell the Patriot Ribbons to shoppers. You should have seen the concoction of bows and ribbons presented in everything from Easter baskets to shoe boxes. Some of the fabric was cut in half; ribbons were tied on the ends and in the middle and looped in long lengths to fly in the wind. Safety pins were stuck through the bow, in the front and on the back. Through it all, people lined up to buy bows. Some gave one dollar, others gave twenty dollars, but everyone gave either a smile or hug, shed a tear or said, "God bless America."

I needed to share the idea with friends. Perhaps it would help them heal a bit, just as it had helped me. I packaged up the bows and shipped them to people requesting them in other states. One person bought a bow and shipped it to a friend somewhere else in America, and now before I knew it, the project was launched in eleven states. My dear friend in Texas said, "I wasn't dealing with the pain and sadness. It was much too hard to bear. So I was denying it instead of trying to help someone else, as this bow has shown me how to do. We must honor the victims."

Within a few weeks, we sent the Relief Fund more than five thousand dollars—or one thousand bows sold for one thousand heroes. Before long, new schools helped, people from other states called from churches and youth groups. People wanted to help in some way; because the "not knowing" part this attack brought makes the helplessness too hard to feel.

One thousand bows, one thousand heroes, more than four thousand additional lives to honor. God bless America.

Lisa Duncan

3

THE WORLD RESPONDS

This is not a battle between the United States and terrorism, but between the free and democratic world and terrorism. We, therefore, here in Britain, stand shoulder to shoulder with our American friends in this hour of tragedy, and we, like them, will not rest until evil is driven from our world.

British Prime Minister Tony Blair

A Fishing Village Opens
Its Heart to Surprise Guests

On September 11, once government officials realized that planes were being used as missiles, thirty-eight international flights were immediately rerouted to the emergency airfield at Gander, Newfoundland, a city of ten thousand on the Atlantic coast of Canada.

Bellevue Police Lieutenant Steve Cercone, who had been in Europe for a family funeral, was one of about 1,000 passengers then driven about twenty-five miles east to Gambo, a fishing village of 2,200.

What was supposed to be a temporary layover—while governments and airlines worked out logistical details of reopening U.S. air space—turned into a five-day adventure for passengers and townsfolk alike.

They huddled around televisions; drank "screech," the native dark rum, at the town's one tavern; ate moose stew and cod filets; and slept in the town's churches and schools. Townspeople quit their jobs that week to attend to the visitors.

"In the midst of this huge tragedy, we were fortunate enough to see the other side of life, the other side of human nature," Cercone recalls. "The kindness of complete strangers who took us in, gave us showers, fed us, did our laundry . . .

"Five days in Gambo. It would make a great movie script."

United Airlines Flight 929—London to Chicago—was 38,000 feet in the air when Cercone heard the news.

The pilot, Captain Mike Ballard, told the 198 passengers that there was a major emergency in New York City and American air space had been shut down.

Fuel was dumped because the plane was too heavy to land otherwise and the emergency landing gear dropped. "Our imaginations were running from A to Z," says Cercone, a twenty-year police veteran and former supervisor of the Bellevue SWAT team.

The small ground crew at Gander, used to a quiet routine as a cargo-plane stopover, was suddenly welcoming 6,500 passengers.

"Around midday, we were told that planes were coming out of the skies and to expect some of them," says Claude Elliot, Gander's mayor. "We had an emergency plan, so we put everything in motion."

Churches, schools and civic organizations opened their doors. Elliot went on radio and television, urging people to donate clothes, bedding, food, pillows and sleeping bags. The city's bus drivers, who were on strike, put down their picket signs and offered to ferry the passengers around.

"Everyone watched the news that morning, everyone knew that these people were stranded from home or had loved ones working at the World Trade Center," Elliot says. "We just tried to make their stay as comfortable as we could."

Gander took in the bulk, about 4,200 passengers. But

some of the burden was shouldered by satellite towns—
Gambo, Glenwood and Benton.

The strangers began arriving in Gambo that afternoon,
four planeloads, still reeling from news of the attacks.

They were divided up quickly among the Society of
United Fisherman, Smallwood Academy, the Lions Club
and assorted other churches and civic groups. Passengers
from Flight 929 slept on cots and pews at the Salvation
Army citadel.

The town's population had just jumped by 50 percent.
And the world had become a little closer.

"We saw it that morning on TV," says Wycliffe Reid,
Salvation Army captain. "But like everything else that
happens in the U.S., it's at a distance. On the same day,
these people are here, right here on our doorstep, and now
we're involved. We're called on to provide a service. We
became a part of these people and what went on."

But first, Reid's immediate concern was: How are we
going to feed them all?

Donations came from grocery stores and restaurants.
Fishermen donated 150 pounds of cod.

The Home League Ladies, two dozen strong, prepared
and served the meals.

"We understood the severity of the situation," says
Kevin Noseworthy, Lions Club president. "We just got
together, pulled down a shift. Someone would cook one
meal, someone would cook another. It was overwhelming
at times. But we got through it.

"When I'm older and in the rocking chair, it will be a
highlight. I did something good for mankind."

The town's only tavern is a single-story bungalow
called the Trailway Pub.

Graham Thompson bought it three months ago and
was remodeling Tuesday afternoon—moving the bar from
one side of the cabin structure to the other. Suddenly,

twenty-five people walked in, then twenty-five more and twenty-five more after that.

"We had 150 people in there, for four nights in a row," Thompson says. "The club was upside down with these people, hectic, warm and hot. We made a lot of good friends out of it."

The television was tuned to CNN, and the frantic staff of seven couldn't serve enough beers.

The bar played host to a ceremony in which outsiders are recognized as honorary Newfoundlanders. They explain it this way: Get on your knees; kiss a codfish on the lips to recognize the area's abundant fishing industry; eat a cake of the local hard bread—so hard it needs to be soaked in water; pound down some "screech," the dark heady rum; and praise Newfoundland.

"That's basically it," Noseworthy says. "You've drank our liquor, you've kissed our fish, you've eaten our bread. Now you're an honorary Newfoundlander."

Locals estimate about 90 percent of the town pitched in. And then just like that, the visitors were gone.

Security checkpoints had been cleared and Flight 929 was ready to come home.

The return flight was quick and everyone uneasy. Captain Ballard pulled Cercone aside and told him: Don't let anyone get through to the cockpit.

Flight 929 landed at O'Hare International Airport in Chicago around 1:00 P.M. September 15, the last of the diverted planes to touch down.

Members of the United ground crew had formed a corridor with their trucks; they were waving United States flags and clapping.

"It just hit you right here," Cercone says, pounding his stomach. "Everyone was hugging, everyone was crying."

Later he had a steak dinner at Gibson's on Rush Street and a good night's sleep at a nearby hotel. On Monday,

Cercone was back in Seattle, back to his life, back to his routine.

Michael Ko

[EDITORS' NOTE: *The visitors have responded by donating $51,000 to the town of Gander, and passengers from one particular flight started a scholarship fund worth $19,000 and "still growing."*]

Smallest Gestures

I expect to pass through this world but once; any good thing therefore that I can do, or any kindness that I can show to any fellow creature, let me do it now; let me not defer or neglect it, for I shall not pass this way again.

Etienne DeGrellet

It's 10:30 P.M. on September 11, and I am pumping up a double air mattress with a manual air pump at Halifax's Exhibition Park. Along with many other Haligonians, I arrived here around 8 P.M. to see if I could help make life a little easier for the stranded passengers. I think it's my fifteenth mattress, and I'm tired, hot and sweaty. An older woman lying on a mattress in a donated sleeping bag looks up at me and says something. All I hear is the word "tea." I stop my pumping and say, "Sure, I'll definitely find you a cup of a tea." She looks up at me and says, "Not for me, for you."

I tell her that I appreciate the offer but that I am fine for the moment. She looks rather solemn as she lies there, by herself, amidst hundreds of other airline passengers who are wandering in and trying to find beds. She is lying on her back and staring up at the ceiling. I comment that it must have been a long day for her.

She is from New York and had been visiting England. She was on a British Airways plane that was rerouted to Halifax in the wake of the terrible events taking place in New York. She begins to tell me about her husband and two daughters who live in New York, and how she would imagine that one of her daughters and her fiancé must be terribly busy as they are both doctors.

Then I ask her the inevitable question, "Have you been in touch with your family?"

Her eyes move from looking at me, to looking at the ground. She says that she hasn't been able to get in touch yet, but that she is confident they're okay, and that they know she's okay. As she talks, I can hear the hesitation and worry in her voice.

I quietly sit next to her and tell her that I work for the local cell-phone company, and offer her my phone to call her husband. A smile spreads across her face as I ask her for the number. It takes us four tries to get through, but finally, I hear ringing on the other end of the phone. I hand her the phone, she takes it, and I don't think I'll ever forget the quivering voice that I heard next. . . .

"Joseph? I'm safe. I'm in Halifax."

She talks for about five minutes and finds out that her family is fine. As Joseph describes the day's events to her, she listens silently with widened eyes and a hand covering her mouth. She asks him to let her daughters know she's okay and before she hangs up, she says, "The Canadians are wonderful. I am so impressed with Halifax." I smile as she hands me the phone. I squeeze her hand, say good-bye and, as I'm walking away, she says, "Thank you so much. Now I can sleep tonight."

As I gather my pump and head towards my next air

mattress, I think about how impressed and proud I am of Halifax, too. I am proud of my mom for helping to find sleeping mats for people at the Dartmouth Sportsplex; I am proud of my brother who stood in line for more than three hours with eight of his colleagues from Mountain Equipment Co-Op to donate blood; I am proud of my boyfriend who helped prepare Mount Saint Vincent University for stranded passengers; and I am proud of my colleagues at MTT Mobility who scrambled around the office all afternoon gathering cell phones to donate to the cause.

In the wake of tragedy like the world experienced on September 11, everyone feels helpless. My experience at Exhibition Park has reminded me of the truth in the old saying, "Every little thing counts." It could be a two-dollar phone call, a thought, a prayer, a donation or a hug—no matter what it is, please remember that it does count.

The smallest gestures clumped together and piled on top of each other can make a world of difference.

Deanna Cogdon

Dear Dad

*Both at home and abroad, we shall persevere
along our course, however the winds may blow.*
Sir Winston Churchill

Sept. 14, 2001

Dear Dad,

Well, we are still out at sea, with little direction as to what our next priority is. The remainder of our port visits, which were to be centered around max liberty and goodwill to the United Kingdom, have all but been cancelled. We have spent every day since the attacks going back and forth within imaginary boxes drawn in the ocean, standing high security watches, and trying to make the best of our time. It hasn't been that much fun I must confess, and to be even more honest, a lot of people are frustrated at the fact that they either can't be home, or we don't have more direction right now. We have seen the articles and the photographs, and they are sickening. Being isolated as we are, I don't think we appreciate the full scope of what is happening back home, but we are definitely feeling the effects. About two hours ago, the junior officers were called to the bridge to conduct ship-handling drills. We were about to do a man overboard drill when we got a call from the *LUTJENS* (D185), a German warship that was moored ahead of us on the pier in Plymouth, England. While in port, the *WINSTON S. CHURCHILL* and *LUTJENS* got together for a sports day/cookout on our fantail, and we made some pretty good friends. Now at sea, they called over on bridge-to-bridge, requesting to pass us close up on our port side to say good-bye.

We prepared to render them honors on the bridge wing, and the Captain told the crew to come topside to wish them farewell. As they were making their approach, our conning officer announced through her binoculars that they were flying an American flag. As they came even closer, we saw that it was flying at half-mast. The bridge wing was crowded with people as the boatswain's mate blew two whistles—Attention to Port—the ship came up alongside and we saw that the entire crew of the German ship were manning the rails, in their dress blues. They had made up a sign that was displayed on the side that read "We Stand By You." Needless to say, there was not a dry eye on the bridge as they stayed alongside us for a few minutes as we cut our salutes. It was probably the most powerful thing I have seen in my entire life and more than a few of us fought to retain our composure.

It was a beautiful day outside today. We are no longer at liberty to divulge over unsecure e-mail our location, but we could not have asked for a finer day at sea. The German Navy did an incredible thing for this crew, and it has truly been the highest point in the days since the attacks. It's amazing to think that only a half-century ago that things were quite different, and to see the unity that is being demonstrated throughout Europe and the world makes us all feel proud to be out here doing our job. I'll write you when I know more about when I'll be home, but for now, this is probably the best news that I could send you. Love you guys.

Megan

Megan M. Hallinan, ENS
Submitted by Thomas Phillips

Photo by PH2 Shane McCoy/U.S. Navy.

Four Simple Words

How wonderful it is that nobody need wait a single moment to improve the world.

Anne Frank

One day after the terrorist attacks in New York, Washington and Pennsylvania, a man stood on the street of a foreign country with an American flag and a sign. I didn't really have time to look; I was busy and in a state of shock over the recent events. Yet something compelled me to stop. What did this man want to say about my country? Would I have to defend mom, apple pie and rock 'n' roll so far from home? I crossed the street. On his sign were four simple words I will never forget: *"Wir alle sind Amerikaner."*

The country was Switzerland, and it is my second home. It is also stubbornly neutral and not even a member of the United Nations. Also neutral, in his own way, is Erwin Handschin, the man with the American flag and the sign. Not a member of any political party, union or club, he has never been to America and doesn't even speak English. This country and this man do not take positions, generally speaking. But on September 12, 2001, Herr

Handschin woke up near Zurich and felt compelled to hold a one-man demonstration. Walking the streets of the largest Swiss city, he carried an American flag over his shoulder and a sign that proclaimed, *"Wir alle sind Amerikaner."* Many people congratulated him or clapped their approval. Because I speak German, I knew immediately what the words meant, but their deeper meaning only became clear a few minutes later.

I introduced myself and a conversation developed. The sixty-year-old had gotten up early that morning and written his feelings down on a piece of paper. He wanted to show that his heart went out to Americans, that he had compassion for them in their time of grief and confusion. As we talked, the deeper meaning of his sign became apparent to me: What America stands for is what most people everywhere stand for. The spirit and the ideals of our country are what is best about being human. They are what men and women all over the world envy and identify with: freedom, democracy, courage, compassion. And yes, even rock 'n' roll.

Today, the streets in Zurich are more or less back to normal. Bankers, barons and businessmen walk these noble *strassen.* Neutrality is secure. But as I stroll through the city these days, Erwin's nonneutral words accompany me: *We are all Americans.* It is one reason why our country will prevail.

The evening after his one-man demonstration, Erwin went back to his apartment, cooked some dinner and went to bed at around midnight. He didn't sleep right away; instead, he lay in bed and thought to himself, *Today you did something good, something that embodies the spirit of people everywhere.* Indeed you did, Erwin.

We are all Americans.

Arthur Bowler

Hope from Abroad

*You cannot spill a drop of American blood
without spilling the blood of the whole world. . . .
We are not a nation, so much as a world.*

Herman Melville

Omaha Beach, France. We'd spent most of the day on
the road and had just sat down for a late dinner—8:30 P.M.
in France, 4:30 P.M. in New York—when we heard the
news.

The couple at the table next to us was from Ireland, and
when they recognized our accents—we were, I believe,
the only Americans in the seafront restaurant—the man
asked if we knew.

Knew what?

And so it began for us: two Americans learning that
more than 5,000 people back home had been murdered by
terrorists.

Two Americans lost in the atrocities of the past—we
were researching World War II for a book I'm writing—
suddenly confronted with an atrocity of the present.

Two Americans who, for the next week, would be

buffered—and frustrated—by being an ocean away from a homeland in mourning.

What a strange juxtaposition: to be listening to the waves wash ashore at Normandy, where fifty-seven years before, Allied troops stormed ashore to liberate northern Europe from the grasp of Germany—and, at the same time, watching CNN images of the World Trade Center collapsing after being attacked by terrorists.

Evil, I was reminded, never goes away. It simply lurks in the shadows of time, morphs to fit the technological advances and springs on another generation. Hitler, bin Laden—the monsters change, the methods change, but the madness that motivates them does not.

Earlier that day, we'd walked through the preserved ruins of a French village, Oradour-Sur-Glane. There, on June 10, 1944, its few hundred residents—like millions of New Yorkers on September 11, 2001—awoke to a place of peace and prosperity. But with the same suddenness as the attack on the World Trade Center, German troops rolled into town and massacred virtually everyone: men, women and children.

By the end of the day, 642 lay dead and the village had been burned to its stone foundations.

"Man's inhumanity to man," I heard a man mutter after witnessing the chilling remains of the village, eerily replete with everything from charred dishes to children's bikes.

The next morning—the day after we'd heard the news from home—we walked among the 9,386 graves at the American Military Cemetery above Omaha Beach.

Chimes played "My Country, 'Tis of Thee." American and French flags, both at half-staff, fluttered in the brisk breeze. And on the beach below, a couple of sand yachts slalomed beside surf once colored with blood.

Now came news of more blood following an attack that,

unlike the Normandy invasion, wasn't done to liberate the oppressed, but to oppress the liberated.

Not until we placed a phone call home did we realize the scope of the terrorist attack. We were traveling France's back roads and didn't see English newspapers and English TV broadcasts until days later.

In a sense, the language barrier protected us from the pain; we weren't barraged, as others were, with constant news reports. Nor, because of the language difference, were we conversing with others about what had happened.

And yet, being thousands of miles away from our friends, family and community also meant a strange sense of disconnectedness tinged with guilt. No matter how far off the beaten path we ventured, sometimes on roads not much wider than our rented Renault, the news from home stalked us.

Meanwhile, though, we sensed that America's pain was Europe's pain. While we were at a D-Day museum, a British schoolmaster cautioned his students to treat Americans with extra respect because of what had happened. On back roads in Luxembourg, the country's flags hung from windows, tied with black "mourning" bands. Once, not far from where Allied troops fought German troops in the bitter Battle of the Bulge, we came across a memorial for the 80th Infantry. It overlooked a beautiful valley and was anchored by two flags, both half-staffed: an American flag and a Luxembourg flag.

We couldn't help but notice the Stars and Stripes had, in the heavy wind, ripped loose from one of its two grommets. It was flying wildly out of control—and yet with a certain amount of tenacity, battered but not beaten, like the country itself.

Finally, on a drizzly Saturday, not far from Liege, Belgium, and the German border, we scanned the white markers of yet another American military cemetery, where more than 7,000 U.S. soldiers had been buried. As I looked at the sea of white crosses and Star of David symbols, I couldn't help but think this was roughly the number of people who had died in the terrorist attacks.

It left me feeling despondent, contrasting the pain of the past with the pain of the present. Would we ever get beyond man's humanity to man? Hadn't the world learned anything in the last half-century-plus?

But just when I had resigned myself to a bleak world in which nobody seemed to care about one another, an incident whispered hope to me.

I'd been interviewing the cemetery's supervisor—the subject of a book I'm writing was once buried on these grounds—when a man with a handful of daisies poked his head in the door.

He was roughly the same age that many of these U.S. soldiers from World War II would have been had they lived. He was German. He spoke little English. And he was, I discerned, seeking a vase.

"Who are the flowers for?" asked the supervisor.

"For New York," he said, "and Washington."

Bob Welch

Did You See Me?

God is known by many different names and many different traditions, but identified by one consistant feeling: love, love for humanity, particularly love for our children. Love does eventually conquer hate, but it needs our help.

Rudolph Giuliani

Did you see me?

I joined with hundreds of my fellow Canadians today, in the shadow of the Detroit skyline, to pay my respects to my American brothers and sisters. I watched as utility workers, stationed in bucket trucks, rose high above the crowd to fly the Stars and Stripes and the Maple Leaf. I shivered as the wind picked up, at just the right moment, and the flags snapped to attention, their colors bright.

Did you see me?

I was the Canadian veteran in full-dress uniform, my military medals shining brightly, whose voice quivered as we sang "O Canada." I thought of the battles we fought together sixty years ago, side by side, united in our common cause. I remembered my comrades, American and Canadian, lost in war, far across the ocean.

Did you see me?

I was the young woman wearing a *hejab* and *bourka*, who held my child's hand. I feared that the intolerance I left behind in my homeland would reappear here, in my chosen country. I wondered if my neighbors would persecute me because of my color and creed. I prayed that my children would not know the hatred my ancestors had known.

Did you see me?

I was the student, only in sixth grade, who marveled that the crowd knew the words to "The Star-Spangled Banner" as well as they knew their own national anthem. I looked across the water, at the Renaissance Center shining brightly, and thought of the U.S. Girl Scouts I had met once. I wondered if they were more afraid than I, or if all children, everywhere, now felt vulnerable. I watched as a dozen bunches of red, white and blue balloons were sent up into the air, floating on the breeze, perhaps later to bring comfort to children in Ohio, Indiana, Illinois.

Did you see me?

I was the businessman, face somber in reflection. I wondered if the thin blue line of the river that divides our countries would now become a barrier. I watched the traffic waiting to cross the border, and I wondered if I would ever go to work again without U.S. Customs' officers searching every inch of my car. I wondered if people I had worked with had lost loved ones, and I mourned their loss as though it were my own.

Did you see me?

I was the young woman, tears in her eyes, who looked skyward during a moment of prayer. A solitary plane flew high overhead, the first commercial flight I'd seen in three days. I thought of the Americans I knew, women just like me. Until Tuesday, we'd concerned ourselves with matters that now seemed mundane. Now we steeled ourselves to smile as we sent our children off to school, calling them back for one more hug, one more look at their innocent faces.

Did you see me?

I was the rabbi who assured the crowd that God had not forgotten us. I said that God was in the heroes, in the people who united in rescue efforts, in the thousands who lined up to give blood around the world, in the hundreds of firefighters who went into the World Trade Center Towers while thousands of people fled. I was the Muslim leader who prayed to Allah, to guide us to the straight way, and to make us understand the beauty of our differences. I reminded all that we are human and asked that Allah unite us in humanity. I was the Baptist preacher who suggested that we must behave like the children of God, as one people.

Did you see me?

My heart swelled with pride as my friends and neighbors leaned over the rail and dropped flowers of red, white and blue into the water. I watched as a sea of blossoms, the symbols of hope, peace and forgiveness, floated past. I listened to our mayor repeat the words that John F. Kennedy spoke about our countries, a decade before I was born: "Geography made us neighbors, history has made us friends. Economics has made us partners, and necessity has made us allies."

I thought of you, my neighbors, my friends, my partners and my allies, and I waved my flag as we sang together, "God Bless America." I prayed that together we would find a way to reclaim hope and healing, and unite together in this time of uncertainty. And with hundreds of my fellow citizens, I offered a wave of support for you and yours.

Did you see me?

Shelley Divnich Haggert

The American Flag

On a Wednesday in September, I traveled south for the funeral of my grandfather. It was a day of sadness, but also one of rejoicing for the wonderful human being I had had the opportunity to know. It was also a time of great sorrow for all Americans. It had been only days since the September 11th terrorist attacks.

Driving along a Canadian prairie road, I saw a long caravan of trucks and other vehicles and, as I got closer, people on horseback. Cowboys and cowgirls were riding horses out in the middle of nowhere! The group was traveling south, toward the border, and they were flying two flags— the Canadian and the American. They were going to meet up with a group of American riders at the border between the two countries. Along the way, the Canadian cowboys were collecting cash, which they were going to give to their American counterparts. They were just one of many Canadian groups who had found a way to help and show they cared after the attacks in the U.S.

Later that day, when I was driving home from my grandfather's funeral, the sky opened and a driving rain poured down from the heavens. Visibility was so bad that I had to slow to a crawl. It was then that I saw it. Large and glorious, whipping in the wind, perched atop an irrigation system, the water still pumping out, flew a flag! It was an American flag, raised to honor the thousands who died on September 11.

I began to cry. I thought about all those lives ending so abruptly. I also cried because I was so touched by the warm act of love demonstrated by a simple Canadian farmer. By flying the American flag he was sending out a message of love and respect to his American neighbors. His actions spoke louder than words ever could: "We are with you, dear friends. We are with you in spirit. We ache for you. We cry for you. We pray for you. We will not forget."

The storm passed as suddenly as it had started, and I found myself driving through the most glorious sunshine. I felt like God was sending a promise for better things to come.

Ellie Braun-Haley

An Ode to America

[EDITORS' NOTE: *This article was written by Mr. Cornel Nistorescu and published under the title "Cîntarea Americii" on September 24, 2001, in the Romanian newspaper* Evenimentul Zilei (The Daily Event).]

Why are Americans so united? They don't resemble one another even if you paint them! They speak all the languages of the world and form an astonishing mixture of civilizations. Some of them are nearly extinct, others are incompatible with one another, and in matters of religious beliefs, not even God can count how many they are.

Still, the American tragedy turned three hundred million people into a hand put on the heart. Nobody rushed to accuse the White House, the Army, the Secret Services that they are only a bunch of losers. Nobody rushed to empty their bank accounts. Nobody rushed on the streets nearby to gape about.

The Americans volunteered to donate blood and to give a helping hand. After the first moments of panic, they raised the flag on the smoking ruins, putting on T-shirts, caps and ties in the colors of the national flag. They placed flags on buildings and cars as if in every place and on every car a minister or the president was passing. On every occasion they started singing their traditional song: "God Bless America!"

Silent as a rock, I watched the "Tribute to Heroes" charity concert—once, twice, three times, on different TV channels. There were Clint Eastwood, Willie Nelson, Robert De Niro, Julia Roberts, Muhammad Ali, Jack Nicholson, Bruce Springsteen, Sylvester Stallone, James Woods and many others whom no film or producer could ever bring together. The solidarity of the American spirit turned them into a choir. Actually, choir is not the word. What you could hear was the heavy artillery of the American soul.

What neither George W. Bush nor Bill Clinton nor Colin Powell could say without facing the risk of stumbling over words and sounds was being heard in a great and unmistakable way in this charity concert.

I don't know how it happened that this obsessive singing of America didn't sound croaky, nationalist or ostentatious! It made you green with envy because you weren't able to sing for your country without running the risk of being considered chauvinist, ridiculous or suspected of who-knows-what mean interests.

I watched the live broadcast and the rerun of its rerun for hours, listening to the story of the guy who went down one hundred floors with a woman in a wheelchair without knowing who she was, or of the passengers who fought with the terrorists and helped prevent the plane from hitting another target and possibly killing many more.

With every word and musical note, the memory of some turned into a modern myth of tragic heroes. And with every phone call, millions and millions of dollars were put in a collection aimed at rewarding not a man or a family, but a spirit which nothing can buy. What unites

Americans in such a way? Their land? Their galloping history? Their economic power? Money? I tried for hours to find an answer, humming songs and murmuring phrases that risked sounding like commonplaces. I thought things over, but I reached only one conclusion: Only freedom can work such miracles!

Cornel Nistorescu
Submitted by Willanne Ackerman

Tribute to the United States

[EDITORS' NOTE: *This timeless editorial, written almost thirty years ago, comes from Toronto by Gordon Sinclair, a Canadian commentator.*]

This Canadian thinks it is time to speak up for Americans—the most generous but possibly least appreciated people on Earth.

Germany, Japan and, to a lesser extent, Britain and Italy, were lifted out of the debris of war by the Americans who poured in billions of dollars and forgave other billions in debts. Today, none of these countries is paying even the interest on its remaining debts to the United States. When France was in danger of collapsing in 1956, it was the Americans who propped it up, and their reward was to be insulted and swindled on the streets of Paris. I was there. I saw it.

When earthquakes hit distant cities, the United States hurries in to help. This spring, fifty-nine American communities were flattened by tornadoes.

Nobody helped.

The Marshall Plan and the Truman Policy pumped a

lion's share of dollars into depressed countries. Today, newspapers in those same countries write about the decadent, war-mongering Americans.

I'd like to see just one of the countries that is gloating over the erosion of the United States dollar build its own airplane. Does any other country in the world have a plane to equal the Boeing Jumbo Jet, the Lockheed Tri-Star, or the Douglas DC10? If so, why don't they fly them? Why do all the international lines except Russia fly American planes?

Why does no other land on Earth even consider putting a man or woman on the moon? You talk about Japanese technology and you get radios. You talk about German technology and you get automobiles. You talk about American technology, and you get men on the moon—not once, but several times, and safely home again.

You talk about scandals, and the Americans put theirs right in the store window for everybody to see. Even their draft-dodgers were not pursued and hounded. They are here on our streets, and most of them, unless they are breaking Canadian laws, are getting American dollars from back home and spending them here.

When the railways of France, Germany and India were breaking down through age, it was the Americans who rebuilt them. When the Pennsylvania Railroad and the New York Central went broke, nobody loaned them even an old caboose. Both companies are still broke.

I can name you five thousand times when the Americans raced to the help of other people in trouble. Can you name me even one time when someone else raced to the Americans in trouble? I don't think there was outside help even during the San Francisco earthquake. Our neighbors have faced everything alone, and I'm one Canadian who is damned tired of hearing them get kicked around. They will come out of this thing with their flag high. And when they do, they are entitled to thumb their noses at the countries who gloated over their present troubles.

I hope Canada is not one of those countries.

Gordon Sinclair

4

RENEWED PATRIOTISM

The world is beginning to understand why we all treasure America so much—our values, our freedom and the strength of the American character.

George W. Bush

The Aftermath

Flags were flying on every house down my block when I realized that my husband and I, who had recently bought our first home, didn't have a flag of our own. Donating blood and money no longer felt like enough.

Immediately, I left on a quest to find an American flag to show my patriotic spirit. After starting up my ancient car, I headed to the local Kmart, Wal-Mart, Home Depot, Lowes, Ace Hardware and even some craft stores. Everywhere I was told the same thing: "We had flags this morning, but we're sold out now. Come back next week, and we'll have more flags."

Next week? Somehow next week didn't seem good enough for this fervent patriot.

I hurried back to my car to proceed to plan B—trying to buy a flag over the Internet. As I drove down the highway, I noticed that nearly every marquee announced, "God Bless America" or "United We Stand." Cars passed me with flag stickers on the bumpers or small flags tied to antennas. Some cars even had flags draped over luggage racks.

This drive was unlike any other I had ever taken. I had known before that Americans were proud, but seeing so many flags today, displayed in such diverse ways, hit me differently than on any Fourth of July or President's Day. This varied display of the nation's colors spoke of unity, courage, determination.

As I stopped at a red light, I heard a familiar tune drifting from a breakfast shop that had opened its doors to welcome customers. "The Star-Spangled Banner" was blasting from a loud speaker.

". . . O say does that star-spangled banner
Yet wave!
O'er the land of the free
And the home of the brave!"

A chill ran down my spine. Although I had heard the words a thousand times before, this day I truly appreciated how Francis Scott Key must have felt as he wrote them. What a welcome sight is the red, white and blue banner flying high. Even though the light had turned green, the cars around me didn't speed off. The lady in the car next to me wiped her eyes and gave me a nod before proceeding on her way. Today, Americans were different, changed. The horror meant to divide us somehow did not. Instead, we were uniting through this tragedy, proud of our heritage.

When I got home I searched the Internet for Old Glory online. I surfed markets in other countries: China, Europe and Australia. Everywhere I searched notices were posted: "Seamstresses working overtime." "Sorry for the delay." "None currently available." All over the world, the American flag supply seemed to have run out.

Still determined, I called family members and asked if they knew where I could find a flag. All were flying their own or didn't know where new ones could be found. My mission seemed hopeless.

Hours passed.

Suddenly, a knock sounded on my door. My grandfather, Jim Pauline, a man who had served in the United

States Army during World War II in the tank division at Normandy under General Patton, held out his hands. In them lay Old Glory.

"Thought you might want this," Grandpa smiled. "Sorry it isn't very big."

I gave him a hug. Even if the flag was just a foot long, I didn't care. The size of the flag couldn't measure the love that I have for my country and for the family and friends who live within its borders.

I walked out into my yard and among the dozens that flew already, I added my very own treasured banner. It seemed a simple gesture, but the meaning was so profound it brought tears to my eyes. I used to think the flag was the symbol of our country, but I now know that what Congress decided on June 14, 1777, rings as true today as it did 224 years ago:

The stars represent each of the United States.

The blue field behind the stars stands for vigilance, perseverance and justice.

The white stripes reflect purity and innocence.

The red stripes symbolize valor and courage.

The terrorist bombers may have murdered five thousand innocent Americans on September 11, 2001, but they couldn't destroy our American spirit.

Approximately eighty-eight thousand flags were purchased in the days after the terrorist attacks—more than at any other time in history. My quest to find a flag wasn't easy. I wasn't alone in wanting to show pride for this beloved country. And for that, I am eternally grateful.

God bless America!

Michele Wallace Campanelli

By permission of Mike Luckovich and Creators Syndicate, Inc.

I Am the Flag of the United States of America

I am the flag of the United States of America.
My name is Old Glory.
I fly atop the world's tallest buildings.
I stand watch in America's halls of justice.
I fly majestically over institutions of learning.
I stand guard with power in the world.
Look up and see me.
I stand for peace, honor, truth and justice.
I stand for freedom.
I am confident.
I am arrogant.
I am proud.
When I am flown with my fellow banners,
My head is a little higher,
My colors a little truer.
I bow to no one!
I am recognized all over the world.
I am worshipped—I am saluted.
I am loved—I am revered.
I am respected—and I am feared.

I have fought in every battle of every war
for more than two hundred years.
I have flown at Valley Forge, Gettysburg,
Shiloh and Appomattox.
I was there at San Juan Hill,
and in the trenches of France,
in the Argonne Forest, Anzio and Rome,
and on the beaches of Normandy, Guam and Okinawa.
The people of Korea, Vietnam and Kuwait
know me as a banner of freedom.
I was there.
I led my troops.
I was dirty, battle-worn and tired,
but my soldiers cheered me
And I was proud.
I have been burned, torn and trampled
on the streets of countries I have helped set free.
It does not hurt, for I am invincible.
I have slipped the bonds of Earth and
stood watch over the uncharted frontiers of space
from my vantage point on the moon.
I have borne silent witness to all of America's finest hours.
But my finest hours are yet to come:
When I am torn into strips and used as bandages
for my wounded comrades on the battlefield;
When I am flown at half-mast to honor my countrymen;
When I lie in the trembling arms of a grieving parent
at the grave of their fallen son or daughter;
When I lie in the arms of a child or spouse who will have
    to go on without one who gave their life to save the life
    of another,
as so many did at the Pentagon and
the World Trade Center on September 11, 2001.
My name is Old Glory. Long may I wave.

Howard Schnauber

Mike's Flag

[EDITORS' NOTE: *This story takes place in a prison in North Vietnam.*]

Mike was a Navy bombardier-navigator who had been shot down in 1967, about six months before I arrived. He had grown up near Selma, Alabama. His family was poor. He had not worn shoes until he was thirteen years old. Character was their wealth. They were good, righteous people, and they raised Mike to be hardworking and loyal. He was seventeen when he enlisted in the Navy. As a young sailor, he showed promise as a leader and impressed his superiors enough to be offered a commission.

What packages we were allowed to receive from our families often contained handkerchiefs, scarves and other clothing items. For some time, Mike had been taking little scraps of red and white cloth, and with a needle he had fashioned from a piece of bamboo, he laboriously sewed an American flag onto the inside of his blue prisoner's shirt. Every afternoon, before we ate our soup, we would hang Mike's flag on the wall of our cell and, together, recite the Pledge of Allegiance. No other event of the day had as much meaning to us.

The guards discovered Mike's flag one afternoon during a routine inspection and confiscated it. They returned that evening and took Mike outside. For our benefit as much as Mike's, they beat him severely, just outside our cell, puncturing his eardrum and breaking several of his ribs. When they had finished, they dragged him bleeding and nearly senseless back into our cell, and we helped him crawl to his place on the sleeping platform. After things quieted down, we all lay down to go to sleep. Before drifting off, I happened to look toward a corner of the room, where one of the four naked lightbulbs that were always illuminated in our cell cast a dim light on Mike Christian. He had crawled there quietly when he thought the rest of us were sleeping. With his eyes nearly swollen shut from the beating, he had quietly picked up his needle and thread and begun sewing a new flag.

John McCain
From Faith of My Fathers

Just Ask Permission

The flag is the embodiment, not of sentiment, but of history.

Woodrow Wilson

Does the First Amendment give us the right to desecrate the American flag? Or is the flag a sacred symbol of our nation, deserving protection by law? Tough call?

I've got the solution.

For those who want to light Old Glory on fire, stomp all over it or spit on it to make some sort of "statement," I say let them do it. But under one condition: They must get permission.

First, you need permission of a war veteran. Perhaps a marine who fought at Iwo Jima?

The American flag was raised over Mount Surabachi upon the bodies of thousands of dead buddies. Each night on Iwo meant half of everyone you knew would be dead tomorrow, a coin flip away from a bloody end upon a patch of sand your mother couldn't find on a map.

Or maybe ask a Vietnam vet who spent tortured years in a small, filthy cell unfit for a dog. Or a Korean War soldier who rescued half a nation from communism, or a Desert Storm warrior who repulsed a bloody dictator from raping and pillaging an innocent country.

That flag represented your mother and father, your sister and brother, your friends, neighbors and everyone at home.

I wonder what they would say if someone asked their permission to burn the American flag?

Next, ask an immigrant. Their brothers and sisters may still languish in their native land, often under tyranny, poverty and misery. Maybe they died on the way here, never to touch our shores. Some have seen friends and family get tortured and murdered by their own government for daring to do things we take for granted.

For those who risked everything simply for the chance to become an American . . . what feelings do they have for the flag when they pledge allegiance the first time? Go to a naturalization ceremony and see for yourself the tears of pride, the thanks, the love and respect of this nation as they finally embrace the American flag as their own.

Ask one of them if it would be okay to tear up the flag.

Last, you should ask a mother. Not just any mother, but a mother who gave a son or daughter for America. It doesn't even have to be in war. It could be a cop. A fireman. Maybe a Secret Service agent. Then again, it could be a common foot soldier. When that son or daughter is laid to rest, their family is given one gift by the American people: an American flag.

Go on. I dare you. Ask that mother to spit on her flag.

I wonder what the founding fathers thought of the American flag as they drafted the Declaration of Independence? They knew this act would drag young America into war with England, the greatest power on Earth. They also knew failure meant more than disappointment. It meant a noose snugly stretched around their necks. But they needed a symbol, something to inspire the new nation. Something to represent the serious purpose and conviction we held for our new idea of individual freedom. Something worth living for. Something worth dying for. I wonder how they'd feel if someone asked them permission to toss their flag in a mud puddle?

Away from family, away from the precious shores of home, in the face of overwhelming odds and often in the face of death, the American flag inspires those who believe in the American dream, the American promise, the American vision. . . .

Americans who don't appreciate the flag don't appreciate this nation. And those who appreciate this nation appreciate the American flag. Those who fought, fought for that flag. Those who died, died for that flag. And those who love America, love that flag. And defend it.

So if you want to desecrate the American flag, before you spit on it or before you burn it . . . I have a simple request. Just ask permission. Not from the Constitution. Not from some obscure law. Not from the politicians or the pundits. Instead, ask those who defended our nation so that we may be free today. Ask those who struggled to reach our shores so that they may join us in the American dream. And ask those who clutch a flag in place of their sacrificed sons and daughters, given to this nation so that others may be free. For we cannot ask permission from those who died wishing they could, just once . . . or once again . . . see, touch or kiss the flag that stands for our nation, the United States of America . . . the greatest nation on Earth.

Tom Adkins

Ragged Old Flag

I walked through a county courthouse square,
On a park bench an old man was sitting there.
I said, "Your old courthouse is kinda run down."
He said, "Naw, it'll do for our little town."
I said, "Your old flagpole has leaned a little bit,
And that's a *Ragged Old Flag* you got hanging on it."

He said, "Have a seat," and I sat down.
"Is this the first time you've been to our little town?"
I said, "I think it is." He said, "I don't like to brag,
But we're kinda proud of that *Ragged Old Flag*.

"You see, we got a little hole in that flag there when
Washington took it across the Delaware.
And it got powder-burned the night Francis Scott Key
Sat watching it writing *Say Can You See*.
And it got a bad rip in New Orleans
With Packingham and Jackson tuggin' at its seams.

"And it almost fell at the Alamo
Beside the Texas flag, but she waved on, though.
She got cut with a sword at Chancellorsville

And she got cut again at Shiloh Hill.
There was Robert E. Lee, Beauregard and Bragg,
And the south wind blew hard on that *Ragged Old Flag.*

"On Flanders Field in World War I
She got a big hole from a Bertha gun.
She turned blood red in World War II.
She hung limp and low by the time it was through.
She was in Korea and Vietnam.
She was sent where she was by her Uncle Sam.

"She waved from our ships upon the briny foam,
And now they've about quit waving her back here at
    home.
In her own good land here she's been abused—
She's been burned, dishonored, denied and refused.

"And the government for which she stands
Is scandalized throughout the land.
And she's getting threadbare and wearing thin,
But she's in good shape for the shape she's in.
'Cause she's been through the fire before
And I believe she can take a whole lot more.

"So we raise her up every morning,
Take her down every night.
We don't let her touch the ground
And we fold her up right.
On second thought, I do like to brag,
'Cause I'm mighty proud of the *Ragged Old Flag.*"

Johnny Cash

Bring Us a Flag

I was involved in a radio contest, which involved twelve contestants living at the state fairgrounds for two weeks in *Survivor*-like conditions: no electronics, little sleep and competitions every day. The contest took place from September 7 to the 21st. Each day a contest member was voted out. The contest prize was ten thousand dollars for the last person left.

There I was, locked up in a thirty-by-thirty-foot cage, playing a silly game that had all of a sudden lost all meaning. The only information we had was from radio news reports heard on the pop station that was running the contest. The only pictures we could see were the ones my lovely wife showed us as she held up a newspaper to the fence. Six of us lived in our little camp, but at that moment we felt alone. My tribemates and I considered walking out and ending the contest. All we could think of was holding our loved ones.

Each day we were interviewed on the radio and shared our thoughts and feelings. Speaking for all of us, one of my tribemates, Jim Severn, made a plea to those listening to bring us a flag. We felt at that time that we needed to see an American flag—nothing else seemed real.

Later that same morning we heard a woman on the radio say she was sending her husband to our camp with a very special flag. She spoke of her grandfather who had been at Pearl Harbor. During the attack, he was responsible for saving many lives. His commander had been so impressed and inspired by this man's actions that he gave him one of the flags from the ruins of Pearl Harbor. His granddaughter now wanted us to have this flag because she was so touched by our simple request.

An hour later we watched as a man walked towards us. In one hand was the flag, holding the other was his son who looked no older than five or six. The pride he felt as he attached the flag to our fence was overpowering. As he finished displaying the flag the most magical thing happened. Where there was once no wind, all of a sudden the flag began to wave as a flag should. At that same moment, the radio began to play "I Will Remember You" by Sarah McLachlan. Her words touched all of us deeply.

Something else magical happened. While the flag was waving proudly, the leaves on the nearby trees were still. It was as if there was a spirit inside this flag causing it to move. Without saying one word during the entire song, we all shared the same thoughts and not a dry eye was to be found.

When we first heard the news of the terrorist attacks we wanted to walk out. When we felt the power of that one flag we wanted to stay and stand strong. By the end of the competition you could hardly see through our fence: It was covered with flags, streamers and decorations brought to us by young and old. People made special trips to visit us and see our flag. Each person expressed the same feelings we had felt as they gazed upon it.

Years from now, people will ask me where I was when the tragedy happened. I will tell them that I was surrounded, not by a chain-link fence, but by the love and patriotism of unfamiliar faces who became a family I will always be part of.

Jon Sternoff

Of Thee We Sing

"Hey, Jennifer!" someone hissed. "Get up!"

Looking up from my doll, I saw that other kids on the playground had dropped what they were doing and froze. Quickly, I rose to full height, clapped my right hand over my heart, and froze like the others, straining to hear the high-pitched trumpet signal the end of the day. Somewhere on our base the United States flag was being lowered, folded with solemn precision, then carried away in a clipped march.

When the last note trailed off, I tried rubbing the goose bumps off my forearms. What little I could hear of the melancholy horn had an effect on me.

Such was a small part of the life of an army brat.

At Saturday matinees, I savored the luxury of a candy bar and soda while waiting for the curtains to swish open. As soon as the screen was revealed, all of us army brats rustled to our feet, palms flat against hearts, and in respectful silence watched a series of patriotic scenes flash across the screen, timed to the rhythm of our national anthem. The last scene of our nation's flag rippling in slow motion burned in my mind as the anthem closed with a rousing flourish.

When I was sixteen, I sat in an off-base public movie theater for the first time. When the lights dimmed, I watched the curtains with anticipation as they parted, then stood up, hand over heart.

"What are you doing, Jenn?" my date asked, yanking on my shirt sleeve.

Scanning the darkness, I saw that I was standing alone—and blocking someone's view. Public theaters, I discovered, did not cater to the national anthem.

"Uh ... I need to go to the bathroom," I mumbled, before escaping to the lobby to nurse my chagrin.

Years later, I married a patriotic man, an Eagle Scout whose tender handling of our flag on Independence Day always brought tears to my eyes. He's never served in any branch of the military, much less been raised in a military family. But scouting ingrained a love of our country in him, and every morning in his school's homeroom he pledged allegiance to the flag.

Living outside the city limits granted us license to shoot off fireworks every Fourth of July. Two years ago, we injected a new family tradition to enhance the celebration. After the last rocket flared, my husband and I broke out singing: "O, say can you see by the dawn's early light. . . ." We sang to our kids who sat open-mouthed in lawn chairs. We sang to the star-stitched sky, to wildlife, to neighbors within hearing distance. We sang "The Star-Spangled Banner," high notes and all. We figured by the time our four kids were old enough to appreciate the words, we would have six times the joy of singing those wonderful words at the tail end of our street.

This summer, our oldest will know how to count all fifty stars on our flag. Before he even dons a scouting uniform, he will be well-versed in the etiquette of handling our nation's flag—like making sure it never touches the ground and that the sun never sets on it.

Not long ago, I was on post late when I happened to glance at some soldiers standing stock-still, their gaze locked onto the horizon. Out of habit born of pride, I stood with my hand over my heart as faint notes spirited me back to my roots.

There they were again.

Goose bumps.

I shivered, knowing it was more than just the song that filled my heart.

It was my country. Sweet land of liberty. Of thee we sing.

Jennifer Oliver

I Pledge Allegiance to the Flag . . . from the Bottom of My Heart

Our local public schoolchildren joined with more than 52 million students nationwide to salute our flag and recite the Pledge of Allegiance on October 12, 2001. I asked these students if they knew the meaning of the words they were saying, and they assured me they did! I asked each of them to share with the class what the words meant to them. Afterwards, I marveled at the precious creative gifts our children possess, especially when one child added the words "from the bottom of my heart" while reciting his pledge.

Children have an uncanny ability to lift our spirits when we least expect it. I am convinced that they are the ideal messengers for the true spirit of peace and patriotism in America.

I pledge allegiance to the flag . . . from the bottom of my heart. . . .

I . . .
The first word in the Pledge of Allegiance is "I," and it means me, an individual. I am one person. I am a

six-year-old American kid, and I am happy to say the pledge to the flag of America at school with my good teacher. It makes me feel safe. When I heard about the sad news that happened to our country I was in a good place: I was sitting on my daddy's lap.

Pledge allegiance . . .

"Pledge" means to promise. "Allegiance" means to do it with love. When you say these words you need to put your right hand over your heart to show that you promise to love America. Some people don't understand what saying the pledge really means. They just mouth the words. I will never forget the brave heroes on the flight that crashed in Pittsburgh on September 11th. One man understood exactly what it means to pledge allegiance to our flag. He made this solemn promise when he turned to the others and said, "Let's roll!"

To the flag . . .

The American flag is like a banner with stars and stripes on it. There is not another flag in the world like the American flag. We have a paper one in our window because they sold out of the real ones at Wal-Mart. Some people have tried to copy the American flag, but they can't get the colors right. Some people have tried to burn it, but they just wind up hurting themselves.

Of the United States . . .

The United States is the name we came up with when we decided to unite the states and get away from the British. We didn't have anything against them, we just wanted to be on our own because we did not believe in some of the things they believed in. For instance, they believed in having a queen, and we looked forward to becoming a more modern country. We wanted George Washington to be the president. Well, we had to fight a war because they had never heard of such a thing! After we won the war, the British people became our good friends, and some of them even moved over here.

Of America . . .

America is a country filled with lots of history. Many books have been written about it. I have read about nine or ten of them so far. Many people died for our country because they wanted freedom for the press. You can be anything you want to be when you grow up in America. It is a free country. When I grow up I want to be a fireman and play a little golf in my *free* time.

And to the republic . . .

Republics are a group of people who work at the White House. They carry briefcases and have lots of important meetings. They swear to tell the truth and nothing but the truth. Republics are not Democrats. My grandpa is one but not my dad. I do not know about my grandma or my mom. They have never mentioned it to me.

For which it stands . . .

When you say this part it means to rise up on your feet. Do not sit down when you are saying the Pledge of Allegiance. It is not proper. Stand up and think about those who died for our country. Me and my family went to Washington, D.C., on our vacation. One day we went to the Vietnam Memorial to look for my uncle's name. When we found it, my dad cried. He said my uncle was one of the brave men for which it stands.

One nation . . .

This means a country filled with praying people. We know this is a true fact because President Bush always says "God bless America" when he speaks to the nation. My mom and my dad say that President Bush is doing a good job. If you want to vote on this you can go to *CNN.com* and talk to Larry King or Dan Rather about it.

Under God . . .

This part means we are below God's roving eye. God is up in heaven and he is looking down on us. We are right here—under him. We can trust God to take care of Americans. If you say "In God we trust" instead of "under God," it means about the same thing.

Indivisible . . .

Indivisible means we cannot see it. It is also called the hidden truth. Only God can see what is going on when things are indivisible, but he will help us see the hidden truth if we only trust and obey. There is no other way, just trust and obey.

With liberty . . .

Liberty is an awesome thing. It means freedom. We even named a bell after it. It is called the Liberty Bell. It got cracked once when someone was ringing it, but that did not stop our country from celebrating the Fourth of July. Americans will never let a cracked bell stop liberty. Let freedom ring!

And justice . . .

Justice means knowing the difference between doing what is right and doing what is wrong. Justice is the word for doing what is right. I do not know the word for doing what is wrong, but someday they will pay for it. President

Bush has warned them that time is running out, and the FBI is closing in.

For all ...

This means everybody is included. It doesn't matter where your family lived before they came to America. Like me for example: I lived in Kentucky before I moved to Missouri. I am half-Mexican, half-Kentuckian, half-Baptist and half-Democrat. But none of that makes any difference because I am an American and I pledge allegiance to the flag from the bottom of my heart.

Jeannie S. Williams

I Am an American

I am a twenty-one-year-old college student from Rockaway, New Jersey. I did not personally know anyone involved in the catastrophe that struck our nation. Still, I feel connected in some way to each and every one of the victims, to their families and friends, and to the brave individuals who helped with the search and rescue. I, like all Americans, was overwhelmed with emotions. I was sad, confused, frustrated and angry—for many reasons. I had so much I wanted to say, but the words refused to come. I wrote the following passage to express my feelings and to make a statement. My thoughts and prayers are always with you. May God bless America.

I am an American. I am free.
I am an American. I am strong. Like our nation's
    foundation, built by our founding fathers over
    two hundred years ago, I will not buckle. I will not
    be broken. I will endure.
I am an American. I have faith. I have looked into
    the eyes of fear, but I am not afraid. I weep
    because I am human, not because I am weak. My

beliefs cannot be taken from me. I will never give up
hope.

I am an American. I have a voice. I speak my feelings
freely because I am free to do so. I will voice my
anger because I am angry. I will shout my frustration because I am confused. I will say my piece. I
cannot be silenced.

I am an American. I am proud. The colors red, white
and blue flow through my veins. Like the torch
that welcomed my ancestors, my soul radiates
freedom and liberty. The flag is my beacon.
Brotherhood and love are what I believe in, truth
and justice are what I stand for.

I am an American. And I am everyone—never just
one. I am everything. I am united. I am the
businessman on Wall Street, the farmer in
Nebraska, the movie star in Los Angeles. I am the
rolling waves of Miami Beach, the blowing wind
of Chicago, the snow-capped mountains of
Boulder and the desert sun of Phoenix. I am not
weakened by cowardly acts of malice; I am
strengthened. I cannot be divided. I will not be
conquered.

I am an American. I will survive. I will stand up and
I will fight and I will defend. I will not sit back and
do nothing when I can do something. I will not
back down. I will overcome. I will prevail.

I am an American. I am free.

Danielle M. Giordano

5

UNITED
WE STAND

'Tis not in numbers but in unity that our great strength lies.

Thomas Paine

One

As the soot and dirt and ash rained over us,
We became one color.
As we carried each other down the stairs of the burning
 building,
We became one class.
As we lit candles of hope and remembrance,
We became one generation.
As the firefighters and police officers fought their way into
 the inferno,
We became one gender.
As we fell to our knees in prayer and strength,
We became one faith.
As we whispered or shouted words of encouragement,
We spoke one language.
As we gave our blood in lines a mile long,
We became one body.
As we mourned together the great loss,
We became one family.
As we cried tears of rage and grief,
We became one soul.
As we shared with pride the sacrifice of heroes,
We became one people.

We are
One color,
One class,
One generation,
One gender,
One faith,
One language,
One body,
One family,
One soul,
One people.
We are the Power of One.
We are United.
We are America.

Cheryl Sawyer, Ed.D.

Chance Encounter

This country sees pain and grief,
But love has tied us together.
Hate tries to destroy,
But love conquers.
Hate tries to separate us,
But love is stronger.
Hate tries to kill,
But love lives.

Annie Perryman, a twelve-year-old in rural Oregon

As the Jewish holidays approached in the middle of September, I went to the local mall to find some outfits for my daughter. I didn't feel much like shopping. Like everyone else, it seemed, I couldn't shake a persistent and pervasive sadness. But I wanted my daughter to have something new for the Jewish New Year. I was looking at little girls' dresses when a young woman stopped me and said, "I notice you are buying girls' clothes. I have to buy something for a little girl, and I don't know anything about sizes. I only have boys. Would you help me?" Drawing on my vast experience as the mother of four daughters, I helped her choose a beautiful dress for a ten-year-old. I couldn't help but notice that the dress was really fancy—velvet and lace—by a company known to be expensive. I remarked casually, "It must be a very special occasion. She's a lucky little girl." But then the woman said, "Well, it's a special occasion. But I don't know how lucky she is. The family is having a big party. Her dad is being deployed to Afghanistan."

It was then that I really looked at this woman. She wore a simple scarf about her head and neck, but what really struck me were her eyes. They were a beautiful brown color, large and sad.

"It's a beautiful gift," I said. I was trying to convey to her how much I sympathized with her concern for those immediately affected by the terrorism, how much I also felt a part of the whole ordeal, how sad I was for all that loss. She clasped my hand for a moment and a silent bond passed between us, the kind of thing only women and mothers understand.

She continued about her business, and I went to the cash register to pay for my items. A woman ahead of me eyed me strangely. I was startled by her stare so I asked her if we knew each other. She said, "No. I heard what you said to that woman over there. How could you even talk to her? Didn't you realize she's one of them?" My shock must have registered on my face because she enlightened me, "That woman is a Muslim. They're all terrorists, you know."

There were three or four people around the cash register at that point, and all of them fell silent. I felt my anger rising. I managed to say tersely, "No, I don't know. I only know that she asked for my help with dress sizes. She was buying a present for a little girl whose father is being deployed." I would have said more, but the woman turned her back on me and walked away.

I was left with the three other women at the cash register. One of them said to me, "Don't feel bad. She's just ignorant."

But, unfortunately, not unique, I thought. I didn't feel bad; I felt angry.

I looked back toward the little girls' department. I saw the Muslim lady holding a dress and looking at me. She dropped her eyes, put the dress back and turned to walk away. I thought she must have heard our exchange. I had an idea.

I asked her out for coffee. I don't know what made me think that a total stranger would go out for coffee, but she said yes. Then, much to my surprise, two of the women at the cash register asked if they could come, too. There we were, four strangers about to become friends!

We only spent an hour together, but it was enough time to reassure this young woman that there are more people with good hearts than hardened ones; at least there were that morning in Nordstrom's department store. We discussed how horrific the attacks had been, how everyone we knew was shocked and saddened, and how we knew that many more people would die as our nation went to war.

As we were leaving, our Muslim friend said, "You are all very kind. You didn't have to do this. It's not the first time someone has reacted to me that way, and it won't be the last. And there probably isn't much anyone can do to change the mind of people like that."

I thought for a moment about how I could explain to this woman why I did what I did. It wasn't really for her. I really did it to make myself feel better. I did it—we all did it—because it felt like the right thing to do. It appealed to our sense of justice, our sense of decency.

We might never be able to influence people like the woman whose remark had unnerved me. But at least I had made myself feel better. If nothing else, I had made three new friends.

That made four of us—four against one—focusing on what unites us, makes us human, instead of what divides us and makes us something less.

I hadn't been quick enough to think of a retort to that one woman's barb. And even if I had, probably nothing I said would have made a difference. But it wouldn't have been enough anyway to simply react. We must also act, and act positively, humanly, showing our best selves.

Going shopping, helping someone find the right size, going for coffee—they were acts that could show at least one nice lady wrapped in a head scarf that those who kill might destroy human beings, but they couldn't touch the human spirit.

It wasn't much, just a cup of coffee. But it was a start.

Marsha Arons

Reprinted with permission of Jimmy Margulies.

The Ominous Sound:
Racist Assumptions

I realize that patriotism is not enough. I must have no hatred or bitterness towards anyone.

Edith Cavell

When you've finally turned off the television because you can't stand any more, when the front door is locked and the cat is fed and the night sky is utterly silent, it's just you and your thoughts.

Late Tuesday night, I recalled my father, about fifty years ago, telling me for the first time about Pearl Harbor.

He described the clenched jaws he saw that afternoon on the streets of New York, the disbelief on every face, the astonishment at how life can deal from the bottom of the deck.

And then, after about twenty-four hours, he saw resolve. Not just to get mad or get even or both. The resolve to go forward by upholding our country's best traditions, our very reasons for existing.

On the Red Line yesterday morning, about twenty-four hours after the horrors of September 11, I saw what I had feared I would see.

A man was sitting near the back door of the fourth car. He was wearing a suit and tie. He was reading the *Washington Post*. He was obviously of Arab extraction.

A woman sat across from him. She was obviously not of Arab extraction.

She stared at the man for about four stops. She was apparently trying to work up the courage to say something to him. Near Cleveland Park, she bolted over and said, accusingly, right in his face, "Why?"

The man was startled. He put down his paper and asked the woman to repeat herself.

"Why? Why did you people do this?"

The man's face flashed through fear, anger, caution and confusion. He said, very calmly, in perfect, unaccented English, "Ma'am, I am an American citizen. I am just as upset as you are."

But of course, what he really meant was, "Please don't blame me or harm me just because I am obviously of Arab extraction."

I fear that many more such confrontations are coming.

I can't imagine a repeat of the internment camps of World War II. In an age of Big Media, in an America that's far more diverse than it was sixty years ago, no broad-brush "security step" could last a day, much less get started.

No, I'm far more worried about the small-scale sort of thing I saw on the subway (and saw aboard a Metrobus in the late 1970s, the day after Iranians kidnapped several dozen employees of the U.S. Embassy).

This isn't the horrid, vicious racism of lynchings and church bombings. But it is just as profound and just as corrosive.

It damns first and asks questions later.

It is dangerously ignorant of our history and our glory.

It is especially galling in a city as varied and as sophisticated as Washington.

Ask your kids about the reflex I saw in the subway. Ask them whether, when they take the measure of someone, they see skin color first, or a swarthy complexion, or a nose that is or isn't broad.

If they are smart—and kids are always smart—they will tell you that race is another generation's hang-up, that it doesn't take you inside someone's soul. When it comes to race, they'll tell you they aren't their fathers' Oldsmobiles.

A fifteen-year-old called me Tuesday afternoon.

He is Iranian-American. He said he was scared to death when he first heard the awful news.

He feared retaliation against himself and his family.

However, he began to feel a lot better shortly after he got home from school. One by one, his buddies from West Springfield High School (all of them white) called to dissect the disastrous day with him.

Not one referred to Arabs as a group or tried to lay the events at his or their doorstep. "It made me feel wonderful," the boy said.

But then, the father of one friend jumped on the line and ordered the conversation terminated right away. The father didn't explain, "But I think I know why," this fifteen-year-old said.

I think I know why, too.

It makes my skin crawl.

This boy was born at Inova Fairfax Hospital. He has spent his entire life in northern Virginia. He told me he wears Nike sneakers and a faded University of Virginia sweat shirt, like thousands of other kids.

But now he is being judged by his ethnic origin—before

the judge even knows whether Arabs were responsible for the horrors of Tuesday.

You will hear an awful lot over the next weeks about how we Americans must come together.

You will see huge increases in church attendance.

You will read stories about people who donate blood six times.

You will see gas station owners who try to charge $5 a gallon shouted back down to $1.45.

But I hope you'll hear shouts, too, about the fundamental strength of our country: the pot that melts us all.

If we are going to summon the will to beat terrorism, we need to check our underpinning first. It won't be very sturdy if we judge books by their covers.

My father made much the same point in that conversation we had fifty years ago.

He told me about an Irish-Catholic fellow who clapped him on the back as they stood on a midtown Manhattan street corner on December 7, 1941.

This man never asked my father if he was Irish, Catholic or Martian. He just said they were all in this together, and they'd all have to stand or fall as one.

True then. True now.

Bob Levey

Long-Distance Call

The power to unite is stronger than the power to divide.

From an AT&T commercial
after September 11, 2001

To say that the events of September 11 changed the world forever is a gross understatement. For many of us adults who had never lived through a war fought on our own soil, it brought home to us our own vulnerability. For our children, September 11 meant fear and the certain knowledge that there was indeed the most heinous kind of evil in the world. I was saddened by my newfound knowledge and angered by my children's loss of innocence.

I watched the images of the World Trade Center collapsing from my home in Chicago. Like everyone else, I was stunned and horrified. But my friend Sharon and I had one more reason to be fearful. Both of us have children at school in New York City. When we were finally able to reach them and were assured they were safe, we hugged each other and cried. Still, both of us heard the fear in our children's voices. As mothers separated from our kids, we ached to reassure them. We couldn't. But one evening as I sat in Sharon's kitchen, she and I learned that sometimes the comfort our children need can come from others.

Sharon was making iced tea. The weather had been unseasonably warm in Chicago. It was hot in New York also as I knew from a conversation I had with my daughter, Rachael, earlier that day. Sharon's phone rang. It was her son, Jake, and thinking that I would enjoy hearing the conversation, Sharon put him on the speakerphone.

But Jake's voice quavered as he said, "Ma, we're in trouble." I reached over to take Sharon's hand.

"What's the matter?" she asked.

"We're in Harlem. Our bus broke down. We're at 135th Street and Amsterdam."

Jake attends Yeshiva University, an all-male college for Orthodox Jewish boys all the way north in Washington Heights. Stern college, Yeshiva University's sister school, is located in midtown Manhattan. The schools provide a shuttle bus so the kids can get together. Typically the boys go to the girls' school because there is so much more for them to do in Midtown.

For the most part, the YU boys had never had any problems with other racial or ethnic groups and were used to traveling freely throughout the city. After September 11, we wanted our kids, as Mayor Giuliani said, to go back to living their lives normally. This meant not being afraid to take the bus into Midtown on a warm summer night to visit friends.

But now Jake was telling his mother that the bus had broken down in the middle of Harlem. To make matters worse, the electricity in the area was on back-up and few stores along Amsterdam were lit. For all that we teach our kids not be prejudiced, when Jake said that a group of about twenty black youths had begun to circle the bus, we were scared.

The bus driver had already called for another bus and notified the police. But the New York City police had their hands full with a city in turmoil. And no crime had been committed.

Sharon and I looked at each other, imagining the scene. She told Jake to keep the doors and windows locked and to wait. She wouldn't let him hang up. We could hear sounds in the background. The Harlem boys were shouting for the Yeshiva boys to open the doors and come out.

"It's so hot in here, Mom." Jake said. "I don't know how much longer we can stay holed up in here."

Eight hundred miles away and only connected by a cell phone, we weren't much use to her son.

Then Jake said, "Ma, one of those kids went and got a lady from one of the buildings. She's coming over. Wait. . . . She's yelling for us to come out." At this point, Jake must have held the phone out so Sharon and I could hear. Sharon's face broke into a wide grin.

"You boys come outta there this minute. Ain't you got no sense? It's a hundred degrees in there. You get yourselves out here and into that drugstore and get yourselves a drink this minute!"

We recognized that tone! We had used it ourselves many times. It was an order any mother would give to a stubborn child!

"Jacob! You do just what she says. And let me talk to her," Sharon said decisively.

Then that mother's voice said, "This here's Bessie. I'm Duane's mama. Duane and his friends was trying to get your boys outta this hot bus. They need to go stand inside where it's cool and get theyselves a soda. What's the matter with them? Ain't they got good sense?"

Sharon laughed softly, "Evidently not, Bessie." She

paused. Then she said, "I'm sorry, Bessie. The boys were scared. They thought your son and his friends would hurt them."

Bessie didn't answer right away. But, I could hear a long exhale. Then her voice cracked a little as she said, "We can't be thinking like that. They's plenty of folks who want that; they's crazy folks in this world. Here comes your boy. They got some soda pop. . . . Mama? You take care, now, hear?"

We heard. We heard New York City turn into a small town where mothers looked after each others' children, chastising them when they needed it; where a group of white Jewish boys and a group of black Harlem boys became just boys enjoying a soda together on a street corner on a hot summer night.

September 11 changed the world forever. New York City and all Americans experienced the worst trauma, the worst horror imaginable. It sickened us all.

That night, at 135th and Amsterdam, a few of us began our recovery.

Marsha Arons

Our American Family

I had been in New York a month before the World Trade Center Towers came down. My family had gathered at a cemetery in Staten Island for the unveiling of my mother's gravestone. The carved granite read "wife, mother, grandmother." She was that, and she was aunt, sister-in-law and friend as well. Once, she was someone's daughter, too. We had come to remember all that.

We looked around for small stones to put on the grave, as is the custom of our religion. I managed to unearth a variety of pebbles, which I held tightly in my hand. Other relatives of mine were buried in that cemetery, and I wanted to remember them, too, by laying memorial stones on their graves. I went from one marker to another in the family plot, laying a symbolic memory on each.

When I finished honoring my relatives, I realized that I had one stone left in my hand. Rather than toss it back on the ground, I looked around for a grave that had no stones, that could use an offering from a stranger. But every grave had at least one stone placed on it. So I put the stone I had been carrying in my purse and thought no more about it.

The Sunday after the terrorist attacks, I was on my way

to New York again, to bring my father to see his sister in Brooklyn. I remembered my last trip to the cemetery. How many more graves there would be now. How many more stones would be needed.

When I returned home, I found the stone I had put in my purse. I took it outside and placed it respectfully in a protected spot in my garden where I could see it as I sat quietly in my back yard. There it would remind me of all the wives, mothers, fathers, aunts, uncles, brothers, sisters and friends who I never knew but grieved for all the same.

The stone was no longer the offering of a stranger. There are no strangers in this country anymore. We are an American family connected by ties of grief, memory and hope.

Ferida Wolff

6

REFLECTIONS

When I despair, I remember that all through history, the ways of truth and love have always won. There have been tyrants and murderers, and for a time they can seem invincible, but in the end they always fall. Think of it. Always.

Mahatma Gandhi

Vintage Voices

Chromed wheelchairs and walkers—parked bumper-to-knee—lined the walls. Dented and scarred from life's battles, silver-haired seniors packed the residents' dining hall at a local eldercare facility. The afternoon's scheduled activity was shoved aside to make room for the topic crowding everyone's minds: the September 11 terrorist attacks on America.

These are their thoughts, their comments, their opinions—ageless wisdom from those nearly forgotten faces in the rearview mirror:

On Fear . . .

- If we feed hope, fear will starve to death.—*Selma, age 74*
- I always thought the Great Depression was the hardest times. But worrying about the future for your grandkids is harder.—*Elsie, age 82*
- At first, I just wanted to pull the covers over my head. Later, I decided to bow my head.—*Bernice, age 75*
- I spent all my working years trying to make life better for my children and grandchildren. Terrorism and war

weren't what I had in mind.—*Henry, age 85*

- In times like these, we need a hand to hold.—*Lena, age 101*
- Worry is like a rocking chair: It keeps you busy, but it doesn't get you anywhere.—*Ava, age 71*
- Why worry when you can pray?—*Trudy, age 89*
- When fear comes in uninvited, just don't give it a chair to sit on.—*Conrad, age 84*

On Courage . . .

- Tragedy is tough, but we're tougher.—*Rosa, age 94*
- Once, I served with the best, for the best. Nothing has changed. *Cordie, WWII veteran, age 79*
- Even in the worst of times, we need to be grateful for our blessings.—*Inez, age 90*
- We've survived hardship and loss. We're a strong generation. The same God who got us through then will get us through now.—*Walter, WWII veteran, age 81*
- It'll feel better when it quits hurtin'.—*Ernst, age 78*
- Americans know a "call to arms" really means my arm in your arm . . . with God's arm around us all.—*Herman, age 83*

On Sorrow . . .

- Some people are gonna be mad at God.—*Eugene, age 82*
- I lost a brother to WWI. I lost a son to WWII. I saw grandnephews serve in Korea, a granddaughter nurse the wounded in Vietnam and a great-grandson board a ship for the Persian Gulf. And I can only shake my head in disappointment . . . just as God must be doing. When will mankind learn?—*Lucy, age 100*

- The more I see how people can hate, the better I like dogs.—*Bill, age 97*
- I've learned it's love, not time, that heals all wounds.—*Selma, age 80*
- War and sin . . . to my way of thinking, they're one and the same. And both corrode the soul.—*Vera, age 88*
- I have old memories, but young hopes.—*Elverne, age 77*

On Hope . . .

- Hope means hanging on even after others let loose. —*Fern, age 75*
- I hope our government ain't all vine and no taters. —*Wilber, age 80*
- We can only hope for the best, prepare for the worst . . . and make do with whatever happens. —*Lillian, age 74*
- Kites rise against the wind. So will we.—*Herman, age 83*
- My favorite words in the Bible are, "And it came to pass." This, too, will pass.—*Marie, age 93*
- Them terrorists barked up the wrong tree. The US of A is made of sterner stuff than they know.—*Wilber, age 80*

On God . . .

- When we think we can't help in some other way, we can always pray.—*Marta, age 96*
- I think God allows dark times so that we'll search for his light.—*Howard, WWII veteran, age 81*
- My momma always said, "Evil stands on one leg; goodness stands on two."—*Hazel, age 92*
- I keep wondering, *Where is God in all of this?* And I keep thinking, *He's waiting to hear from you.*—*Edna, age 103*
- God is as tough as a pine knot.—*Mary Margaret, age 77*

• We need to look to God in prayer. My knees don't work anymore, but I'm kneeling in my heart just the same.—*Marie, age 93*

Carol McAdoo Rehme

Time to Pray

More things are wrought by prayer than this world dreams of.

Abraham Lincoln

On the morning of September 11, 2001, my family woke to the sounds of metal crashing and a person screaming. I ran for the phone to call 911, while my son hurried to the corner. He returned with a report that a motorcyclist had broadsided a left-turning car and had been thrown twenty feet along the pavement. Emergency vehicles arrived promptly, and everyone seemed to be all right. But still, the event rattled me. It reminded me that our lives can be dramatically changed in a single moment.

A short time later my husband called from work and told me to turn on the news.

What? I thought. *That neighborhood accident made the news?*

"What channel?" I asked.

"Pick one," he said flatly.

I hurried to the living room and punched the power button. Immediately, I saw a strange and terrible sight. A skyscraper with fire and smoke billowing out a few stories from the top. Sketchy blurbs scrolled across the bottom of the screen as flustered newscasters spoke in shocked tones about the World Trade Center. A passenger jet had flown directly, purposefully, into the North Tower, instantly killing everyone on board and many inside the building. Another plane flew into the South Tower. One tower had collapsed. As I watched, the second one fell.

Hours passed as I watched the reports, updates and corrections in stunned shock. The Pentagon had also been hit. Another plane had crashed in a field in Pennsylvania. At the time, no one knew if there was a connection between the plane that crashed "in the middle of nowhere" and the others. Later, it was determined that it had also been hijacked, apparently intended for the White House or Air Force One.

What kind of a world do we live in? I thought. Ignoring the work I had scheduled to do that day, I spent hours glued to the television. The newscasts on every channel showed videos of the planes slamming into the towers over and over again. Every once in a while, new footage was found and shown, displaying the gruesome scenario from different angles.

We had just been in New York. Eleven days before, on August 31, my husband and I had flown out of Newark Airport to visit relatives in Pennsylvania and Kentucky for a week and a half. On Sunday, September 9, we drove back to Newark Airport. We arrived in New Jersey well ahead of schedule, so we drove around, looked at the sights and took pictures—including photos of the New York skyline! We ended up missing our original return flight, as well as a connecting flight, so we didn't get back home until about five o'clock Monday evening. The next morning, as we watched the news, I thanked God that we had made it home, and I prayed for the many who hadn't.

All day Tuesday, most of Wednesday and a good portion

of the days thereafter, I watched the news on television, listened to news radio and even checked the news pages of the Internet for updates. I watched the many faces of people who had been directly affected by this unspeakable tragedy—those whose loved ones had died or been severely injured.

In the midst of the tragedy, stories of bravery and heroism surfaced. One story described a man on the Pennsylvania plane who tried to call home, but ended up reaching an operator. After making her promise to call his wife and children to tell them he loved them, he asked her to recite the Lord's Prayer with him. She did. Then he, with the help of a few other passengers, somehow thwarted the hijackers' intentions and ultimately saved the lives of countless individuals who had been targeted for attack on the ground.

As the days passed, I did my best to return to my usual routine—especially to my work, as the president had urged us to do. But life no longer felt "normal." Like most people in the country, my emotions were much closer to the surface. I only left the house to get groceries or other necessities. And I was not making plans for another cross-country vacation any time soon.

But the most noticeable difference in my life was an obsessive compulsion to watch the news. I have never been one to tune in regularly or even to read the newspaper (other than the entertainment and coupons sections). But after September 11, I started listening to the news several times a day to catch all the late-breaking updates. We listened to news reports every night just before bed. The television was turned on first thing every morning, even before breakfast, to find out what had happened while we were sleeping. Throughout the day, I checked Internet news sites and flipped madly from local stations to CNN, MSNBC and back again. I didn't want to miss anything new, and I was ready to grab the phone and call friends and loved ones if something happened they might have missed.

One day, as I sat glued to the television, something occurred to me. Wouldn't it be wonderful to have that same obsessive compulsion about spending time with the Lord—praying with him, listening for his voice, reading and studying his word? Not that it wasn't important to find out if CNN had anything new. But shouldn't it be even more important to make sure I didn't miss anything God might have to say to me? How different would my life, and the lives of my friends and loved ones, be if I called them immediately every time I received a new tidbit of wisdom from the Lord?

In that moment, I made myself a promise. Whenever I felt the urge to pick up the remote and turn on the news to find out what was going on, I would pray. Pray for my country. Pray for President Bush and his advisors. Pray for those who had lost loved ones in the attacks. Pray for the rescue workers at the disaster sites. Pray for the Arab-Americans who were experiencing the backlash of prejudice. Pray for the innocent civilians of Afghanistan. Pray for the reservists who had been called to report for duty. Pray for those who might be planning further attacks against the United States or other peace-loving countries. Pray for the Taliban and even for Osama bin Laden himself. Pray for all the individuals who had been so deceived by evil that they believed they were doing God and the world a favor by eliminating the "spiritually bankrupt" people of America from the face of this planet.

Today, after I have spent time in prayer, I allow myself to watch the news, but only long enough to see if anything major has occurred. Then I turn it off and pray some more before going back to my duties. This self-imposed regimen has brought me peace in this time of terror. My focus is no longer on the tragedy, but on the God of the universe, the Lord of my life.

Do I have time in my busy schedule to pray that many times in the day? I had time to watch the news compulsively for many, many days.

There has never been a more important time to pray than right now.

Kathy Ide

THE FAMILY CIRCUS   **By Bil Keane**

"Daddy says you've been 'stremely busy since September 11th, but . . ."

Reprinted with permission from Bil Keane.

Putting Things into Perspective

Nothing like a terrorist act against several thousand innocent people to put your life into perspective. I was worried about a lot of things a week ago, but for the life of me, I can't seem to remember what those things were. Something about money and not having enough of it, I suspect. One of our credit cards is a little high. I was probably worried about that. But then I saw the millions of pieces of paper blown out of the World Trade Center offices, representing the financial lives of thousands of people. The Manhattan streets looked like the devil threw a tickertape parade. Except, instead of confetti, the sky was filled with stock orders, inventory lists, personal checkbooks, savings accounts and, who knows, maybe even a laundry list. And as important as those little pieces of paper had been just days before, they were the farthest things from the minds of the victims' families, friends and the rescuers.

So I must be wrong. I couldn't have been worried about one little credit card statement. One piece of paper. That would be absurd.

Maybe I was worried about the heat. It has been awfully hot in Hawaii the last few weeks. But watching those firemen clad in stifling, heavy, protective coats, climbing up and down tons of cement and steel rubble, frying in the heat at Ground Zero, I knew I must be wrong. I couldn't possibly have been worried about our heat. Maybe I was worried that we had not had a good heavy rain in a long time. We need rain badly. But then I thought about the people trapped below the rubble in New York and the worries there that it would start raining. The rain would interfere with the rescue operation, possibly making a dangerous situation even worse. Suddenly, lack of rain seemed like a good thing.

I might have been worried about my health. I used to be a pretty good hypochondriac. As I've gotten older, I'm not really able to focus as well, at least not the kind of focus it takes to convince yourself that you've got a tumor growing somewhere on your body or are going through the early stages of mad cow disease. That's a young hypochondriac's game. But how could I have been worrying about my health at all when, unlike the thousands of victims of the World Trade Center destruction, I was still alive.

Being alive is good. Being alive is something to be thankful for. You shouldn't waste being alive worrying that you might be putting on a few pounds, or feeling guilty about having an extra slice of pizza.

I might have been worried about some argument I had with my wife. But is that possible? When two people live together for more than twenty years, someone's going to get on someone else's nerves, especially if that first some-one is me. But a long, loving relationship is something to celebrate, and only an idiot would worry about a few bumps along the way.

A week ago, life was one big worry. Funny, today it's a blessing.

Charles Memminger

What I've Learned

Unfortunate events, though potentially a source for anger and despair, have equal potential to be a source of spiritual growth. Whether or not this is the outcome depends on our response.

The Dalai Lama

After the tragedies of September 11 the world changed. We awoke to a different world on September 12—no doubt about it. Despite our losses, our heartache and our fears, some positive outcomes have resulted from these events, outcomes that the terrorists who wished to destroy us could never have anticipated or comprehended. There is renewed patriotism in America. Our flag is flying proudly from churches, businesses, homes, cars and schools. Neighbors are taking an extra moment to wave to each other. Hurried citizens are slowing down, spending a little more time with family and friends, and being a little more kind.

In times of sorrow, we realize what is truly important. Here's what I learned about the important things in life, during the sorrowful days that followed September 11:

- Life is too short to stay in an unhappy marriage, a job you loathe or a town you hate. If something doesn't make you happy now, you need to move forward and find something that does make you happy. You may never get another chance. Live your life today! Be happy today.
- Value your family and friends as much as possible. Sometimes we get so busy in life that we think we "don't have the time" to spend with family and friends that we should. But there is nothing more important than our relationships with our loved ones. Turn off the television and the computer, put down your book, and talk to those you love. They may not be here tomorrow.
- There are heroes all around us. A hero is someone who is willing to crash an airplane into a field, knowing that he is going to die, just to save the life of others—strangers he doesn't even know. A hero is someone who runs into a burning building to help scared strangers to safety and pays for it with his own life.
- People really do care about each other, and they really care about what is happening in the world. People can put aside their differences and work together for the good of mankind.
- True leaders and true heroes emerge in times of crisis.
- In times of adversity, you learn who your true friends are. A friend of mine, who I have known since childhood, wrote me to say she wanted to tell me how much she has valued our friendship over the past twenty years. She wanted to say it now, just in case she never got another chance. That's a true friend!
- Everyone around the world must overlook their differences and work together if we are ever to enjoy a truly peaceful world.
- Renewing our relationship with God cannot be put off until tomorrow. Tomorrow may be too late!

Finally, I've learned that all we need to do is reach out and help our neighbors, even when they don't ask for help. Imagine what a better world this would be if everyone performed one random act of kindness every day.

Victoria Walker

Familiar Strangers

On Tuesday September 11, 2001, at 8 A.M., I boarded a flight in New York headed for Los Angeles. Shortly we rolled out onto the runway, lurched back, fired down the runway, and soared into the sky. It must have been almost 8:30 A.M. when I looked over my shoulder and gazed out at the New York skyline noting the clear view from Columbia University, my alma mater, all the way down to the World Trade Center. *What a beautiful day,* I thought to myself. *I wish I wasn't leaving.* I then closed my eyes and drifted off to sleep.

A little over ninety minutes later I awoke when the pilot's voice came over the loudspeaker. "Ladies and gentlemen," he announced in a calm voice, "we are making an emergency landing in Cincinnati because of an apparent terrorist attack in the New York area. Please stay calm."

There was a nervous murmur throughout the cabin. The journalist in me demanded immediate information, and I reached for the phone. I quickly ran my credit card through the phone, waited for the dial tone, and dialed our news desk in Los Angeles. The phone cackled, but when the other line picked up, there was no mistaking the panicked tone in one of my colleagues.

"Are you okay?" she asked.

"I am." I asked for further information.

"Two planes crashed into the World Trade Center. They've come down. They've come down."

The phone cut off and went dead. I frantically redialed. No luck. I tried my sister in Los Angeles. No luck. I slowly sat back in my chair and began to panic. I knew my father had flown out of New York on a different flight about an hour before me. I knew my mother was on a flight originating in London destined for San Diego. I tried to meditate and tell myself that everyone would be okay. Tears burned my eyes.

When we touched down twenty minutes later, the pilot instructed us not to turn on our cell phones. He gave us instructions to immediately evacuate the plane and follow the instructions of security personnel. We did.

Finally in the terminal, I reached for my phone and turned it on. There I stood huddled with hundreds of other interrupted passengers and gazed up at the television. The fresh images of two smoldering stumps—the remains of the towers of the World Trade Center—played on the screen. Finally, I got in touch with my sister, Mallika, who was sobbing on the other end of the phone.

"I'm okay. Where's Papa? Where's Mom?"

Mallika supplied all of the answers—everyone was safe. I placed my next call again to the office. I knew that there was work at hand. Sure enough, I already had a car reserved and was destined back for New York. At the rental agency, there was a great shortage of cars. People in line started shouting out their destinations and everyone began carpooling. I joined two other men from the New York area and we were off. Over the next twelve hours we listened closely to the radio as details of the terrorist attack emerged.

Every five minutes the name of another family member or friend popped into my head and I dialed the number frantically. Most New York numbers were jammed or out of service. One friend I was able to contact informed me that he was unable to contact a mutual friend of ours. He worked in the 105th floor of one of the towers. He was scheduled to attend an 8:30 A.M. meeting.

Someone from the meeting had called to say they had survived the initial attack and were waiting for a rescue team. No one had heard from any of them since.

Finally, just after midnight, we made it just to the edge of New York City, in Fort Lee, New Jersey. There would be no crossing into Manhattan Island—all the bridges and tunnels had been sealed. I spent the night in New Jersey unable to sleep much, and by 6 A.M., I was dressed and ready to get in.

The only way to get across was via the commuter train that was offering limited services. As we pulled toward the station in Hoboken, New Jersey, the trains slowed to a stop. There on the other side of the river they stood, like ashen smoking gravestones, the ruins of the Twin Towers. The train car was silent as everyone stood hushed and gazed out the window. A young woman beside me began to whimper. Another man lowered his head into his hands and muffled his sobs.

Back in the city, people walked around in a daze. The streets were empty of cars but full of wandering pedestrians, walking directly down the middle of Broadway and Fifth Avenue. As we made our way downtown (I had already hooked up with a television crew), we noticed small cafés open and people filling the outside sidewalk seats. People sat mostly in silence gazing upwards at the thick plume of white smoke still snaking its way westward. At West 4th Street, a group of kids played basketball. At one point the ball rolled out of play. A young shirtless boy ran after the ball and bent down to pick it up. When he lifted his head he looked up at the air at the same thick trail of smoke. He shook his head and wiped away something from his eyes—either sweat or tears—and turned away.

Walking home, I stopped and talked to a police officer. After chatting a few minutes, the officer asked me if I would like to see Ground Zero. I agreed to stay just at the edge away from the workers. The pictures on television of the devastation caused by Tuesday's attack do the scene of the crime absolutely no justice. In real life it appears as if an asteroid has hit the lower part of Manhattan. There are charred, twisting slabs of metal and concrete in every direction. It is unfathomable, unspeakable, incomprehensible. The tragedy today is in its infancy. For the thousands who lost their lives, there are thousands more—friends and family—who will never sleep a restful night. There are parents, children, siblings, friends and neighbors who walked out of their buildings one morning and have not returned. This is a national tragedy but also a very personal one.

On Wednesday night while in a cab returning from work to my apartment, I noticed the Muslim name of my driver. He noticed the tone of my skin in the rearview mirror. He nodded at me. On the radio, the commentator was relaying a warning to all men of Middle Eastern and South Asian descent—to be wary of unwarranted violent reprisals from agitated residents of the city.

The taxi driver again looked at me through the mirror and smiled ironically, "We love America. It is our home."

About a month ago, I rode up with two colleagues to the Northwest Frontier region of Pakistan bordering Afghanistan. We were covering a story on Islamic militancy training grounds based in Pakistani religious schools.

In the West they have widely been reported to be the training ground for the grooming of young Muslim boys into hostile anti-Western terrorists. In Pakistan, both the government and the men at the school hotly contested these claims, castigating the West for generating such racist propaganda. I traveled to this lost area with as little bias as possible—but with a certain and undeniable fear in my heart.

In the school itself, the chancellor was most kind and hospitable. He had us tour the grounds of the school, meet teachers and some of the boys—though at first we weren't allowed to talk to them. We were then escorted into his private residence. The first thing I noticed on the center table was a bowl of big yellow mangoes and a picture. The picture was of our host—an older Muslim mullah wearing a traditional white turban and a stained orange beard and his friend, Osama bin Laden, the number-one man on the FBI's list of Most Wanted. I asked our host if we could interview him. He agreed but insisted first that we share mangoes with him. I agreed and he took out a long knife and proceeded to slice the fruit for me. We slurped and chatted for a while and finally were permitted to turn on the camera.

I asked the mullah a wide array of questions: Did he hate the U.S.? Why is there such anti-Americanism in this part of the world? Should Americans be afraid?

He answered them all eloquently and without hostility. He talked about the history of the U.S. and Afghanistan, how during the Cold War they were allies, united fighting a war against the Soviets.

"You gave us weapons and trained our men. You built our roads, fed our people. Do you realize, young man, that your government helps to create and to fund the Taliban because it was in their interest to use guerilla warfare and terrorist tactics against the Russians? You made us your friend.

"But then your Cold War ended and you deserted us." At this point, there was a hint of animosity in his voice. "Because it was no longer in your selfish interest to have us as your allies, you abandoned us, left our people, hungry and hateful. You turned your friends into foes because you used us like whores."

There was a silence between us.

Finally I asked him about the picture, about the nature of his relationship with Mr. bin Laden.

"He's an old friend. And a good man."

I shook my head. "Is he a terrorist?"

"We don't call him that here." The mullah made it clear he was not interested in talking any more. We shook hands. I thanked him for his hospitality.

On the way out I thought about that hospitality. I knew that the mullah himself had endorsed a *fatwa*, or religious order, by bin Laden several years ago urging Muslims to kill American civilians. But here was this man cutting mangoes for us and being very gracious.

"Today you are our guest. If we were not hospitable, we would be very ashamed. But in times of war, yes, you would be an enemy and we may kill you. Today a friend, tomorrow, *inshallah* [God willing], there will not be one."

Today, Friday, September 14, 2001, four days since the terrorist attack, it appears we may be on the threshold of war. Our president has called it the first world war of the 21st century. I am not sure whom we will be fighting. I would like to go to my favorite café in the city—a small Egyptian place on the Lower East Side that I have been going to since college. The waiters—mostly young Middle Eastern guys who like to talk about basketball and soccer, who come and sit at your table and share a puff on the sweet tobacco hook as they serve there—they are my friends.

But I'm not sure when it will open again, if it will open again. There's a mosque next door that has been closed since the attack.

The weeks and months and perhaps even years ahead

promise to be complex and wary. Hopefully our leaders will be judicious, precise and compassionate in the difficult decisions that lay ahead. But it is each of us that now must rise up and be the true warriors in this difficult time. Does that mean seizing weapons and braving the threat of death out on a battlefield?

Precisely not. Because the battlefield is invisible. The enemy is elusive.

The web of evil is too complex. Today there are no answers. It is too early for solutions, for remedies. For now we each have our stories—where we were on the day that the Twin Towers toppled. Each one is dramatic; each one is tragic. From this day forward, every day I shall observe a quiet remembrance for the victims of this calamity. Each one of us may choose our own way how to memorialize this moment but I believe we are all obligated to reflect for a moment, to care about our neighbor, to meditate for peace and tolerance because ultimately the only forces that can defeat such profound evil are compassion and hope.

I ask everyone to join me in prayer for the healing of our wounded civilization (if we can call it that). Let us pray every day to our gods remembering, as my dad has taught me since childhood, that Christ was not a Christian, Mohammed was not a Mohammedan, Buddha was not a Buddhist and Krishna was not a Hindu.

Gautam Chopra

Can't We Call Game?

At first I was hopeful. Colin Powell seemed to be creating a police action against terrorists, perhaps a new way of thinking about defense. No longer bombs and ground troops but detective work and international collaboration aimed exactly at the sources of terror. I have been so disheartened since we have actually started to deploy troops to Afghanistan. I have been so disheartened since anthrax has been the daily headline. I have been so disheartened since security has been the focus of all travel, the security of body searches and X-ray machines and M-16s at boarding gates.

Now at Logan Airport there are even machines being installed smart enough to scan faces and locate possible matches. And with a curtailing of civil liberties, who knows, I may end up being held for questioning instead of flying to my friend's wedding on a non-stop to Los Angeles.

I remember my first week teaching public kindergarten in Brookline, Massachusetts. A slight boy with a freckled face and a quiet manner was afraid because a bully followed him to school. Well, this jolted me; I was no longer working in the sheltered environment of private schooling. I was no longer teaching in a place where parents dropped off their kids at the classroom door and picked them up at the end of the day and did almost everything else they could think of to make school life smooth in between. But I was mistaken.

Jason's parents were also at the ready to do whatever was needed. The question, of course, was to decide just what that was. His mother talked with me, she talked with the principal, she talked with the guidance counselor, she talked with the perceived bully's teacher, who in turn talked with the perceived bully. I talked with Jason, my students and with students in other classes. Meanwhile his father took the pragmatic approach of hopping along behind Jason as he made his way to and from school, hiding against telephone poles, hovering in doorways, stooping behind shrubbery, watching over Jason as an omnipotent presence ready to spring and wrestle with harm whenever it arose. Of course, we all knew we couldn't manage all of this activity forever.

The second week of school Jason came in transformed, arm in arm with his bully. I observed, Something's changed, what happened? "Oh," said Jason, "I just said, 'Want to be friends?' And he said, 'Yes.' So we are. And that was that."

Since that day, Jason has been one of my handful of heroes. What he did was so direct, so appropriate, so right. Why had we adults made things so complicated? Why had we been so fearful? Of course, I recognize that some of what we did may have laid the groundwork for the resolution, but I always feel the world is in good hands when I listen to NPR and hear the byline, "This is Jason Beaubien reporting from . . ." But NPR isn't the whole world and Jason has a limited sphere of influence.

I am worried that learning to distrust will be, in the long run, more harmful to all of us than simply living by trust. I am worried that learning to be afraid is more harmful than simply trusting. I am committed to educating people about risks, even statistics, to prepare them for making choices only they can make. But I am not in the business of bullying them into being afraid, being terrorized, no longer trusting they can finding the goodness in other people. I am taking on the political stance of not giving in to being afraid. I am choosing to ignore the reign of terror imposed on us in the name of patriotism, in the name of justice. I choose to live from love, to work on garnering goodwill.

Last weekend, my seven-year-old granddaughter, Keely, invited me for the first time to watch her play soccer. I was enchanted, all these six- and seven-year-old girls in their matching black-and-white shorts and cleats practicing their moves. There were six girls on the team; four would play while two warmed up—the Galaxies versus the Milky Ways. The coaches encouraged passing, stressed it was all about working as a team. It was not about *anyone* but rather about *everyone*. Each girl played every position and for equal time slots throughout the game. Late in the game, three girls on the Milky Way team fell down hard in quick succession. The referee said, "They are getting tired." And so he called "game." The Milky Ways huddled and chanted, "One, two, three, four, we don't care about the score. Five, six, seven, eight, who do we appreciate—the Galaxies!" And then the Galaxies cheered the Milky Ways. Two lines formed and each girl slapped the palm of each opposing team member, saying "Good game" to each. When I congratulated Keely on kicking in two goals for her winning team, she said simply, "I got good passes; it was a good game."

I've been wondering what would happen if, in our war on terrorism, we asked, "Want to be friends?" If that did not get an affirmative response, how about asking some kindly referee to step in with, "People are starting to get

hurt; I'm calling game." Or maybe a neighborhood parent
could simply take away the war toys for good.

Molly Lynn Watt

Reflections from a New Father

Rather than fearing death, we're embracing life—life is now seen as more precious, more meaningful than it seemed before that tragic fall day.

Laura Bush

My second daughter was born on September 11, 2001, at 4:41 P.M. I wrote the following article for our church bulletin.

I have looked forward to writing this article for about nine months, and I hoped that it would be filled with joyous words devoted totally to my gratitude to the Father for bestowing the same title upon me . . . again. Indeed, I am thankful that Anna Belle Skidmore was born on September 11, 2001 (seven pounds, thirteen ounces and twenty inches long, with red hair and blue eyes like her sister), but my heart is heavy that as our family added a member, so many other people lost those who they had brought into this world. Although the world Anna Belle was welcomed into is a different world than the one that awaited her a day earlier, let's reflect on the words of the doctor as she held my daughter for her first unaided breath while a nearby television relayed the unfolding tragedy. Turning to everyone in the room, the doctor said, "May this child be a reminder of who is really in control of our world."

The day of my daughter's birth will always be connected with memories and memorials of death, but on 4:41 P.M. on Tuesday, as images of death engulfed our minds, God made his way into the world . . . in our midst . . . among us . . . as he did so many years ago . . . in the image of a child. My friend shared a very poignant thought, reminding me that although the date of Anna Belle's birth might forever be associated with the events of that day, it would be a blessing to know that it might also be the same day that marked the beginning of a rebirth of an awareness of God in our nation, in our schools and in our homes.

On the way to the church to write these words, I heard "The Star-Spangled Banner" being played on the radio. Flags hung on the front doors of many houses on both sides of the road—one was even hand-drawn by a child. I have to trust that we gained a greater allegiance not only to the flag this day, but that we also became aware of our need as a nation to truly be "under God." If July 4 is our Independence Day, perhaps September 11 should become our "Dependence Day"—a day in which we as a nation come to realize that our collective hope, future and lives were placed more securely in his hands.

I, too, began a new life on Tuesday, just as my daughter, Anna Belle, began a new life.

And just as Anna Belle, I was pulled from a place of safety, security and peace into a tragic, scary, unpredictable and hostile world.

Even though Anna Belle was born into uncertainty, she was immediately placed into the hands of a father whose main desire is to protect her, provide for her and promise her a rich future. Her story is my story . . . and yours. We are all frail, tiny and vulnerable, and our physical lives come with no guarantees. Yet that part of us most carefully created in his image is safe in the hands of a protecting, providing and promising Father. September 11 will always, in one special way, be a celebration of life for this particular father. My prayer is that history will look back and one day celebrate it as a day of renewed life toward our Father.

Another friend sent me these words in a simple but powerful note:

On a day in which everyone is asking, "Why would God ever let this happen?" perhaps we should look at you holding your daughter and ask the very same question.

David Skidmore

The Mustard Seed

Seeds of faith are always within us; sometimes it takes a crisis to nourish and encourage their growth.

Susan Taylor

In the darkest of days, we sometimes have to dig deep for the faith that will carry us through. It's not always easy, as I recently learned.

Like all Americans, September 11, 2001, is a day that I will never forget. My day started out with a promise to clean the house with my dear husband. Following the long illness of a loved one, we had neglected our most monotonous chores. It was time now to engage in this long-overdue task as even the cat was sneezing from all the dust.

This Tuesday we were up early and worked diligently, even skipping our lunch. At 1 P.M. the phone rang. Our son-in-law was working at Roosevelt Field, a large shopping mall here on Long Island, and he was calling to ask if he could stay with us if he couldn't get across the bridge to his home in Westchester that night.

My husband spoke to him, and I watched as his face turned white. "What's wrong?" I asked.

"Anne, quick, turn on the television set. New York City has been attacked!" he yelled.

"What? Who? Where?" I stammered.

"Just turn the set on," he repeated.

I ran to the living room, put on the TV and watched in horror. I stood in shock, watching the recast of the Twin Towers collapsing, the clouds of smoke billowing skyward, people running for their lives, screaming in terror. America was under attack! Soon, I started crying. My entire body shook. I kept saying, "Oh my God," until I couldn't believe it was my own voice I heard. My husband held me, and we sat in silence for the next hour, listening to the tragic reports. It was unreal, a science fiction movie—it just couldn't have happened to our beautiful New York City. "All the people who worked in the towers, the rescue workers, the police, the firemen, all lost," I cried.

We quickly began to account for our own family members—who was where, who might be at risk. After a while, we discovered they were all safe. In the next few days we accounted for all our close friends and were extremely grateful. We heard stories from neighbors, friends and family about how the attack had affected them.

We continued to watch the reports, praying for a miracle for the missing. It did not come. I fell into a depression, becoming deeply saddened by the loss of so many, enraged at the destruction of the city where I had been born and raised. When Sunday came, my husband dressed for church and I felt the tears come to my eyes. "I can't go with you," I said. He went alone. I stayed and lamented the sheer terror I felt within myself. *What kind of world are we living in?* I thought. *Our poor grandchildren. Is this their inheritance: a world gone mad?*

For the next several Sundays, my husband attended

services by himself. I tried to pray, I tried to have faith; it just wouldn't come. I pushed myself each day just to get out of bed. I felt empty, lost and very confused.

I'm not sure why, but on October 7 I told my husband that I wanted to go to church with him. He smiled and said he was pleased, and that I would be happy to know that Father Jim would be saying Mass that day. He knew I enjoyed this priest's down-to-earth sermons. The theme of the service was the need for us to rekindle our convictions. It spoke of having faith if only the size of a mustard seed. Now, a mustard seed is very small, almost difficult to see on a normal basis. I cried through the entire service, yet when we left the church I felt a new resolve.

That night I told my husband that I needed to show him something. From a box yellowed with age, I removed a small, round glass ball the size of a marble. I put it in his hand, and he asked, "What's this?"

I replied, "My mother gave that to me thirty-seven years ago when the baby died."

An infant son had passed away from a lung infection and I had gone into a deep depression. I couldn't fathom the reason that God would allow something that unthinkable to happen. I lost all my faith and stayed away from church. Nothing was real for me at that time and no one could reach me to help. My heart was broken, my desire to live lost. My dear mother had pressed the small object that my husband now held in his hand into mine one evening. "My darling daughter," she said, "all you've faced recently has been tragic, and there are no answers to the questions of why, but you must go on. I know it's hard, almost impossible, but if you can have faith, if only the size of that mustard seed, you will begin to heal."

I stared at this person that I loved with all my heart and wondered how she expected me to believe what she was saying. She put the small glass object in my hand and said, "Just try, Anne."

That evening I continued to roll the ball over and over in my palm. I concentrated on the tiny brown speck in the middle of it. I felt myself get stronger. I felt the desire to believe that things would return to normal, that life would hold joy for me once again. *I can have faith the size of that speck. I can do that, I can,* I kept repeating it to myself.

Thirty-seven years later, I held the round sphere that held the mustard seed in my hand. I prayed that night and once again, I felt stronger. We all need to hold on to the thought that we can also have the faith, the spirit, the resolve, if only the size of that small speck, to see us through this crisis. I know it won't be easy, it never has been. However, in our country's history, our darkest moments become our finest hours.

Anne Carter

Ground Zero

Three months after September 11, 2001, I found myself walking the perimeter of Ground Zero in lower Manhattan with four other women. My cousin, Karen, and I had flown from Wisconsin to New York to attend the opening of my daughter Jeanne's art show at a gallery in mid-Manhattan. Karen, a nurse, wanted to see Ground Zero because she planned to return for three weeks as a Red Cross volunteer to help care for the police and fire-fighters who would be working there twenty-four hours a day for at least another year.

On that clear crisp December day, Jeanne, Karen and I invited my dear friend, Mary Ann, the executive editor of *Guideposts Magazine,* a New Yorker by love and by choice, to join us. Mary Ann and I have been friends since 1982, have stayed at each other's homes and are counting the years until her retirement so we can travel together and nourish our friendship more often.

The fifth woman with us that Sunday was Ellen, who taught art with my daughter at Long Island University. Ellen lived in an apartment just blocks from the World Trade Center area and actually witnessed both planes crashing into the towers and the buildings imploding.

Like hundreds of others she dialed 911 the moment it happened.

None of the five of us had been to Ground Zero before that day and somehow we knew it was something we needed to do as a group. We walked and walked around the perimeter, stared, wondered, shook our heads, shed tears and watched the firefighters working to put out the fires deep underground. We breathed in the acrid air that filtered up from below the streets and smelled like burning plastic. We saw hundreds of people filing by St. Paul's Chapel where tall fences were installed to hold thousands of flowers, notes, letters, posters and the pouring out of love and grief from a nation of people who cannot comprehend what happened on those sixteen acres in New York City's oldest section.

We walked down the street where a half-dozen huge dump trucks lined up to take their turn removing the steel and the ashes of the dead. We five women understood that the air was filled with toxic chemicals and perhaps everyone should wear masks to protect themselves but we didn't. Somehow it seemed that if we physically breathed it in, we would understand it better. Ellen mentioned that by breathing we became a part of the dead.

Ground Zero is a holy place. People are quiet, respectful. On one narrow street where we had to step over broken sidewalks and makeshift wooden walkways, there were a dozen handmade signs begging, "Please, no photographs or videos." But around the corner, down another street there were people taking snapshots and filming the hubbub in and around the gaping hole. The mind cannot comprehend such devastation, nor remember the details, so photos are necessary.

I wanted to remember the coarse, black, wet ashes in front of the church two blocks from where the towers stood. I wanted to remember the chain-link fences that protected the workers and the people who flocked to that neighborhood.

Most of all, I need to remember how it felt to walk south a few blocks to Battery Park at the very tip of Manhattan where we could see the Statue of Liberty in the harbor. We five women stood on the dock where people board the ferry that takes them to the statue and then on to the immigration museum on Ellis Island. We arrived at the park just at sunset. The colors over the ocean screamed with red-orange brilliance as if all was well in New York.

There was a huge photographic mural covering a building at the dock with enormous photos of Gandhi and Martin Luther King, reminding visitors of lives dedicated to peace. To the left was the sunset, the statue, the ocean. To the right, a view of the skyscrapers of lower Manhattan, New Amsterdam, the oldest section of New York, where the Trade Center for the world once stood. Only the skyline was missing its two most dramatic pieces. The gaping space between buildings was obscene, unfathomable, especially if you'd been to New York before and could remember exactly where the Towers stood. Sixteen acres, gone.

As we five women took in that sunset, punctuated with the Statue of Liberty to the south, and then looked north to where the giant towers once stood, each of us experienced muddled thoughts about the world and about our lives before and after September 11. To see that much death and destruction up close, or to live and work near where America was attacked, does something to your soul.

As we walked toward the subway, my daughter put her arm around my waist. I reached for Mary Ann's hand. Karen and Ellen walked close together, sharing their feelings about life after September 11.

We five women in our thirties, forties, fifties and sixties, together for one afternoon, represented a scattering of different relationships. But for three hours that day we were sisters who experienced awe, fear, anger, depression, amazement, loyalty, patriotism and the friendship that comes when people share their emotions. We saw a skyline that was different than before. But we also saw the Statue of Liberty and the sunset. We saw wet ashes and mangled steel on one side of a street and a sunset of enormous brilliance and beauty on the other. It was good to see them both together and to know that even though the skyline of New York will never be the same, the work and hope arising from the ashes in lower Manhattan is the stuff of liberty and sunrises and sunsets so beautiful you simply can't define them. You need to go there to understand.

Patricia Lorenz

Make It Green

If there is to be a memorial, let it not be of stone and steel. Fly no flag above it, for it is not the possession of a nation but a sorrow shared with the world.

Let it be a green field with trees and flowers. Let there be paths that wind through the shade. Put out park benches where old people can sun in the summertime and a pond where children can skate in the winter.

Beneath this field will lie entombed forever some of the victims of September 11. It is not where they thought to end their lives. Like the sailors of the battleship *Arizona*, they rest where they fell.

Let this field stretch from one end of the destruction to the other. Let this open space among the towers mark the emptiness in our hearts. But do not make it a sad place. Give it no name. Let people think of it as the green field. Every living thing that is planted there will show faith in the future.

Let students take a corner of the field and plant a crop there. Perhaps corn, our native grain. Let the harvest be shared all over the world, with friends and enemies, because that is the teaching of our religions, and we must show that we practice them. Let the harvest show that life prevails over death, and let the gifts show that we love our neighbors.

Do not build again on this place. No building can stand there. No building, no statue, no column, no arch, no symbol, no name, no date, no statement. Just the comfort of the Earth we share, to remind us that we share it.

Roger Ebert

7

WHERE NEXT?

America has suffered a great loss, but what has not been lost is our spirit, our resiliency as a society.

Colin L. Powell

THE FAMILY CIRCUS   By Bil Keane

"Don't worry, PJ, we'll rebuild!
It's the 'Merican way."

Reprinted with permission from Bil Keane.

Celebrate Life

*Life presents as many opportunities for happi-
ness as it does for tragedy.*

Rudolph Giuliani

Last night I attended a bar mitzvah that would have
been inspirational at anytime, but for the three-hundred-
plus who attended in the aftermath of the events of
September 11, 2001, it was an amazing, life-affirming experience. I am sharing this story because I believe that many
will find comfort from the stories shared with our congregation by a thirteen-year-old boy.

Like many citizens across the nation, my husband and I
felt the need to be with people immediately following
September 11, and planned to attend the Friday night
Shabbat service at the Birmingham Temple of Farmington
Hills, Michigan. During the drive, I read from the temple
bulletin that a bar mitzvah would be celebrated. I was surprised and hoped it would be postponed, preferring the
focus of the evening to be on making sense of the week's
events. Tragically, the adult son of a favorite temple friend
had been on the ninety-fourth floor of the World Trade

Center, and I knew it would be a sad night as we all struggled to digest this personal and national tragedy.

We arrived to find the parking lot filled and the temple crowded. Many apparently felt the need to come together. The service began with beautiful, mournful music. Then Rabbi Sherwin Wine spoke at length about the horrors of the terrorist attacks. He stated that we had two purposes for being there this night. The first was to mourn the victims, including the son of Skip Rosenthal, Joshua Rosenthal, a fine man who had grown up worshipping at the temple and was well known to many present. The second purpose was to thwart the terrorists' desire to demoralize us by continuing to celebrate life-cycle events—in this case, a bar mitzvah, the "coming of age" of a Jewish boy.

Next, family members of the bar mitzvah boy read passages about milestones, family, dignity, power and peace.

Then Rabbi Wine introduced Jackson, the bar mitzvah boy. At our Humanistic Judaism temple, it is the custom of bar and bat mitzvah students to spend the year prior to their thirteenth birthday researching the life of a Jewish hero or heroine, and apply lessons from their hero's actions to their own life. Tonight, the Rabbi stated, Jackson would be our teacher.

Jackson climbed the box placed behind the podium and faced the packed room, grinning. Proudly he announced that he had chosen to share the story of the life of Solly Gonor. Jackson had read his book, *Light One Candle: A Survivor's Tale from Lithuania to Jerusalem,* about how, as a twelve-year-old boy in Germany, Solly had endured unspeakable hardships to keep himself and his father alive during the Nazi regime. Jackson had managed to locate Solly, now a seventy-four-year-old living in Israel, and began a year-long e-mail correspondence.

Jackson told us how Solly, as a twelve-year-old himself,

enjoyed sports and hanging out with friends, when suddenly he was no longer free and was in danger because of
his Jewish identity. Solly's family missed a chance to leave
the country, and after they were forced from their home,
hid briefly with five other families in a barn. In the middle
of the night, Solly's father woke them and led them out of
the barn just as soldiers arrived. The family watched in
horror as everyone in hiding was forced out, forced to dig
their own graves, and shot, one by one.

Jackson shared a story about how the Gonor family
lived for a period in the Kaunas ghetto, where Solly
endured hunger and cold. Solly was bravely able to
retrieve food thrown over the ghetto wall by a boy who
had been a friend before the war, each risking his life to
make a midnight run to the barbed-wire fence when the
guards were not looking. Boredom was another hardship,
as the Germans banned one of the Jews last remaining
pleasures by ordering the collection and destruction of all
books. Knowing he risked his life, Solly and a friend hid
books in a forbidden part of the ghetto. Solly grieved
when his former math teacher was found with a book and
shot. Solly attributes his ability to stay alive in the ghetto
to his friendships with two other teens, both of whom
later died in concentration camps.

Solly's family was sent from the ghetto to a work camp,
and then to a concentration camp. It was there that he was
separated from his mother, and promised that he would
keep his father alive. Jackson told us about Solly's heart-
wrenching experiences at the camp, but also about how
Solly used his wits to keep himself and his father fed and
clothed.

Finally, the Germans had an idea that the Jewish pris-
oners would build them a fort, and sent them on a death
march through miles of snow-covered roads. Here Solly,
in his fatigue, lost track of his father. Eventually, Solly

collapsed beside a tree, where he truly believed he would die. He fell asleep. A Japanese American soldier, who awakened him and lifted him out of the snow, told him he was free. Solly was later reunited with his father, who had been taken to a hospital. Just five years ago, Solly was reunited with the soldier who found him in Israel. This reunion brought back many memories that Solly had long suppressed, and that was when he began to write his book. Jackson stated that he had committed himself to telling Solly's story of courage.

When Jackson finished speaking, the entire congregation stood and loudly applauded his moving presentation. As the clapping finally slowed, Jackson announced that he had one more part to his bar mitzvah. He stated that, "Due to the closing of the airports this week, none of the out-of-towners has been able to come in for this night, except for one. That person is . . . Solly Gonor!" A gasp went through the entire room. Jackson proceeded, "Since Mr. Gonor was not able to celebrate his bar mitzvah when he was thirteen, I would like him to join me now."

A white-haired man in the front row stood and slowly made his way up to the podium next to Jackson. The crowd stood and applauded wildly. For several minutes, Mr. Gonor stood with his hand over his eyes, struggling to regain his composure. Then Jackson and Mr. Gonor read together, first in Hebrew, then in English.

After the reading Mr. Gonor addressed us, stating that he never expected that his experiences would one day be an inspiration to a thirteen-year-old boy. He stated that he was glad he had been able to make the journey from Israel and meet his e-mail pen pal.

Mr. Gonor's story reminded us that evil in the world is not new, but that the human spirit and will to survive is strong. At a time when many of us were asking how we could bear the sadness of the days following September

11, we were reminded of those who suffered through years of Nazi cruelty, as well as people in countries all over the world where terrorism is a way of life. We were reminded by thirteen-year-old Jackson that we must, indeed, continue to celebrate life.

Our evening ended by standing together and singing *Ayfo Oree*. The words, translated from Hebrew, are as follows:

> *Where is my light? My light is in me.*
> *Where is my hope? My hope is in me.*
> *Where is my strength? My strength is in me.*
> *And in you.*

Caroline Broida Trapp

What Is It?

Darkness cannot drive out darkness; only light can do that. Hate cannot drive out hate; only love can do that. Hate multiplies hate, violence multiplies violence; toughness multiplies tough-ness in a descending spiral of destruction. . . . The chain reaction of evil—hate begetting hate, wars producing more wars—must be broken, or we shall be plunged into the darkness . . . of annihilation.

Martin Luther King Jr.

The simple question continues to echo through my mind hours later.

"What is it, Mommy?" my nine-year-old Katherine asked. "What is it that makes some people do something so awful! What is it?"

The day was dawning as she questioned me. We were standing in our front yard, the sky turning from gray to blue as we prepared to take her to school. She looked up at me, her deep blue eyes round, her innocent face waiting expectantly for an answer. Her expression said,

"Mommy will know the answer. My mommy can take care of anything."

I paused, looking toward the sky. The same sky that had just turned passenger planes into weapons of destruction that plowed into American targets. Targets I had seen personally. Targets I could remember being built as a child in New Jersey. Targets that are visual icons of New York and Washington, D.C.

"Fear. Hatred. Misunderstanding. And the desire to keep people in fear, hatred and misunderstanding." I looked at my daughter, who at nine is wise beyond her years. She was slowly nodding. I continued, "These people know that if you are afraid, you cannot feel love. If you cannot feel love, you cannot feel peace. These people do not want us to feel peace or love. They want to control us. We won't let them do that, though, will we?"

In a very short conversation, Katherine had brought my resolve firmly back. She reminded me of a very important lesson that lives deep within me.

In the moments after I heard of the devastation that was occurring so close to where I had grown up, I was frightened to the point of near hysteria. I paced, frantically worried about my children, my friends, my safety, my country, my world. But Katherine reminded me that I could not feel fear and feel love at the same time. As I listened to reports from survivors, I saw gratitude in their words. I heard an unusual peace. I saw light among the tragedy.

We can love as we grieve the senseless loss of so many lives. We can love as we pray. We can love as we donate time, blood and money to the Red Cross and other charitable organizations. We can love as we talk to complete strangers, sorting out our own feelings about the tragedy. We can love as we hug our children, friends and neighbors. We can love as we take an extra moment to simply feel grateful for each breath. For each moment. For each person whose lives we touch positively. We can love as we put one foot in front of the other. We can love as we choose to trust. We can love as we serve our fellow world citizens.

Later that day I was with Emma, my four-year-old daughter, at the park. She came to me and I gave her a big hug. She looked at me and stated simply: "A plane flew into a building. Lots of people died. Let's talk about it."

So we did. Plainly, and with the vocabulary of a preschooler, we talked about what had taken place in New York City. She went back to playing.

Soon she returned to me and said, "Mommy, give me a nice big hug so the bad guys can't get me."

And I did. Hug. Love. Keep the bad guys away. And when the bad guys come anyway, remember to hug. To love. To trust. To feel peace deep within you.

Hug. Love. Live.

Julie Jordan Scott

STAHLER. ©*UFS. Reprinted by permission.*

Something Special

"I would do something special for her. Not take out the trash without being reminded. Something special, something I wouldn't ordinarily do." With tears streaming down his face, the gentleman had just answered the reporter's question, "What would you do differently if you had known you might not see your wife again?"

Now, I personally think that is a pretty crappy question to ask anyone, much less the husband of a victim of a terrorist attack. The reporter seemed to have no compassion for this man whose wife's plane had been flown into the World Trade Center.

"I'm just glad I kissed her good-bye and told her I loved her this morning," he managed to choke out.

Of course, we would all act differently if we knew time together with our spouse was running out. My anger at the insensitive reporter simmered along with the disbelief and fear that had become part of my life since watching the results of the attack on America. "Stupid guy," I muttered to myself, switching off the television. Maybe I needed a break. I have that luxury. I can turn off the pictures of the devastated buildings, despondent relatives and harried rescue workers.

But could I turn off my feelings? My husband Alan and I farm. He was cutting a field of soybeans that afternoon. I decided to go take pictures of the American flag he had mounted on the back of our combine. With terrorists trying to cripple our nation, we wanted to show our support: The American farmer was still hard at work.

Back at the house, starting a load of laundry, I found myself thinking about that interview. *I would do something special,* played over and over in my mind. That gentleman would never have that opportunity now, but I did. I hope Alan and I have another forty years together. But there are no guarantees. Tomorrows are not guaranteed.

Something I wouldn't ordinarily do. Well, his pickup could sure use a good cleaning. So I got to it. After about thirty minutes of vacuuming and scrubbing the interior, I was ready to wash the outside. I had one little problem: Starting the power washer was a bit tricky. You had to choke the motor just enough, and the idle had to be set just so. The possibility of getting jerked on the recoil was significant. *Something special. . . .* Grabbing the pull rope I tackled it head on. Suddenly it was very important to me to accomplish this surprise for Alan. Several attempts later, with no success and an aching arm, I thought I might not succeed. *Lord,* I prayed silently, *I could sure use your help. I want to get this started so I can finish this for Alan. I really want to do this for him.*

The guilt hit immediately. How could I bother our Lord at a time like this? Thousands were praying for their loved ones. Much more important prayers needed his attention right now. "I'm sorry, Lord," I whispered. How could I be so selfish? I had spent a lot of time in prayer over the past three days, asking for comfort for the victims' families, strength for our nation's leaders and healing for all of us. My request for help now was automatic. I always ask for help when facing a difficult task. But it just didn't seem right to do so today.

Defeat didn't seem an option either, so I pulled the rope one more time. The motor sputtered to life.

Yes, Alan was surprised and grateful when he saw his pickup. And I was surprised and grateful for the important lessons I learned that day. First of all, despite his tactless approach, the reporter brought home a very important point. Through his pain, the man who lost his spouse taught me to cherish mine. I will look for those "special" things to do for Alan.

Secondly, and maybe more importantly, God does care about us, all of us. He hears the prayers of those whose suffering seems unbearable. He cares. And he hears those of us who need a little boost when we have set out to do something special for someone we love.

Pam Bumpus

Why Are You Waiting?

The more you praise and celebrate your life, the more there is in life to celebrate.

Oprah Winfrey

I get many e-mails, and every day I sort through a host of funny pictures, ribald jokes and forwarded chain letters that I read, enjoy and summarily delete. But every once in a while I receive an e-mail of significance—a collection of words important enough to compel me to share it with my cyberspace amalgamation of family and friends. Which is exactly what happened on Tuesday morning, September 11, 2001.

A writer friend of mine sent me a most thought-provoking e-mail, which she entitled, ironically enough, "Some thoughts for a happy day." The theme of the composition was the need to "seize the moment and live life to the fullest."

I read it, reread it and realized that the electronic transmission perfectly matched my own personal philosophy. Further, it provided a needed reminder that life is short so we need to play hard and enjoy it. I tapped into my lengthy e-mail address book and began forwarding the worthy correspondence to family and friends. In the process, I retitled it "Life as it should be lived."

In one of those serendipitous life moments, as I hit send and put my group mailing on its merry way, my phone rang.

It was my husband urging me to turn on the television. Within moments, my mind was reeling as I watched the incredulous turn of events play out in New York City and Washington, D.C. Conflicting emotions of fear, anger, sorrow and compassion pulsed through my body, while the relentless journalism queries of who, what, when, where and why tortured my writer's brain.

The last time I visited the Big Apple, I went to the World Trade Center. I sat at the bar in the rooftop Windows on the World restaurant and felt as if I was truly on top of the world. It was a memorable evening that is forever captured in a group picture I have hanging on my office wall. And now, in a matter of moments, the picture and the people in it are all that remain of that magical evening. Moving my glance from that celebratory photo to the devastating reality unfolding on the television screen, I felt suddenly isolated. I wanted, and needed, to reach out and touch another human being, to assure myself that no matter how shattering this incomprehensible event might be, my family and my friends were still alive and well, and my sense of normalcy was going to survive.

At about that same moment, e-mail messages began filling my inbox—all referring to the same subject—"Life as it should be lived." I looked at the senders' names and discovered many of the family and friends that I had just written to moments earlier.

As I opened their letters, a flood of grief and fear filled my computer screen, along with phrases that spoke of the value of family and friendship.

At the same time, my phone began ringing. My husband, my daughter, my sister-in-law, my friends, fellow writers—people from New York to California—called, one after another. Everyone was responding to the same need to reach out and ensure the stability of their lives. When, at last, each of our senses and sensibilities had been soothed, we said our loving good-byes, promising to talk more often and get together soon.

I refocused on the day's terrible events as they continued to unfold. I also returned to the e-mail that had so innocently started my morning. I read it again, this time with a new focus and understanding, lingering over the final line that read, "If you were going to die soon and had only one phone call you could make, who would you call, what would you say and why are you waiting?"

For the countless numbers in those four airplanes, three office buildings and random city streets, that question is now irrelevant. For the rest of us, perhaps of greater import than the question is how will we decide to answer.

Christina M. Aht

Standing in Solidarity

Cultivation of tolerance for other faiths will impart to us a true understanding of our own. For me, the different religions are beautiful flowers from the same garden, or they are branches of the same majestic tree.

Mahatma Gandhi

Five miles from our home in LaVerne, California, are two Muslim schools that I did not realize were there until the days following the terrorist attacks in September. Then came that day, September 11, 2001, that changed every American's life in some way. It is interesting to notice that the 911 in its dateline is the emergency telephone number throughout our country. It is a reminder of how so many felt helpless and threatened during the tragedy.

It became a time to watch the unbelievable scenes on the television news. Later, a question came to my mind. What could I ever do to help ease the pain in this tough situation? One answer came very unexpectedly.

My husband, Chuck, a pastor in the Church of the Brethren, was invited by a Muslim acquaintance to an interfaith meeting on the Friday following the attacks. There, one idea presented was to give support to the Muslim schools, which had closed upon hearing the news of the terrorist attacks.

A few days later, a phone call came asking us to go stand in front of these schools when they reopened. All we were expected to do was to be a "presence" there, to show our support for the Muslims as human beings and fellow Americans, not as terrorists. It sounded simple enough.

With some uncertainty, I arrived at the gated school the morning it reopened, September 19. Several other Brethren, as well as people from other denominations came. Our waving, smiling and greetings began to be returned to us immediately by the parents and teachers as they drove into the drop-off area. Many expressed their appreciation for us being there. As days passed, we were given donuts, flowers, letters of thanks from the students, a breakfast and a thank-you luncheon where plaques were presented to the LaVerne and Pomona Fellowship Churches of the Brethren. These plaques state that we are united under the same God.

We have become acquainted with these dear Muslims who are more like us than I could have imagined. Never have they tried to convert us or terrify us. They have been very accepting of who we are. In fact, it was an amazing moment when one Muslim stated that some of them wanted to come to our worship service in LaVerne. Her faith encouraged learning about other faiths, she reported. The date of October 14 was set for their visit, and thirty of these new Muslim friends were warmly greeted by our congregation.

The following Monday, we heard that their attendance at our church had been a meaningful time for them. They sent a note of gratitude to the LaVerne congregation.

For us, a relationship with the Muslim community is

just beginning. We have been invited to attend their worship service. We have scheduled a planning session to determine how we can work together. Out of tragedy has emerged a Christian-Muslim relationship that is exciting and fulfilling. Little did I dream of what blessings were in store for us from being just a "presence" at the Muslim City of Knowledge School, and little did I know how much our presence would mean to the teachers and students. A thank-you note from a fifth-grader said it all:

Dear People,
   You make me feel safe. Without you, I wouldn't feel safe. I like how polite you are. With you I won't feel suspicious. This is a thanks from my best friends and me.
Love,
Hassan

                                    Shirley Boyer

Neighbors Knowing Neighbors

Eternal vigilance is the price of liberty.

Lendil Phillips

We were waiting. All of us. Since September 11, 2001, we were waiting for another attack. We had been warned by our President, and now we were wondering when it would come and where it would come. Though we were told to go about our lives as we ordinarily would, it seemed impossible to forget that somewhere in the country, a terrorist or a group of terrorists, was about to strike again. And they hated us enough that they would eagerly die so that we might die.

And so we met, a group of us, at a neighbor's house. We went to talk. To express our feelings about what had happened and what might happen. At first we just discussed the events and shared our shock and anger. We asked questions of one another. Why did this happen? Why didn't we know? Why are we hated like this? The fear circled the room as we discussed our helplessness. Most of us had met before, but this was a different kind of meeting. We were asking each other for help. We were neighbors getting to know one another.

And then someone asked, "What can we do?" She didn't mean the country or the state. She meant our community. She meant herself. What could she do to take back the control and fight the helplessness? What could we all do in that room, she asked, that would take away the control from the terrorists and bring it back into our own hands?

It was then the group decided to take action. We would form a neighborhood watch program, only this one would not just include crime in the community, but we would also be concerned with terrorism and the vigilance it demanded in order to be defeated. We might meet in a church or synagogue, where we could keep a survival kit with blankets, water, first-aid supplies, battery-operated radios, anything that might become necessary during an emergency. We could meet with the police, firefighters and emergency crews and let them know we were there to help them. We would work together and join the community in caring about one another. We would fight the fear and the helplessness by getting to know our neighbors. Old neighbors had moved away. New neighbors moved in every day. We would get to know them also. We would introduce ourselves, bring a plant, welcome them to the community.

There were elderly people in our town. Through this program, we could watch out for them. Our block captains could have their phone numbers and contact them if we needed to be evacuated. They would know they were not alone. There were mothers who worked outside the community. We could have their work phone numbers and if there was an emergency, we would get in touch with them so that they would not worry about their children. We could have "safe houses," marked so that the children would know which house to stop at if a problem arose on their way home from school. We could meet once a week or once a month to discuss the news and upgrade our own program. We could get to know each other and each other's needs. No one would be a stranger in our town.

The terrorists settled their nests in communities where neighbors didn't know neighbors, or if they did, they didn't care. They knew our habits but we didn't know theirs. We worked, we played, we enjoyed life. We were unaware we were being watched. They watched us but we didn't watch them. They thought they knew us. They thought we were unchangeable. That night we discovered our most important weapon against them: neighbors knowing neighbors. Neighbors caring about one another. Neighbors helping one another.

And if terrorists are looking for a place in which to settle, they'll have to find another town.

This one isn't available.

Harriet May Savitz

Is This Normal?

I learned that it is possible for us to create light and sound and order within us, no matter what calamity may befall us in the outer world.

Helen Keller

September 11, 2001. Four thousand gathered for midday prayer in a downtown cathedral. A New York City church filled and emptied six times that Tuesday.

The owner of a Manhattan tennis shoe store threw open his doors and gave running shoes to those fleeing the towers. People stood in lines to give blood, in hospitals to treat the sick, in sanctuaries to pray for the wounded.

America was different this week.

We wept for people we did not know. We sent money to families we've never seen. Talk-show hosts read scriptures, journalists printed prayers. Our focus shifted from fashion hemlines and box scores to orphans and widows and the future of the world.

We were different this week.

Republicans stood next to Democrats, Catholics prayed

with Jews. Skin color was covered by the ash of burning towers.

This is a different country than it was a week ago. We're not as self-centered as we were. We're not as self-reliant as we were. Hands are out. Knees are bent. This is not normal.

And I have to ask the question, do we want to go back to normal? Are we being given a glimpse of a new way of life? Are we, as a nation, being reminded that the enemy is not each other and the power is not in ourselves and the future is not in our bank accounts? Unselfish prayerfulness is the way God intended for us to live all along.

Maybe this, in his eyes, is the way we are called to live our entire lives. And perhaps the best response to this tragedy is to refuse to go back to normal. Perhaps the best response is to follow the example of Tom Burnett. He was a passenger on Flight 93. Minutes before the plane crashed in the fields of Pennsylvania he reached his wife by cell phone. "We're all going to die," he told her, "but there are three of us who are going to do something about it."

We can do something about it as well. We can resolve to care more. We can resolve to pray more. And we can resolve that, with God being our helper, we'll never go back to normal again.

Max Lucado

Reprinted with permission of Bruce Beattie. ©2001 *Copley News Service.*

Act Two

The date is June 24, 1859. Atop a hill overlooking the plain of Solferino, Jean-Henri Dunant has a box seat view as Napoleon's troops prepare for battle with the Austrians below. Trumpets blare, muskets crack and cannons boom.

The two armies crash into each other as Dunant looks on, transfixed. He sees the dust rising. He hears the screams of the injured. He watches bleeding, maimed men take their last breaths as he stares in horror. Dunant doesn't mean to be there. He is only on a business trip—to speak to Napoleon about a financial transaction between the Swiss and the French. But he arrived late and now finds himself in a position to witness firsthand the atrocities of war.

What Dunant sees from his hill, however, pales in comparison to what he is soon to witness. Entering a small town shortly after the fierce encounter, Dunant now observes the battle's refugees. Every building is filled with the mangled, the injured, the dead. Dunant, aching with pity, decides to stay in the village three more days to comfort the young soldiers.

He realizes that his life will never be the same again. Driven by a powerful passion to abolish war, Jean-Henri

Dunant will eventually lose his successful banking career and all his worldly possessions to die as a virtual unknown in an obscure poorhouse.

But we remember Dunant today because he was the first recipient, in 1901, of the Nobel Peace Prize. We also remember him because of the movement he founded—the Red Cross.

Act One of Jean-Henri Dunant's life closed June 24, 1859. Act Two opened immediately and played the remainder of his eighty-one years.

Many people's lives can be divided into two acts. The first act ends when one decides to follow a new direction or passion. Dunant's old life, driven by financial success, prestige and power, no longer satisfied him. A new Jean-Henri Dunant emerged in the second act of his life, a man who was now motivated by love, compassion and an overriding commitment to abolish the horrors of war.

The second act of some people's lives may begin with a conversion or a major turning point. Others speak of a defining moment. The old self is laid to rest and a new self is born—one governed by principle, spirit and passion. You may be ready for Act Two. It is the final scene of a life that counts.

Steve Goodier

We shall go forward together. The road upward is strong. There are upon our journey, dark and dangerous valleys through which we have to make and fight our way. But it is sure and certain that if we persevere, and we shall persevere, we shall come through dark and dangerous valleys into sunlight broader and more genial and more lasting than mankind has ever known.

Winston Churchill

More Chicken Soup?

Many of the stories and poems you have read in this book were submitted by readers like you who had read earlier *Chicken Soup for the Soul* books. We publish at least five or six *Chicken Soup for the Soul* books every year. We invite you to contribute a story to one of these future volumes.

Stories may be up to twelve hundred words and must uplift or inspire. You may submit an original piece, something you have read or your favorite quotation on your refrigerator door.

To obtain a copy of our submission guidelines and a listing of upcoming *Chicken Soup* books, please write, fax or check one of our Web sites.

Please send your submissions to:

Chicken Soup for the Soul
P.O. Box 30880, Santa Barbara, CA 93130
fax: 805-563-2945
Web sites: *www.chickensoup.com*
www.clubchickensoup.com

We will be sure that both you and the author are credited for your submission.

For information about speaking engagements, other books, audiotapes, workshops and training programs, please contact any of our authors directly.

In the Spirit of Giving

Since 1995, Health Communications, Inc., and authors Jack Canfield and Mark Victor Hansen and their coauthors, have made it a practice to assist the less fortunate by donating part of the proceeds of each book to various charities. These organizations have included: the American Red Cross, The Wellness Community, Habitat for Humanity, Covenant House, Save the Children, Children's Miracle Network, Boys & Girls Clubs of America, The American Society for the Prevention of Cruelty to Animals, YMCA of the USA, Special Olympics, as well as forty-five other worthy organizations. In all, over $3.4 million has been donated to these groups.

In the spirit of *Chicken Soup for the Soul,* we have always felt it important to give back to the community and inspire others to turn their lives around. We will continue this long tradition with each new book in the series. Please know that, as a reader, you are doing your part to make the world a better and brighter place through your purchase of books in the *Chicken Soup for the Soul* series. We thank you for your ongoing support.

Who Is Jack Canfield?

Jack Canfield is one of America's leading experts in the development of human potential and personal effectiveness. He is both a dynamic, entertaining speaker and a highly sought-after trainer. Jack has a wonderful ability to inform and inspire audiences toward increased levels of self-esteem and peak performance.

He is the author and narrator of several bestselling audio and videocassette programs, including *Self-Esteem and Peak Performance, How to Build High Self-Esteem, Self-Esteem in the Classroom* and *Chicken Soup for the Soul—Live.* He is regularly seen on television shows such as *Good Morning America, 20/20* and *NBC Nightly News.* Jack has co-authored numerous books, including the *Chicken Soup for the Soul* series, *Dare to Win* and *The Aladdin Factor* (all with Mark Victor Hansen), *100 Ways to Build Self-Concept in the Classroom* (with Harold C. Wells), *Heart at Work* (with Jacqueline Miller) and *The Power of Focus* (with Les Hewitt and Mark Victor Hansen).

Jack is a regularly featured speaker for professional associations, school districts, government agencies, churches, hospitals, sales organizations and corporations. His clients have included the American Dental Association, the American Management Association, AT&T, Campbell's Soup, Clairol, Domino's Pizza, GE, ITT, Hartford Insurance, Johnson & Johnson, the Million Dollar Roundtable, NCR, New England Telephone, Re/Max, Scott Paper, TRW and Virgin Records. Jack is also on the faculty of Income Builders International, a school for entrepreneurs.

Jack conducts an annual eight-day Training of Trainers program in the areas of self-esteem and peak performance. It attracts educators, counselors, parenting trainers, corporate trainers, professional speakers, ministers and others interested in developing their speaking and seminar-leading skills.

For further information about Jack's books, tapes and training programs, or to schedule him for a presentation, please contact:

Self-Esteem Seminars
P.O. Box 30880
Santa Barbara, CA 93130
Phone: 805-563-2935 • Fax: 805-563-2945
Web site: *www.chickensoup.com*

Who Is Mark Victor Hansen?

Mark Victor Hansen is a professional speaker who in the last twenty years has made over 4,000 presentations to more than 2 million people in thirty-two countries. His presentations cover sales excellence and strategies; personal empowerment and development; and how to triple your income and double your time off.

Mark has spent a lifetime dedicated to his mission of making a profound and positive difference in people's lives. Throughout his career, he has inspired hundreds of thousands of people to create a more powerful and purposeful future for themselves while stimulating the sale of billions of dollars worth of goods and services.

Mark is a prolific writer and has authored *Future Diary, How to Achieve Total Prosperity* and *The Miracle of Tithing*. He is coauthor of the *Chicken Soup for the Soul* series, *Dare to Win* and *The Aladdin Factor* (all with Jack Canfield), and *The Master Motivator* (with Joe Batten).

Mark has also produced a complete library of personal-empowerment audio and videocassette programs that have enabled his listeners to recognize and use their innate abilities in their business and personal lives. His message has made him a popular television and radio personality, with appearances on ABC, NBC, CBS, HBO, PBS and CNN. He has also appeared on the cover of numerous magazines, including *Success, Entrepreneur* and *Changes*.

Mark is a big man with a heart and spirit to match—an inspiration to all who seek to better themselves.

For further information about Mark, write:

MVH & Associates
P.O. Box 7665
Newport Beach, CA 92658
Phone: 949-759-9304 or 800-433-2314
Fax: 949-722-6912
Web site: *www.chickensoup.com*

Who Is Matthew E. Adams?

Matthew E. Adams has extensive media and journalism experience and is an accomplished public speaker. He began his career working in radio while still in high school. After graduating from college he worked for ESPN in the production department where his assignments were SportsCenter, the NHL and the NFL. In addition to his media activities, he has spent the last twelve years as an executive in the golf and sporting goods industry. He also can be seen as a regular contributor on The Golf Channel.

Matthew has written numerous stories for the *Chicken Soup for the Soul* book series. *Chicken Soup for the Soul of America* is the first *Chicken Soup* book that he has coauthored. While researching for the book he toured Ground Zero and interviewed many people directly affected by the events of September 11, 2001. Matthew said the trip to the World Trade Center site, within weeks of the terrorist attacks, "Was an incredibly emotional experience. The scale of destruction and loss devastated me. Yet, at the same time, the people of New York were so strong and resolute. I found them to be inspiring. They are true heroes."

Matthew found the experience of coauthoring a *Chicken Soup for the Soul* book to be very rewarding. "I am humbled by the dedication of all of the people who worked tirelessly to pull this book together. I am particularly thankful for the patience and support of my wife Donna and my family."

Matthew Adams is available for professional speaking engagements and can be reached by e-mail at *mattadams422@aol.com* or by mail at the Chicken Soup for the Soul offices.

Chicken Soup for the Soul
P.O. Box 30880, Santa Barbara, CA 93130
fax: 805-563-2945
Web sites: *www.chickensoup.com*
www.clubchickensoup.com

Contributors

Several of the stories in this book were taken from previously published sources, such as books, magazines and newspapers. These sources are acknowledged in the permissions section. If you would like to contact any of the contributors for information about their writing, or would like to invite them to speak in your community, look for their contact information included in their biography.

The remainder of the stories were submitted by readers of our previous *Chicken Soup for the Soul* books who responded to our requests for stories. We have also included information about them.

Christina M. Abt is a newspaper columnist, magazine profiler and radio commentator. Her work has also been featured on the *Heartwarmers.com* Web site as well as in *Heartwarmer's* books and *Petwarmer's* CD. She is the wife of one awesome husband, Thom, the mother of two terrific kids and will always be her mother's daughter. E-mail: *christinaabt@hotmail.com*.

Tom Adkins resides in King of Prussia, Pennsylvania. As executive editor of *CommonConservative.com*, Tom is often published nationally and frequently appears as a pundit on various political television shows. With deep appreciation, he dedicates this article to the men, women and families who served and sacrificed in America's Armed Forces.

Marsha Arons is a freelance writer and video producer. Her stories and articles have appeared in *Good Housekeeping, Reader's Digest, Redbook, Woman's Day* and *Woman's World.* She has contributed to eight of the books in the *Chicken Soup for the Soul* book series. She is married and the mother of four daughters.

Lynn Barker, member of the Writers Guild of America, has written for print, television, film and the interactive market. Credits include, *The Twilight Zone* (1986), *Amazing Stories* and *Star Trek: Deep Space Nine.* She is a film critic and entertainment writer for several Web sites and is content producer at *www.agirlsworld.com.* E-mail: *lynbark@earthlink.net.*

Kimi Beaven grew up on Kauai and met Alan in India in 1990. She has a beautiful daughter Sonali and two wonderful stepsons. Kimi and Alan are known for their enthusiasm for life and deep commitment to the uplift-ment of humanity. Kimi can be reached at *Bheaven@aol.com.* More informa-tion can be found at *www.Alanbeaven.org.*

Erin Bertocci holds a bachelor of arts from Columbia College, Columbia University and is a manager at Accenture, the world's leading provider of management and technology consulting services and solutions. She is proud to be a native of New York City. She was born, raised and currently lives in Manhattan.

Arthur Bowler, a graduate of Harvard Divinity School, is a writer, speaker and part-time minister in Switzerland. He is the author of the forthcoming book *A Prayer and a Swear,* a funny, inspirational look at life. You can reach him at *bowler@bluewin.ch.*

Shirley Boyer recently retired after thirty years of teaching in elementary education. Shirley enjoys reading stories to children, flower gardening, swimming, traveling and being a hostess in her home. She keeps busy with occasional substitute teaching, reading and being with friends.

Ellie Braun-Haley is the author of *A Little Door, A Little Light,* an uplifting collection of stories about, angels, heavenly intervention and after-death communication. She is currently gathering stories for the sequel and pub-lishing related stories on the Web. Contact her at *shaley@telusplanet.net* or *www.eaglecreek.org.*

Helice Bridges, creator of the "Who I Am Makes a Difference" Acknowledgement Ceremony and Training Programs, has positively impacted the lives of over 23 million children and adults worldwide in corporations, organizations and schools. To order Blue Ribbon products or invite Helice to speak, please reach her at *ablueribbn@aol.com.*

Pam Bumpus and her husband, Alan, farm in east central Illinois. Writing is her hobby. She plans to publish a book, *Backside of the Storm,* a collection of inspiring and humorous events from a family journal she keeps, in the near future. Please e-mail her at: *pamela@mcleodusa.net.*

Michele Wallace Campanelli is a national bestselling author and published novelist of Hollis Books. She is assisted by editor Fontaine Wallace, English professor at Florida Institute of Technology. Her cousin, Amberley Wallace, is on the USS Carl Vinson, an aircraft defending US in Enduring Freedom. To contact Michelle, go directly to *www.michelecampanelli.com* Michele sends all the families affected by the 9/11 tragedy her prayers. God bless America!

Anne Carter, a native New Yorker and retired teacher, dedicates this story to her daughter, Donna, whose middle name is courage. May the world of our "Sweetest 13" always be proud and free. She sends her love to Daniel, Dylan, Alexander, Cameron, Maclaine and Matthew, Katie, Jack, Douglas, Alexandra, Shane, Christian and Michael. Contact Anne at: *carteracdc@webtv.net.*

Deanna Cogdon is a wireless marketing communications manager with Aliant Telecom (serving the four Atlantic Canadian provinces). She holds an undergraduate degree from Careleton University, a diploma in public relations from Algonquin College and is completing a diploma in marketing and international business. She is an aspiring writer. E-mail: *deannacogdon@hotmail.com.*

Fred O. Cox was born March 18, 1941, in Pleasantville, New York, grew up in Pittsfield, Massachusetts, and graduated from Duke University, in 1963. He began his career in banking in New York City and then worked for thirty years in resort and golf development and management. He is a co-founder of Boulders in Carefree, Arizona, has served on several boards of directors. Today Mr. Cox acts as a consultant and resides in Palm Beach, Florida.

Terri Crisp has been involved in helping animals during disasters since 1983. She is the author of two books, *Out of Harm's Way* and *Emergency Animal Rescue Stories,* which tell of her experiences in over fifty major disasters. She can be reached at: *cri655@aol.com.*

Mike Daisey's monologues include *Wasting Your Breath* and *I Miss The Cold War.* His first book, *21 DOG YEARS: Doing Time @ Amazon.com,* will be published in spring 2002 by *The Free Press.* He lives in Brooklyn with his lovely wife, Jean-Michele. You can find him online at: *www.mikedaisey.com.*

Elizabeth Danehy currently resides with her parents and sisters in Duxbury, Massachusetts. She is presently working toward a bachelor's degree in social work at Marist College in Poughkeepsie, New York. She is a member of The Sirens, an a capella group whose CDs are available to the public.

Michael D'Antonio is a writer who lives on Long Island, New York. He is the author of ten books on subjects as varied as religion, golf, atomic science and the pesky mosquito. He can be contacted at *mdant92290@aol.com*.

Michael De Adder, artist, was born in New Brunswick, Canada. He received his bachelor of fine arts degree from the province's Mount Allison University. Michael currently draws daily editorial cartoons for a major East Coast newspaper. Michael is also an accomplished painter. Please view samples of his cartoon work online at *www.artizans.com*.

Lisa Duncan is a professional speaker and trainer. She teaches "Investment Dressing: How to Build a Professional Wardrobe on $5 a Day" to colleges and national corporations. She also offers inspiring speeches and seminars on the benefits of stress management and on having an "Attitude of Gratitude." She may be reached at Duncan and Duncan Enterprises LLC; 303-512-7638; e-mail: *lisa.duncan@prodigy.net*.

Meredith Englander graduated from the University of Michigan with a BA in psychology from Columbia University with a master's in clinical social work, and Bank Street College of Education with a master's in special education. She is a cofounder and director of MATAN: The Gift of Jewish Learning for Every Child. For more information, visit: *www.matankids.org*.

Captain Aaron Espy is a firefighter/paramedic who works and lives southwest of Seattle. He is best known throughout the fire service for his unique brand of firehouse poetry. Espy is a columnist, freelancer and author of *Standing in the Gap,* a book of firehouse poetry.

Marc Farre is a New York-based composer, singer and songwriter with three CDs released so far. His most recent, *Man on the Sun* (available on Amazon.com), has been hailed by critics as "fantastic," "mesmerizing" and "joy and ecstasy." He's also composed more than a dozen scores for modern ballet, as well as special music for healing. Marc can also be heard occasionally on public radio. "Prayer Flags" will appear on Marc's next album. In the meantime, you can download it for free (and contact Marc) on his Web site: *www.marcfarre.com*.

Robin Gaby Fisher has been writing for *The Star-Ledger,* New Jersey's largest circulation newspaper, for seven years. She was a finalist for this year's Pulitzer Prize for her seven-part series *"After The Fire"* which chronicled nine months in the lives of two students recovering from critical burns in the Seton Hall University dormitory fire. Recently she wrote a five-part series about two World Trade Center widows and their struggle to recovery from the September 11 tragedy. Please reach her at *rfisher@starledger.com.*

Danielle Giordano is a twenty-one-year-old college student from Rockaway, New Jersey. She is a special education major and aspiring writer. Her passage was written directly following the tragic events on September 11, her goal is to express our unity and show that we will not help to feed the fear which terror thrives on. Please reach her at: *danig627@hotmail.com.*

Teri Goggin, R.N., is a writer, reiki master and mother of two remarkable children. Her book, *Strong & Wise: Four Keys to Transforming Life's Pain,* unlocks the secret to finding powerful gifts beneath painful challenges. For information on her book, or the *Strong & Wise* workshops, visit Teri's Web site: *www.StrongWise.com.*

Steve Goodier is the publisher of the Internet newsletter *Your Life Support System.* He sends his e-zine of hope and encouragement to people in over 100 nations daily. He left his position as senior minister in a Denver, Colorado, church to write and publish his newsletter and has since written numerous books. Steve and his wife (and best friend), Bev, now work together, in their home in Colorado, publishing the daily e-zine and inspirational books. You can only get Steve's books here: *www.LifeSupportSystem.com* or call 877-344-0989.

Maria Miller Gordon is a trade organization's newspaper editor-in-chief, a freelance writer and a photographer. She is the cofounder of her local writers club and is currently working on her first novel. Maria lives in rural northwest Ohio with her husband and two children. Contact her at: *maria_miller_gordon@hotmail.com.*

Steven M. Gorelick, Ph.D., is a college administrator and sociologist at the City University of New York. His specialties are the press coverage of crime and violence, social panic, and the history of propaganda. His commentaries have appeared in *The Washington Post, Los Angeles Times, Christian Science Monitor, International Herald Tribune* and in many other publications.

Shelley Divnich Haggert is a freelance writer and the editor of a local parenting magazine. Shelley has three children and enjoys living on the Canada-U.S. border. She loves history and literature and plans to publish children's picture books one day. Please reach her at: *shelley@thewritesideup.com.*

Megan Hallinan received her bachelor's degree from Trinity College in Dublin, Ireland. She is a native of Cape Cod, Massachusetts, and received her commission as a naval officer on March 17, 2000. After the navy, she will spend the rest of her life traveling.

Susan Halm, when not donating blood, is saving lives through communications. Visit *www.2000online.com*.

William Harvey studies at The Juilliard School in New York City. He is the director of Music for the People, soon to become a nonprofit organization, which will send young classical musicians around the world to play for people who need the solace music provides, starting with soldiers stationed at overseas bases. For more information, please contact him at *williamrharvey@hotmail.com*.

HeroicStories is a free online newsletter that publishes true stories of "heroes in everyday life," inspiring their readers to act to help others in need. *HeroicStories* also publishes reader reactions to the moral issues raised in the stories. Thus, *HeroicStories* creates a global dialog about humanity's incredible capacity to act to benefit others. Free e-mail subscriptions are available at: *www.HeroicStories.com*.

Bill Holicky is an architect who lives in Boulder, Colorado, with his wife Kelley and their son Jackson. His passage is dedicated to the memory of Jackson's older brother, I.B. He can be reached at *bckc@frii.com*.

Kathy Ide lives in Brea, California, with her husband, Richard, and two sons, Tom and Mike. She is a full-time freelance author, coauthor, editor, and proofreader. She works with both authors and publishing houses, including Moody Press, Thomas Nelson Publishers and Honor Books. E-mail: *kayide@pacbell.net*.

David Jacobson is an award-winning cartoonist currently working for *The Journal News*, a Gannett newspaper in Westchester, New York, where his cartoon appears daily. His sports cartoon, "Offsides," was syndicated through United Features.

Bil Keane created "The Family Circus," based on his own family, in 1960. It now appears in well over 1,500 newspapers and is read daily by 188 million people. The award-winning feature is the most widely syndicated panel cartoon in America. Check out The Family Circus Web site: *www.familycircus.com*.

Carol Kline, coauthor of the bestselling *Chicken Soup for the Pet Lover's Soul, Chicken Soup for the Cat and Dog Lover's Soul* and *Chicken Soup for the Mother's Soul 2*, has been a pet lover her entire life. Currently she is on the board of directors for the Noah's Ark Animal Foundation located in Fairfield, Iowa, a unique, cageless no-kill animal shelter that saves lost, stray and abandoned cats and dogs. Write Carol at: P.O. Box 1262, Fairfield, IA 52556, or e-mail: *ckline@lisco.com.*

Rosemarie Kwolek works in Manhattan as a legal secretary and lives in Bardonia, New York, with her husband, Edward, a design engineer for the Port Authority of New York and New Jersey where he was assigned to Tower One of the World Trade Center. They have two daughters in college and one in medical school. Rosemarie can be reached at *NYR001@aol.com.*

Patricia Lorenz is an art-of-living writer and speaker and the author of three books, over 400 articles; a contributor to ten *Chicken Soup for the Soul* books; thirteen *Daily Guideposts* books; numerous anthologies; and an award-winning columnist for two newspapers. For speaking engagements phone 1-800-437-7577 or e-mail: *patricialorenz@juno.com.*

Gordon MacDonald is an author and speaker among business and non-profit organizations on the subject of leadership and the organization of the inner life of the person. Author of fifteen books, he is best known for *Ordering Your Private World.* A book centered on his experiences and observations of life at Ground Zero is due later in 2002. He lives with his wife, Gail, in Canterbury, New Hampshire.

Jimmy Margulies is the editorial cartoonist for *The Record* in New Jersey. The recipient of international, national and local awards, his cartoons are syndicated by King Features. A graduate of Carnegie Mellon University, he and his wife Martha have two children, Elana and David. *JimMarg@aol.com.*

Charles Memminger, a National Society of Newspaper Columnists award-winner, is a newspaper columnist and screenwriter in Honolulu, Hawaii. His column, "Honolulu Lite," is published in the Honolulu Star-Bulletin and can be read online at *www.starbulletin.com.* You may e-mail him at *71224.113@compuserve.com.*

Mary Mooney began writing after the age of forty. Living in Jakarta, Indonesia, for three years gave her a new appreciation for her family, country and world. She is certified as a multicultural, diversity trainer and hopes to have her first children's picture book dealing with diversity, *Happy Family Cookies,* published soon.

Cornel Nistorescu, fifty-three, is one of Romania's most influential journalists. During a career spanning almost thirty years, he worked as a reporter, columnist and senior editor. He has published three books, founded a press group and a radio station. He has written for publications in Belgium, Holland, France and the United States. Currently he is the managing director of the daily newspaper, *Evenimentul Zilei,* in which he is publishing his daily column. Contact him at: *corneln@expres.ro*; fax: +4 01 202 20 10.

Jennifer Oliver, wife of househubby, Stephen, and four beautiful children, is a Webmaster for a government organization in central Texas. Her stories have appeared in several e-zines and in "Heartwarmers of Love." She is currently writing a fictional romance novel and managing a Web site for inspirational stories. E-mail: *fourears@hotmail.com*.

David Page is an elementary school principal in the suburban Philadelphia, Pennsylvania, area. He is a writer of poetry, short stories, TV scripts and plays. Two of his most well-known pieces are the comedy, *If I Only Knew Then*, and the musical, *Resisting Gravity* (starring Grammy Award-winner, William Warfield.) David lectures nationally.

Jeff Parker has been editorial cartoonist at *Florida Today* since 1992. His cartoons are distributed to newspapers throughout the United States by *Cagle.com*. Jeff also assists Dean Young and Denis Lebrun with the art chores on the renowned comic strip, "Blondie," for King Features

Annie Perryman is a twelve-year-old, born and raised in rural Oregon, who loves Father-Mother God, family and friends, Sunday school, America, school, tap and jazz dancing (ten years), horses (especially at Grammy's farm and Cedars Camps), karate (Green Belt), soccer (four years), storytelling (County Hall of Fame), speech (first place), modeling, acting, reading, fishing, and her dog and cat. E-mail: *perryman@cdsnet.net*.

Judith Simon Prager, Ph.D., clinical hypnotherapist, trains first responders, pediatric interns and psychiatric nurses in verbal first aid. With Judith Acosta, LCSW, she has written *The Worst Is Over: What to Say When Every Moment Counts* about words that can calm, relieve pain, promote healing and save lives. Web site: *www.theworstisover.com*.

Carol McAdoo Rehme, a frequent contributor to *Chicken Soup for the Soul* and other inspirational books, is a full-time storyteller, speaker and author. Her latest passion is a pilot program, "Silver Linings for Golden Agers." It is the recipient of several grants and provides highly interactive, multi-sensory presentations at eldercare facilities. Contact her at: *carol@rehme.com* or *www.rehme.com*.

Harriet May Savitz was born in Newark, New Jersey, and grew up during the depression. She is the award-winning author of twenty-one books and two essay collections, *Growing Up At 62* and *Messages from Somewhere: Inspiring Stories of Life After 60* (Little Treasure Publications, Inc.). To learn more, visit *www.harrietmaysavitz.com*.

Cheryl Sawyer is coordinator of the Counselor Education Program at the University of Houston Clear Lake. Cheryl enjoys traveling, camping and playing with her children. As a nationally recognized speaker in educational fields, Cheryl is available for conference or workshop presentations. She has recently been honored as the Clear Lake City, Texas, *Barnes & Noble* author-of-the-month. Please reach her at: *Sawyer@cl.uh.edu or Sawyeredd@aol.com.*

Howard Schnauber is a retired state park manager and real estate agent. He was Marine Sgt. from 1941 to 1946, and fought on Guadalcanal and Peleliu. Joined the 40th Div. 160th Reg. Tank Co. during the Korean War and was the recipient of four Purple Hearts. Past Commander and active in the D.A.V. for over 15 years. He has written articles for the *Fort Collins Coloradoan*. Neva and Howard have been married for forty-five years.

Raised in the Midwest, **Joyce Schowalter** gardens, e-mails, and markets drinking water purifiers via her Web site: *www.AlwaysPure.com.* She invites you to check out inspiring true stories of heroes in everyday life at *HeroicStories.com,* where her signature is "Co-Conspirator to Make the World a Better Place."

Julie Jordan Scott is a Passionate Living coach, writer, speaker and Mom extraodinaire who lives with her four children in Bakersfield, California. She has taught thousands of people worldwide to live with passion everyday. To contact Julie, call 661-325-4116, e-mail: *julie@5passions.com* or visit her Web site: *http://www.5passions.com.*

David Skidmore, his wife, Melissa, and daughters, Daisy Sue and Anna Belle, live in Tennessee, where he serves as youth minister for the North Boulevard Church of Christ. He speaks often to teens, and enjoys watching his daughters entertain the world. He can be reached at *jdskidmore@aol.com* or at 615-893-1520.

Jon Sternoff's goal is to inspire others to inspire others. Since 1992 he has maintained his own romance related inspirational Web site, Romance 101 (*www.rom101.com*). His source of inspiration can be found with his wife, Janel, and his two basenjis, Tosh and Zoe. He can be reached at: *jon@rom101.com.*

Ann Marquerite Swank is eighteen, majoring in fine art and child psychology. She still works with children in her family's in-home childcare, and helps care for her disabled father. By auctioning her artwork, she raised over two thousand dollars for September 11 relief funds. Digital portfolio available and commissions accepted via: *justswank@aol.com.*

Dave Timmons is a motivational speaker, singer and songwriter, specializing in leadership and personal growth. His background includes twenty-five years as an innovative leader in the banking industry. His mission is inspiring people to aim higher and achieve more in their personal and professional lives. Please contact him at: *dave@davetimmons.com*.

Caroline Broida Trapp is a member of the Birmingham Temple of Farmington Hills, Michigan, a humanistic Jewish Congregation. An initial circulation of this story by her mother resulted in e-mail requests from around the world for Solly Ganor's book. Contact: *www.birminghamtemple.org* or *www.rongreen.com/solly.html* for information on humanistic Judaism or Holocaust survivor Solly Ganor.

Victoria Walker resides in Fort Myers, Florida, with her teenage son, Jeremy. She is a freelance writer, the owner of WordWalker Publishing, a company that specializes in business copywriting and informational e-books, and she is proud to be an American! For more information, visit her online at *http://worldwalkerpublishing.com* or *http://victoriawalker.com*.

Tina Warren is a mother, writer and Web designer. Her work can be found at *http://www.unifiedspirits.com*. Tina enjoys the simple pleasures in life such as playing peek-a-boo with her son or making a stranger smile. E-mail her at: *unifiedspirits@yahoo.com*.

Molly Lynn Watt divides her writing life between Antrim, New Hampshire, and Cambridge, Massachusetts. She is published in newspapers, magazines, journals and elsewhere. She is a forty-year veteran teacher, workshop leader and national consultant on school improvement. She lives with her husband, Dan, and is a grandmother of five.

Bob Welch is a columnist at *The Register-Guard* newspaper in Eugene, Oregon and author of six books, including *The Things That Matter Most* and the Gold Medallion award-winning *A Father for All Seasons*. He can be contacted at *bwelch1@concentric.net*.

Jeannie S. Williams is a prolific author, lecturer and consultant in the field of education. She conducts dynamic staff development, parenting and student workshops and has more than twenty-five years' experience working with teachers and parents. She is a frequent contributor to the *Chicken Soup for the Soul* books and the *Stories for the Heart* book series. Jeannie shares the joy of working with children in her two newest books, *What Time Is Recess?* and *I Pledge Allegiance . . . From the Bottom of My Heart*. She can be reached at P.O. Box 1476, Sikeston, MO 63801 or e-mail: *mageni@semo.net*.

Ferida Wolff is the author of *Listening Outside Listening Inside,* an inspirational book for adults, as well as fourteen books for children. She was both a student and teacher of yoga for twenty-six years and now facilitates meditation workshops. Please visit her Web site: *www.feridawolff.com* or contact her at *fwolff@erols.com*.

Permissions *(continued from page iv)*

Two Heroes for the Price of One, New York Cabbies, No Words, Chance Encounter and *Long-Distance Call.* Reprinted by permission of Marsha Arons. ©2001 Marsha Arons.

FYI. ©2001 by *The New York Times Co.* Reprinted by permission. Originally published in *The New York Times,* November 6, 2001.

What Can Be Said? Reprinted by permission of Mike Daisey. ©2001 Mike Daisey.

Twin Saving at the Twin Towers. ©2002 *The Star-Ledger.* All rights reserved. Reprinted with permission. Appeared in *The Star-Ledger* September 27, 2001.

More Than Chocolate. Reprinted by permission of Terri Crisp and Carol Kline. ©2001 Terri Crisp and Carol Kline.

E-Mails from Manhattan. Reprinted by permission of Meredith Englander. ©2001 Meredith Englander.

Prayer Flags. Reprinted by permission of Marc Farre. ©2001 Marc Farre.

Anxiously Awaiting. Reprinted by permission of Rosemarie Kwolek. ©2001 Rosemarie Kwolek.

A Day in D.C. Reprinted by permission of Maria Miller Gordon. ©2001 Maria Miller Gordon.

Last Call. Reprinted by permission of David A. Timmons. ©2001 David A. Timmons.

The Vigil. ©2001 by *The New York Times Co.* Reprinted by permission. Originally published in *The New York Times,* November 6, 2001.

A Picture and a Friendship. ©2001 by *The New York Times Co.* Reprinted by permission. Originally published in *The New York Times,* October 23, 2001.

Memento. Reprinted by permission of Mary Sue Mooney. ©2001 Mary Sue Mooney.

Dust. Reprinted by permission of David C. Page. ©2001 David C. Page.

A Night at Ground Zero. Reprinted by permission of Erin Bertocci. ©2001 Erin Bertocci.

The Only Thing We Could Think Of. Reprinted by permission of Elizabeth M. Danehy. ©2001 Elizabeth M. Danehy.

Playing for the Fighting 69th. Reprinted by permission of William Harvey. ©2001 William Harvey.

Reflections from the Pit. Reprinted by permission of Thomas Gordon MacDonald. ©2001 Thomas Gordon MacDonald.

Dear Mr. Cox. Reprinted by permission of Michael D'Antonio. ©2001 Michael D'Antonio.

Dear Mike. Reprinted by permission of Fred O. Cox. ©2001 Fred O. Cox.

A Patriot to the End. Reprinted with permission of *The Associated Press.*

Beep If You Love America and *Neighbors Knowing Neighbors.* Reprinted by permission of Harriet May Savitz. ©2001 Harriet May Savitz.

The Face of America and *How the Children Help.* Reprinted with permission of *HeroicStories.com,* ©2001.

Answering His Country's Call. Reprinted with permission of *The Dallas Morning News.*

His Dream Came True. The Miami Herald, Issue November 5, 2001 by Linda Robertson. ©2001 by *The Miami Herald.* Reprinted by permission of *The Miami Herald* via the *Copyright Clearance Center.*

The Unity of Strangers. Reprinted by permission of Lynn Barker. ©2001 Lynn Barker.

The Cops from Madison, Alabama. Reprinted by permission of Steven M. Gorelick, Ph.D. ©2001 Steven M. Gorelick, Ph.D.

Given the Choice. Reprinted by permission of Aaron Espy. ©2001 Aaron Espy.

Operation Teddy Bear. Reprinted by permission of Tina Warren. ©2001 Tina Warren.

Send Beauty. Reprinted by permission of Theresa M. Goggin. ©2001 Theresa M. Goggin.

Repaying an Old Kindness. Reprinted with permission of *The Associated Press.*

The Crumpled Blue Ribbon. Reprinted by permission of Helice Bridges. ©2001 Helice Bridges.

BOWS Across America. Reprinted by permission of Lisa Duncan. ©2001 Lisa Duncan.

A Fishing Village Opens Its Heart to Surprise Guests. ©2001, *Seattle Times Company.* Used with permission.

Smallest Gestures. Reprinted by permission of Deanna Cogdon. ©2001 Deanna Cogdon.

Dear Dad. Reprinted by permission of Megan Michaela Hallinan. ©2001 Megan Michaela Hallinan.

Four Simple Words. Reprinted by permission of Arthur Wilson Bowler. ©2001 Arthur Wilson Bowler.

It's All American

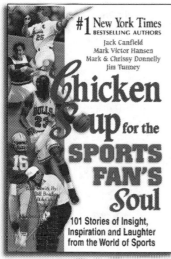
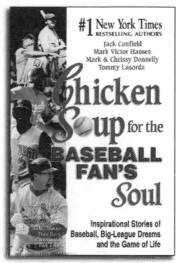
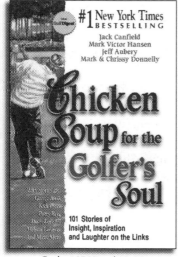
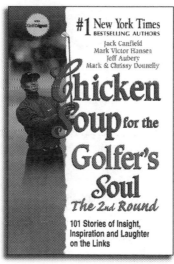

Saluting
America's Best

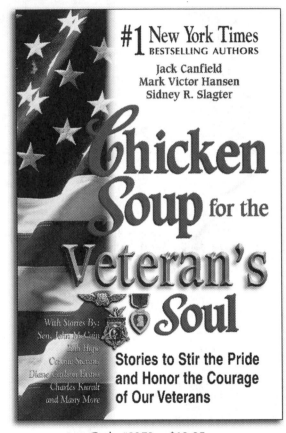

#1 New York Times
BESTSELLING AUTHORS

Jack Canfield
Mark Victor Hansen
Sidney R. Slagter

Chicken
Soup for the
Veteran's Soul

With Stories By:
Sen. John McCain
Bob Hope
Connie Stevens
Diane Carlson Evans
Charles Kuralt
and Many More

**Stories to Stir the Pride
and Honor the Courage
of Our Veterans**

Code #9373 • $12.95

Exercise Your
Freedom to Travel

#1 New York Times
BESTSELLING AUTHORS
Jack Canfield
Mark Victor Hansen
Steve Zikman

Chicken Soup for the TRAVELER'S Soul

Stories of Adventure,
Inspiration and Insight to
Celebrate the Spirit of Travel

Code #9705 • $12.95

Also Available